# Visual Research and Indonesian Ethnography

This book focuses on how visual records—mainly on film or video—can provide data for research and presents a variety of visual projects drawn from ethnographic fieldwork in Indonesia.

Karl Heider argues for the expansion of visual anthropology—or anthropology with a camera—beyond descriptive ethnographic film into actual use of the camera as a research tool. The chapters explore several ways in which camera-generated materials can complement and support what anthropologists already do in their research. Heider includes samples from fieldwork in Indonesia conducted over a number of years, particularly in New Guinea and Sumatra with groups including the Dani and Minangkabau. His studies combine visual and psychological anthropology and provide insight into the analysis of emotions in particular.

Intended to inspire new approaches to the ethnographic enterprise, the book is valuable for scholars of visual anthropology and Southeast Asia.

**Karl G. Heider** is a Carolina Distinguished Professor of Anthropology (Emeritus) at the University of South Carolina, Columbia, SC, USA.

## Anthropology and Cultural History in Asia and the Indo-Pacific
Series Editors: Pamela J. Stewart and Andrew Strathern

This series offers a fresh perspective on Asian and Indo-Pacific Anthropology. Acknowledging the increasing impact of transnational flows of ideas and practices across borders, the series widens the established geographical remit of Asian studies to consider the entire Indo-Pacific region. In addition to focused ethnographic studies, the series incorporates thematic work on issues of cross-regional impact, including globalization, the spread of terrorism, and alternative medical practices.

The series further aims to be innovative in its disciplinary breadth, linking anthropological theory with studies in cultural history and religious studies, thus reflecting the current creative interactions between anthropology and historical scholarship that are enriching the study of Asia and the Indo-Pacific region. While the series covers classic themes within the anthropology of the region such as ritual, political and economic issues will also be tackled. Studies of adaptation, change, and conflict in small-scale situations enmeshed in wider currents of change will have a significant place in this range of foci.

We publish scholarly texts, both single-authored and collaborative as well as collections of thematically organized essays. The series aims to reach a core audience of anthropologists and Asian studies specialists, but also to be accessible to a broader multidisciplinary readership.

Recent titles in series:

**Honour, Mana and Agency in Polynesian-European Conflict**
*Annette Wilkes*

**Visual Research and Indonesian Ethnography**
Beyond Description
*Karl G. Heider*

www.routledge.com/Anthropology-and-Cultural-History-in-Asia-and-the-Indo-Pacific/book-series/ASHSER1241

# Visual Research and Indonesian Ethnography
Beyond Description

Karl G. Heider

LONDON AND NEW YORK

First published 2021
by Routledge
2 Park Square, Milton Park, Abingdon, Oxon OX14 4RN

and by Routledge
605 Third Avenue, New York, NY 10158

*Routledge is an imprint of the Taylor & Francis Group, an informa business*

© 2021 Karl G. Heider

The right of Karl G. Heider to be identified as author of this work has been asserted by him in accordance with sections 77 and 78 of the Copyright, Designs and Patents Act 1988.

All rights reserved. No part of this book may be reprinted or reproduced or utilised in any form or by any electronic, mechanical, or other means, now known or hereafter invented, including photocopying and recording, or in any information storage or retrieval system, without permission in writing from the publishers.

*Trademark notice*: Product or corporate names may be trademarks or registered trademarks, and are used only for identification and explanation without intent to infringe.

*British Library Cataloguing-in-Publication Data*
A catalogue record for this book is available from the British Library

*Library of Congress Cataloging-in-Publication Data*
A catalog record has been requested for this book

ISBN: 978-0-367-76481-4 (hbk)
ISBN: 978-0-367-76558-3 (pbk)
ISBN: 978-1-003-16752-5 (ebk)

Typeset in Sabon
by MPS Limited, Dehradun

# Contents

*Acknowledgments* vii
*Foreword by Series Editor* viii

Introduction: the place of visuals in anthropological research 1

## PART I
## Visual research projects 11

1 Microcultural incidents in Minangkabau children's emotion behavior 13

2 *Dead Birds* revisited: rethinking emotion in a New Guinea Dani funeral 33

3 Comparing styles of teaching and learning in some South Carolina and West Sumatra kindergartens: video-cued multivocalic ethnography (by Karl G. Heider and Louise Jennings) 39

4 Three styles of play: New Guinea Dani, Central Java, and Micronesia 55

5 Nonverbal studies of Dani anger and sexual expression: experimental method in videotape ethnography 64

## PART II
## Exploring Indonesian cinema 81

6 National cinema, national culture 83

| | | |
|---|---|---|
| 7 | Analyzing emotion in scenes from Indonesian cinema | 93 |
| 8 | Culture and cinema in Indonesia: Teguh Karya's *Doea Tanda Mata* | 131 |
| 9 | Banana peels: visual conventions in Indonesian movies | 137 |
| 10 | Anger in Indonesian cinema | 141 |
| 11 | Order and disorder in Indonesian genre films and national politics | 146 |

Appendix
Other uses of visuals: fragments and suggestions  148

*Bibliography*  162
*Index*  168

# Acknowledgments

So many people have helped with one or another of the investigations described in this book that I could fill another book just doing justice to their work. But here I must at least thank especially Eleanor Rosch, Louise Jennings, Janet Elashoff, Paul M. Heider, Robert Gardner, Paul Ekman, and the colleagues in his shop, as well as Malie, Mary Winn, and John B. Heider.

# Series editors' foreword
Seeing and Understanding: Visual Components of the Anthropological Project

It is a pleasure to add Prof. Karl Heider's book to our *Anthropology and Cultural History in Asia and the Indo-Pacific* series that we founded, encompassing 18 titles to date. We encourage authors to join this series by contacting Pamela J. Stewart and Andrew Strathern (pamjan@pitt.edu).

Karl Heider is well-known for his long-standing and innovative work in the field of visual anthropology, starting with his pioneering ethnographic fieldwork from 1960 onward among the Dani people of West Papua and his collaborations with the filmmaker Robert Gardner that produced, inter alia, the famous film *Dead Birds*, on Dani warfare. *Dead Birds* has long been a classic ethnographic film, challenging stereotypes about "primitive" warfare and describing the improvised and opportunistic strategies of fighting wielded by the Dani. Karl's work on Dani ethnography in general helps further to contextualize the understanding of land use, intermarriage, and exchange relations.

The present book puts on display the great range of projects that Professor Heider has developed and followed up since those early days of path-breaking work among the Dugum Dani. One of the main directions his work has taken has been among the Minangkabau of West Sumatra in Indonesia, where he carried out field studies of emotion concepts and their roles in ethnopsychological contexts. Emotion concepts are often a key to understanding cultural themes and patterns, and because of the difficulties of developing verbal ways of identifying emotions, visual materials can be crucial. Professor Heider moves in a direction important for his book: the incorporation of visual materials into ethnography as a specific research tool, going beyond the category of "ethnographic film."

Further, what we call "emotion concepts" are often pivotal cultural markers of social relations and processes, as, for example, the concept of popokl, "anger/frustration" in the culture of the Melpa-speaking Mount Hagen people of the Western Highlands Province in Papua New Guinea. Popokl features as a vital transducer in community relations in Hagen, helping both to constrain and explain trajectories of conflict and peacemaking in domestic and wider contexts. Professor Heider's handling of emotions in Minangkabau focuses on how emotions are displayed in interactions among children, in ways that must surely also enter into interactions among adults. He took videotape records of events and shows here, as elsewhere, how these videos can be used as a research tool. This is a demonstration that he replicates with several other studies in this book.

In the midst of these careful expositions, we find gems of discussions of themes that have attracted notice in anthropology over time. One such gem is his reference to the media response to his finding that among the Grand Valley Dani there was a postpartum taboo on sexual intercourse between spouses lasting four to six years. Heider reports that American audiences expressed disbelief about the findings. How could spouses refrain from intercourse for such a length of time? Heider's comment is laconic. He notes that observation of this taboo did not seem to produce undue stress. Indeed not: it would relieve stress on the wife, because the taboo operated as long as she breastfed their child. What is extraordinary here is that this taboo is also widely found in Highlands Papua New Guinea and is a stock-in-trade of ethnographic accounts. Anthropology's role as a means of dispelling ethnocentric notions is well illustrated here.

A comparable effect is achieved in the deft exposition of different styles of play among the Dani, Central Javanese, and Micronesian peoples. Culture enters into the minutiae of behavior, including among children, and the Dani style of free play contrasts with both Micronesia and Java, in line with the hierarchical elements of society in these places by contrast with the Dani. Professor Heider also revisits the putative theme of sexual anxiety or the lack of it among Dani, finding here some differences between Grand Valley and Western Dani in expressions of emotions such as "disgust."

This book eloquently parses the author's immense contributions to visual anthropology over a long and distinguished career. In addition, however, it probes new methodological themes and interpretations of data, giving it an exploratory and innovative, forward-looking tone, and making it attractive for both mature scholars in the field and scholars earlier in their careers. Backward- and forward-looking at the same time, the book is a fitting tribute to Professor Heider's creative mind. We are delighted that this book is included in our *Anthropology and Cultural History in Asia and the Indo-Pacific* series.

As we have noted, this book extends the topic of visual anthropology well beyond the established category of "ethnographic film." As a footnote, it is interesting to note that classic ethnographic film can still generate interest and appreciation. We experienced this ourselves in 2019 when we were visiting Fudan University in Shanghai and giving lectures there. We found that our colleagues there had never had the opportunity of watching the well-known film "Ongka's Big Moka," dating back to 1975. We showed them a copy, and we received a host of interesting comments seeking to understand the character of leadership in the Mount Hagen society.

Pamela J. Stewart and Andrew Strathern[1]
University of Pittsburgh, November 2020

## Note

1 Pamela J. Stewart (Strathern) and Andrew J. Strathern are a wife-and-husband research team who are based in the Department of Anthropology, University of Pittsburgh and codirect the Cromie Burn Research Unit. They are frequently invited international lecturers and have worked with a number of museums to assist them with their collections. Stewart and Strathern have published over 50 books, over 80 prefaces to influential books, over 200 articles, book chapters, and essays on their research in the Pacific, mainly Papua New Guinea (Mount Hagen, Duna, and Wiru areas primarily) and the South-West Pacific region (e.g. Samoa, Cook Islands, and Fiji); Asia (mainly Taiwan, and also including Mainland China, Inner Mongolia, and Japan); Europe (primarily Scotland, Ireland, Germany, and the European Union countries in general); and New Zealand and Australia. One of their strengths is that, unlike some others working in the Mount Hagen area among the Hagen people, they learned the language, Melpa, and used it to understand the lives of the local people. Their most recent coauthored books include *Witchcraft, Sorcery, Rumors, and Gossip* (Cambridge University Press, PostHoondert_Final.indb 17 8/20/19 12:58 PM xviii | Series Editors' Preface 2004); Kinship in Action: Self and Group (Prentice Hall, 2011); *Peace-Making and the Imagination: Papua New Guinea Perspectives* (University of Queensland Press with Penguin Australia, 2011); *Ritual: Key Concepts in Religion* (Bloomsbury Academic, 2014); *Working in the Field: Anthropological Experiences Across the World* (Palgrave Macmillan, 2014); *Breaking the Frames: Anthropological Conundrums* (Palgrave Macmillan, 2017); and *Sacred Revenge in Oceania* (Cambridge University Press, 2019). Their recent coedited books include *Research Companion to Anthropology* (Routledge, 2016, originally published in 2015); *Exchange and Sacrifice* (Carolina Academic Press, 2008); and *Religious and Ritual Change: Cosmologies and Histories* (Carolina Academic Press, 2009), including the updated and revised Chinese version (Taipei, Taiwan: Linking Publishing, 2010). Stewart and Strathern's current research includes the topics of Cosmological Landscapes; Ritual Studies; Political Peace-Making; Comparative Anthropological Studies of Disasters and Climatic Change; Language, Culture, and Cognitive Science; and Scottish and Irish Studies. For many years, they served as Associate Editor and General Editor (respectively) for the Association for Social Anthropology in Oceania book series and they are coseries editors for the *Anthropology and Cultural History in Asia and the Indo-Pacific* book series. They also currently serve as coeditors of four book series: *Ritual Studies, Medical Anthropology, European Anthropology*, and *Disaster Anthropology*, and they are the long-standing coeditors of the *Journal of Ritual Studies* (on Facebook at www.facebook.com/ritualstudies). Their webpages, listing publications, and other scholarly activities are: http://www.pitt.edu/~strather/ and http://www.StewartStrathern.pitt.edu/.

# Introduction: the place of visuals in anthropological research

Visual anthropology includes a wide range of ways in which anthropologists use visuals—usually film or video—in their research, analyzing cultural behavior, their straightforward descriptions of cultural behavior, and their teaching about cultures. By far, the most common activity has been the making and using descriptive ethnographic film. But this book goes beyond the description of ethnographic film, to focus on research: how can visual records—mainly on film or video—provide data for research.

This book is a collection of essays which explore several ways in which camera-generated materials can complement and support what anthropologists already do in their research. Part 1 includes five chapters describing how I have used different visual projects to enhance my research in Sumatra, New Guinea, and the US. Part 2 includes six chapters that complement my research on Indonesian cinema. And Part 3, Odds and Ends, includes six chapters on my own fragmentary projects from my own fieldwork intended to stimulate other anthropologists with visual minds, cameras, and spare time during their own field trips.

Anthropologists—especially ethnographers—have been using cameras in their research and reporting since the 19th century. Photography and anthropology have grown up together. Great anthropological ancestors of present-day anthropology like Franz Boaz, the Torres Straits Expedition members, and Bronislaw Malinowski all incorporated some photography in their work. But I would begin a serious history of visual anthropological research with the famous work in Bali carried out during the late 1930s by Gregory Bateson and Margaret Mead. Each had already established themselves with important ethnographies—Mead in Samoa (Mead 1928) and Bateson in New Guinea (Bateson 1936). Then, together they carried out ground-breaking research in Bali, concentrating on a small upland village in 1936 and 1937. Bateson did extensive photography, both still and movie work. From this came the Bateson and Mead book "Balinese Character" (Bateson and Mead 1942), which used 759 photographs (out of a corpus of some 25,000 stills), laid out in facing pages, on one side five to nine annotated photographs on a particular theme, on the other side text describing the topic and further analyzing the photos. Later, under Mead's

2  *Visuals in anthropological research*

direction, Bateson's cinema footage was edited into several films released in the 1950s. Some were descriptive of Balinese subjects ("Karba's First Years" and "Trance and Dance in Bali"), one included New Guinea footage, another juxtaposed Balinese, New Guinea, and US footage and one showed a Balinese dance master and a dance master from India trying to teach each other their dance moves. Sadly, this research never got the attention it deserved. Soon after leaving the field, Bateson and Mead went their separate ways and World War II claimed the attention of anthropologists. (Actually, Bateson, Mead, and many of their close colleagues turned to research national character through the analysis of feature films from different cultures.)

In 1951, Mead and Frances Cooke Macgregor published a second study analyzing 380 of Bateson's photos of eight of the Balinese children in terms of the Gesell-Ilg developmental stages identified for American children. Working with the Gesell-Ilg group at Yale, Mead and Macgregor were able to contrast the Balinese development patterns with the American patterns.

A third study, of the Fore of Papua New Guinea by E. Richard Sorenson (with a foreword by Margaret Mead) (Sorenson 1976) used a similar layout—pages of multiple still photo sequences—to describe and analyze the environment and culture, focusing especially on children's behavior.

But such presentations of data through multiple arrays of still photos were not widely emulated. There have been some presentations of ethnographically informed photographs by anthropologists. Frank Cancian, who had been a professional photographer before becoming an anthropologist, published several collections of photographs on the Mayans whose culture he had analyzed in print. Robert Gardner and I published a selection of photographs of the New Guinea Dani, using 337 photographs out of some 26,500 that were shot by the seven members of the Harvard-Peabody Expedition during the six months of the expedition, but this was more a coffee table book than a scholarly research treatise (Gardner and Heider 1968).

In recent years, there has been a tremendous increase in the visual anthropological literature. And presentations at conferences, particularly at the annual Society for Visual Anthropology sessions followed immediately by the American Anthropological Association meetings, as well as the biennial visual conference in Great Britain of the Royal Anthropological Society—all vital venues for presentation and discussion of new visual projects.

I also call attention to recent innovative publications on visual anthropological research. For example, the monograph *Jero Tapakan: Balinese Healer: An Ethnographic Film Monograph* written by Linda Connor, Patsy Asch, and Timothy Asch (1986; second revised edition 1996). Timothy Asch, one of the most important anthropological filmmakers, had collaborated with John Marshall on Kalahari Bushman films, then collaborated with Napoleon Chagnon on Yanomamo films, and finally with his wife

Patsy Asch and the anthropologist Linda Connor on filming a Balinese healer, Jero Tapakan. Their book (Connor, Asch, and Asch 1996) is a detailed ethnography of Balinese healing practices as well as an analysis of the four films on healing that were produced by that partnership.

Also in 1996, Ronald C. Simons, professor of Psychiatry and Anthropology, published a comprehensive account of the Startle Reflex as a wise-spread cultural pattern. His own research focused on the Malay syndrome of latah, which is also the title of the film by Simons and his collaborator, Gunther Pfaff.

The most ambitious recent development in visual anthropology research is reported in Robert Lemelson's book *Afflictions: Steps Toward a Visual Psychological Anthropology* (Lemelson and Tucker 2017). Lemelson describes at length his take on visual anthropology, where it has been and how it has developed. The core of the book describes his own research on mental illness in Bali, focusing on six particular cases, each of which is described in a short film (*The Affliction Series*). This all represents a huge time-consuming project, but it lays down a challenge. Is it worth it? And one thinks back on the Bateson-Mead project in Bali, which for all sorts of reasons was never really completed.

Finally, I want to flag a relatively new area of interest: the remarkable emergence of what one book has called "global indigenous media." At least since the Second World War projects, when American anthropologists studied German and Japanese feature films, there has been some anthropological interest in the ways that cultural patterns were pictured in feature films from industrialized countries—including my own mining of Indonesian films for cultural patterns. But now, with film equipment so available and convenient, there are films made by the same "tribal" peoples that anthropologists pictured in "ethnographic films" (see Wilson and Stewart 2008 and Ginsburg, Abu-Lughod, and Larkin 2002).

It is fair to say that no other social science has used photography so much and to such good effect as anthropology. John Collier Jr.'s *Visual Anthropology: Photography as a Research Method* (Collier, 1967, second edition 1986) may have been the first book to use the term "visual anthropology" and to deal with anthropological photography in a programmatic way. Since then, "visual anthropology" has boomed. We have a Society for Visual Anthropology, two journals called *Visual Anthropology*, books on *Rethinking Visual Anthropology*, *Doing Visual Anthropology*, *The Future of Visual Anthropology*, *Reflecting Visual Anthropology*, and *Applied Visual Anthropology*. A recent book, Viewpoints. *Visual Anthropologists At Work*, edited by Mary Strong, a past president of the Society For Visual Anthropology, and Laena Wilder (Strong and Wilder 2009) has 15 chapters by various anthropologists exploring the field in the broadest terms.

For years, "Visual Anthropology" meant mainly descriptive ethnographic film. There was a brief surge of research on nonverbal communication in the 1950–1970 period using still and 16-mm movie film and video, but except among some linguistic anthropologists, it has died down. With the availability of synch sound videotape followed by digital technology, ethnographic film-making boomed and attention was focused on descriptive reporting about cultures through the use of ethnographic films. But by the 21st century, a new generation of anthropologists was thinking and writing about a wide range of visual approaches to anthropological research.

My own first involvement in visual anthropology was in the summer of 1960 when I was a graduate student specializing in archeology. That spring, Robert Gardner and I had many conversations while smoking cigarettes on the front steps of the Peabody Museum at Harvard. Gardner was working on film footage in the basement of the museum and our conversations often centered on film. When I announced that I was going to spend the summer on a University of Pennsylvania dig at the classic Mayan site of Tikal in Guatemala, he suggested that I shoot footage for a film on Tikal. I readily agreed. Penn shipped a camera up to Cambridge, Gardner checked me out on it, and so I spent the summer supervising excavations of a Mayan house mound and shooting footage. That Fall, I used the equipment in Gardner's lab to edit my film "Tikal." Meanwhile, he was putting together a Harvard-Peabody team to visit the Grand Valley Dani of Netherlands New Guinea, where he would shoot footage for what would turn out to be his first major film, *Dead Birds*. Suddenly, his plans for a ethnographer on his team fell through and he invited me to become the official ethnographer. The other members of the expedition stayed in New Guinea for six months but I stayed on to work on the ethnography of the Dani, which would become my doctoral dissertation. During my second year with the Dani, I shot footage on technology for a school curriculum project: "Dani Houses" and "Dani Sweet Potatoes." These are both straightforward descriptive ethnographic films based on my endless hours of observing Dani construction and horticulture activities, as carried out by the same people described so personally and dramatically in Gardner's film "Dead Birds."

The most controversial conclusion in my Dani ethnography was my claim that Dani couples observed a four- to six-year-long postpartum sexual abstinence. And not only did both father and mother refrain from sexual relations with each other for years after the birth of a child, but they were not stressed by it. These claims were based on my fairly good command of the Dani language, my extensive genealogies of every one in my neighborhood as well as my yearslong knowledge of my Dani neighbors.

But when I mentioned it to my American audiences, I was met with flat-out disbelief. My claims were picked up in the American press, in Playboy magazine, and I was interviewed on the Good Morning America television show. Since my descriptive account of Dani sexuality clearly did not suffice, I began to think about more formal research approaches. The video approach described in Chapter 6 does not completely resolve the issue, but I present it here as an attempt to move from simple descriptive reporting toward a more visual anthropological research-based ethnography.

*Visuals in anthropological research* 5

By the 1980s, I was doing most of my fieldwork among the Minangkabau in West Sumatra, Indonesia on psychological issues, most having to do with emotion. Whereas in the 1960s, I had to shoot 16-mm film without synchronous sound and then had to wait until having it processed at home, now with video technology, I could shoot in the morning and review the footage in repetitive detail with my research assistants the same afternoon.

I lived with my family in the small mountain city of Bukittinggi. In the evenings, I could view rented copies of Indonesian movies. I soon realized the research possibilities of these films. Of course, they were fictional, but they were written and acted by Indonesians for Indonesian audiences. In 1968, I spent six weeks in Jakarta, in effect doing ethnography through Indonesian cinema, viewing newly released films as well as older archived ones, and interviewing actors, actresses, and directors. Out of all this, came my book Indonesian Cinema as well as Chapters 6–11 in this book.

So, here I present a variety of visual projects I have done as part of my ethnographic research since 1960. I have focused mainly on two Indonesian cultures: the Grand Valley Dani of Papua (West New Guinea) and the Minangkabau of West Sumatra as well as on ethnographic film and Indonesian cinema. I had begun my dissertation fieldwork by looking at the material culture of the Dani and moved on to consider emotion and folk psychology of the Minangkabau. Although I did not start out to "do visual anthropology," I often found ways of using visual records in my research. These visual approaches produced important background information and sometimes were actually included as part of the published results. These chapters in Part I have not been published previously, but are related to my books on specific research (particularly Heider 1970 and 1997 on the Dani, and Heider 1991a and 2011 on the Minangkabau). The chapters in Part II relate to my book on Indonesian cinema (Heider 1991b). In the process of making these books reasonably succinct, I had left out some related studies of peripheral relevance. I never got around to submitting them as journal articles but now I realize that there are variations on the present theme, the use of visuals in anthropological research. The third part of this book describes various fragments of visual materials that suggest other projects, fragments of video projects that could have been carried out while I was in the field. This collection demonstrates some of the ways in which visuals can enhance the ethnographic research enterprise. Although elsewhere, I have written much about descriptive ethnographic film, which has always been an important part of visual anthropology, here I want especially to emphasize research possibilities in anthropology. It is convenient to think of three major areas of visual anthropology activity:

1. Research itself analyzing behavior captured in visual records;
2. Reports of research using photographs and other visual records, including descriptive ethnographic films;
3. Teaching anthropology with visuals.

6  *Visuals in anthropological research*

These are certainly overlapping uses. None of the examples in this book are limited to only one category. But each puts different demands on the same materials.

## Some principles of visual anthropology

The goal of this collection is not to define visual anthropology, but rather to explore various approaches and to inspire greater use of visuals in field research. Like many or most of us who claim the label of visual anthropologist, I became a camera buff at an early age, discovered anthropology soon thereafter, and have been alert to the possible connections between these interests ever since. We can begin with the following four basic and intentionally provocative precepts.

1. **The secret: "Visual Anthropology" is a particularly problematic label.** That is, I cannot imagine what a nonvisual anthropology might be. All anthropology is potentially visual. To be sure, there have been ethnographic books and articles without pictures of any sort, only words. But in every such case, the words at times are used to evoke visual scenes. From this assumption that any anthropological enterprise lacking visuals is somehow incomplete comes the next precept.

2. **The assumption: every anthropologist can use visuals to enhance their research, to report their research, or to teach anthropology.** This is the great challenge of visual anthropology and makes missionaries of us all. Actually, I am continually impressed by ways in which anthropologists who have shown little interest in incorporating visuals in their work, suddenly on their own, "discover" visuals. A goal of this book, beyond contributing to the ethnographic record, is to focus in on visuals in research, to demonstrate a wide variety of such uses and, ultimately, to encourage other anthropologists to think how visuals might enhance their own anthropological research in ways both carefully designed as well as unanticipated research projects.

3. **The prerequisite: the anthropology must drive the visuals, not the other way around.** The strongest argument for this tenet is in the case of ethnographic film. It is there also that the most disagreements arise, for this is where two traditions, two disciplines, converge: people trained as filmmakers and people trained as anthropologists. This can lead to extreme judgments. In the two editions of my *Ethnographic Film*, published 30-year apart (Heider 1977, 2006), I struggled to develop criteria by which films would be more "ethnographic," yet in the eight editions of *Films For Anthropological Teaching* I tried to include many films that were useful for teaching anthropology whether or not they were by these criteria "anthropological." Most films are about people,

and anthropology studies people. So far so good. But it does not then follow that most films are anthropological. Over more than a century, anthropology had developed theories and methods to study humans and other primates. Universities award PhDs to people who have spent years of studying and applying these theories and methods. As our work has been successful, other disciplines like sociology, geography, and psychology have adopted our tools, and often it is difficult—and unnecessary—to distinguish them from anthropology. When I have served on selection juries for ethnographic film festivals in the US and abroad, we have always seen films that are brilliantly made from a cinematic standpoint, and would serve well in anthropology courses for an instructor who could frame the films in anthropological terms. And these compete with films made by students or professors who are less adept cinematographers but who deliberately address authentic anthropological issues. Juries usually reward some of each kind of film but secretly wish that the anthropologists knew a bit more cinematography, and the cinematographers had more inkling of anthropology. And afterward, we defend each camp to the other. One long-term solution presumably lies in those ethnographic film or visual anthropological programs that provide training in both anthropology and film production.

Interestingly enough, still photography in anthropology has generated nothing like the attention paid to ethnographic film despite the pioneering work of Bateson and Mead's research in Bali, mentioned above. Still photographs have long been used in monographs and textbooks (and now, increasingly, in journal articles and even on journal covers.) But despite all the critical fury around text and film, still photographs seem to have been given a pass. Perhaps they have just been accepted as irrelevant nice additions. But surely still photographs deserve the same critical consideration as other visuals.

4. **The claim: no visual (photograph, film, or video) can stand by itself without accompanying text.** Photos cannot speak for themselves. Here is a thought experiment challenge: could a photograph alone reliably and replicatably communicate an anthropological message? Sol Worth used to say in this connection that no photograph alone could state a negative. I think that he was right. Ethnographic films pose a more complex problem. Even an ethnographic film uses some text, spoken or narration or written as title. There have been attempts to produce textless messages: Robert Gardner's India film, *Forest of Bliss*, has only a couple of lines by Yeats at the beginning, but nothing more (in English at least). Gardner assumed that his visuals alone would carry messages. But he finally relented and 16 years after the film was released, published the book *Making Forest of Bliss (2001)* in which he

and his ethnographer, Akos Ostor, discussed the film, shot by shot. Until then, very little of the visuals in that film were accessible to most Western viewers. Turning to the Collier and Collier volume, Visual Anthropology, we find many stunning photographs. The final photograph, "Navajo family meal," has a typical note: "The camera provides us with access to both infinite detail and infinite qualitative depth, both hardware of culture and the full dimension of human character" (Collier and Collier 1989: 237). I don't think so. This is claiming too much. And we circle back to the second tenet: visuals can enhance anthropology, but cannot substitute for text; they cannot alone do anthropology.

## The scope of visual anthropology

There is no authorized definition of "visual anthropology." It really depends on the interests of the writer. The essays in this book represent my own interests. These are all projects that I have been involved in over half a century of anthropological research and teaching. There are major omissions. A recent President of the Society for Visual Anthropology, Mary Strong, works in the anthropology of art and her recent book, subtitled Visual Anthropologists at Work, includes chapters on art (Strong and Wilder 2009). I have no objections to this, but my feeling is that the anthropology of art covers such a vast area that it deserves to be considered on its own: the graphic arts, from Paleolithic cave paintings to the present, architecture, music, dance, and theater—all together fill many volumes and feed into some common problems. The anthropology of art may be now reemerging from undeserved obscurity. (This obscurity was not always a problem. Long ago, Franz Boas (1927), one of the founders of American anthropology, actually wrote a book called *Primitive Art*).

This book is deliberately broadly inclusive within a fairly narrow reading of "visual anthropology." It is meant to inspire and provoke but not to read anyone out of either "visual" or "anthropology." There is room for many enterprises within those labels. On its web site, the Society for Visual Anthropology spreads a wide net, claiming its interest in:

> "all aspects of production, dissemination, and analysis of visual forms ... film, video, photography and computer-based multimedia ... all visual aspects of culture, including art, architecture, and material artifacts ..."

Each of the following chapters deal with visual subjects and each involves the use of cameras. I had thought of titling this book something like *Through a Camera's Eye*, or *Anthropology With a Camera* or *Photographic Visual Anthropology* but finally settled for the present title. But cameras are the common thread, whether using film or electronically stored images.

## Locating the visual data

At one point, I hoped to put the visual data for each chapter online, in The Cloud, so that any reader could have free and easy access while reading the printed text of a chapter. This would be an important innovation for a field like visual anthropology. Certainly, it is now, at last, technically possible. But there are two major problems. First, many of these chapters analyze clips from ethnographic films or feature films that are copyrighted and in commercial distribution. Negotiating the rights to send clips from these films to my Cloud for the use of my readers would raise unprecedented problems. But at least such films clips are available.

The second problem is ethical. I shot much of this footage during my research in recent decades. I was careful to explain my research as far as possible to my informants and subjects, directly and through my research assistants, routinely showing the footage to the subjects shortly after shooting it. But my real analysis of the behavior, coming much later, revealed aspects of that behavior that might well have been embarrassing to the subjects today. This is true for my footage from Sumatra, and even more so for the South Carolina footage in Chapter 3. The extraordinary advances in technology allows research unthinkable in the 1939s but also raises ethical problems unanticipated by earlier scholars.

# Part I
# Visual research projects

# 1 Microcultural incidents in Minangkabau children's emotion behavior

In my research among the Minangkabau of West Sumatra, Indonesia, most of the data that I analyzed come from Minangkabau talk addressed to me the ethnographer, what Minangkabau said or wrote in response to my interview questions or questionnaires (see Heider 1991a and 2011). But during my first two years of field research, in the 1980s, I also made extensive observations of 16 Minangkabau children. I made notes of what I saw and heard and also shot two hours of video on each child twice for a total of 64 hours of taping. In the days immediately following each tape session, I made a rough transcription of the tape with the aid of my research assistants. This taping turned up some extraordinarily rich interactions. Ray Birdwhistell termed such events as "microcultural incidents" (see his film, *Microcultural Incidents in Ten Zoos*). This is the sort of behavior that passes so quickly that it is almost impossible to capture by the usual pencil-and-notebook style of recording, but careful sifting through the videotape record allows one to identify these gems of data. We can begin with a particularly telling 60 seconds of interaction that comes from the videotape of Eva, one of the older girls in my sample. (I use pseudonyms for each child.) It was shot in 1983, when she was four years old. In this passage, anger and aggression are expressed and diverted in many different ways.

Here, I begin with an analysis of the brief clip of Eva, offering it as a model of what one can find in such "microcultural incidents." Then I go on to describe the entire study to demonstrate how analysis of the video record can turn up much more data than one could recognize with ordinary observations.

I was following Eva with my video camera for two hours one afternoon. She was playing with several other children from the neighborhood in and around her aunt's house. Not much happens: Eva has a minor fight with another girl and the aunt separates them. Here is the transcript, with my analysis on the right:

14  *Visual research projects*

|  |  | My Comments |
|---|---|---|
| Aunt: | Who's being naughty? (shakes right finger at Eva)<br>*Sia nan jahe?* | 1. Disingenuous |
| Eva: | *Si Budi!* | 2. Lies |
| Aunt: | (to Eva) Move on over there!<br>*Aniak kien!*<br>(to other girl): Sit here!<br>*Siko duduak!*<br>(to Eva): You can't do that!<br>*Indak buliah.*<br>It's naughty, not right.<br>*Nakal, ndak cap jempol.*<br>[literally: thumbs up brand] | 3. Direct command |
|  | I'll give you a flick<br>(e.g. with my finger, a mild punishment)<br>*Den jentil cie.*<br>(to other girl): Sit here.<br>*Siko tagak.* | 4. Threat |
| Eva: | Hit her one, Indra (to her little brother)<br>*Tinju no cie, Indra* | 5. Agent of a third party enters |
| Aunt: | I'm not going to take you to the ceremony (to Eva)<br>*Evam indak bau baleh.* | 6. Empty threat |
| Eva: | Esi can't go to the ceremony (taunting)<br>*Esi ndak bau baleh!* | 7. Empty threat passed on |
| Aunt: | Oh, just great! | 8. Sarcasm, verbal, and nonverbal |
|  | *bagus, cap jempol!*<br>(to other girl): Stand over there!<br>*siko tagak*<br>To Eva: Why are you following?<br>*ko ka marl je?*<br>I'll hit you.<br>*'bu lacui* | 9. Empty threat |
| The aunt now leaves the frame. Eva approaches the other girl, raises her right arm, then as the aunt returns to the scene, Eva's hand moves into a clasped position of innocence. || 10. Nonverbal dissimulation |

Note: the aunt speaks a mixture of Minangkabau and Indonesian, two closely related languages.

There are the following ten significant moves in this interaction.

1. **Disingenuousness.** The aunt enters, knowing full well that her niece Eva has caused the other little girl to cry, so her question "who's being

naughty?" is an indirect way of declaring "Eva has been being naughty." Shaking her finger in reproof is a gesture made to the general audience, but especially directed toward Eva.

2. **Lie.** Eva redirects the accusation in 1, above, blaming the crying on Budi, a boy standing nearby. (In fact, Budi rarely ever gets into fights except, as we shall see later, when he is at school.)
3. **Direct command and comment.** The aunt tells Eva that she can't do that, it's naughty. Here, she first uses a word for naughty, *nakal*, and follows it up with the verbal label for an emblem as she says that is not "*cap jempol*," or "thumbs up brand."
4. **Direct threat.** The aunt threatens to give Eva a finger flick to the ear, a mild form of punishment.
5. **Third party.** Eva enlists her little brother, Indra. She pulls Indra, who is now just two years old, between herself and the other girl and tells him to hit her.
6. **Empty threat.** One of the aunt's stock phrases for controlling the children of her neighborhood is to offer to take them or refuse to take them to some unspecified ceremony. But in fact there is no ceremony, and everyone knows that.
7. **Empty threat passed on.** Eva passes on the empty threat, disingenuously pretending that it is Ela, another girl, who will be deprived of the ceremony.
8. **Sarcasm.** The aunt says "good," using again the label for the thumbs up emblem which means good, and actually makes the thumbs up emblem with her right hand. But the words are said with a clearly sarcastic tone which reverses the meaning of both verbal and nonverbal messages.
9. **Nonverbal dissimulation.** The aunt briefly leaves for another room, Eva raises her hand as if to hit the other girl, but then as the aunt returns, Eva smoothly alters her arm position into a nonthreatening clasp of her hands.

So, here we have it. A 60-second slice of interaction between aunt and niece, with nine different sorts of anger and aggression, most of them quite indirect. This was hardly an atypical moment. Aunt and niece had been practicing this style of interaction for months and continued to hone it as long as I observed them.

Of course, my purpose in following Eva was to observe how she was being acculturated into Minangkabau patterns. But here we see her, at age four, already in masterful control of indirection. And, in fact, even as she is using her two-year-old brother Budi in her script, she is training him in indirection.

The segmentation of behavior in this way has a certain intrinsic logic. We begin as the aunt enters the scene and end when the aunt removes the other little girl from Eva's grasp. But of course, the other children were also involved in the preceding moments and continued to move about the house

16  *Visual research projects*

afterward. The frame of the video camera creates a somewhat artificial boundary to the event. And of course, long before that afternoon, the main characters had developed their roles as scolding aunt, naughty niece, complicit little brother, innocent bystander, and victim.

## Kilek jo bayang—the Minangkabau pattern of indirection

The main impression of this interchange is the intensity of ploys used by the girl and her aunt, and the variations which they play on indirection. I chose it to examine because it is such an elegantly condensed summary of typical Minangkabau interaction. The redirection of emotion, especially such a dangerous emotion as anger, is accomplished in a variety of ways through a variety of channels, verbal as well as nonverbal. There is a Minangkabau phrase, *kilek jo bayang*, which describes this indirection even as it itself is illusory. Literally, *kilek* (Indonesian: *kilat*) refers to the flash of lightning. And *bayang* refers to a reflection (which is an image arriving indirectly). The late Dr Khaidir Anwar, the leading Minangkabau linguist, once suggested to me that *kilek jo bayang* was like the strategy in billiards where, in order to get a ball to one destination, one banks it off the side in another direction. (He had lived in England.)

In fact, the interaction during this same two-hour period includes other examples of both direct and indirect statements:

| | |
|---|---|
| Direct: | Aunt to Eva: "don't be naughty" |
| | "you can't be naughty" |
| Indirect: | Older girl: "Budi will break the glass (if he doesn't watch out)" |
| | Aunt to children: "you'll fall" |
| | "you'll break your foot" |
| | Older girl to younger girl: "you'll fall down if you run like this" |
| | Older girl to Budi: "I'll be angry with you" |

## Engagement

It is especially noteworthy that each of the statements got no answer. They were not part of a dialogue. In fact, the passage describing the interaction between the aunt and niece is unusual because it does not represent a sustained give and take, however momentary.

## Videotaping versus pencil and notebook records

The brief example of interaction with which I opened this chapter gives an idea of the sorts of data that can be retrieved through a video record that would have been hardly noticeable, not to say accessible, with pencil and notebook. Now, I shall expand on the video project, culling from the many hours of video that I made of a few other Minangkabau children.

The ethnographic study of the role of culture in shaping emotion behavior invites a variety of approaches, each of which brings out aspects of emotion which slip past other approaches. In addition to the other more formal experiments and elicitations, in some of which I collaborated with psychologists (in particular Paul Ekman and Robert Levenson) to explore the more cognitive aspects of Minangkabau emotion (Heider 1991a; Ekman et al. 1987; Ekman and Heider 1988; Levenson et al. 1992; Heider 2011), I carried out these systematic observations of 16 Minangkabau children for two years over a period of three years. This was a longitudinal study designed to explore the ways in which the children acquired appropriate adult Minangkabau emotional behavior. These observations included as well the 130-minute videotape records of each child in the first and third years of the study. Now, I shall draw on five more of these videotapes.

The task was designed to combine the broad holism of naturalistic ethnographic observations with the systematic rigor of a more experimental approach. In my previous ethnographic research, on the Dani of Irian Jaya (Papua), Indonesia, I lived adjacent to a settlement with a population fluctuating around 50 people. I observed what happened in that area as I visited homes and strolled around the neighborhood. Over the years, I built up an overall idea of Dani life and behavior, which I formalized into two ethnographies (Heider 1970, 1997). Although I did some focused interviewing and systematic collecting of data, most of my time was spent wandering around watching, listening, and talking, following the flow of Dani life.

I designed this Minangkabau project very differently. Since so much had already been written about Minangkabau over the last century by foreigners, as well as Minangkabau themselves, there was no need to gather data for a first ethnographic description. My research was concerned with the cultural patterning of emotion, and it was possible to approach the problem directly.

I lived with my own family in a large rented house in the middle of Bukittinggi, which is a small mountain city in the Minangkabau heartland in West Sumatra. On weekends, I did things with my family, and one day a week I made the two-hour trip to Padang, on the coast, where I taught an anthropology course at Universitas Andalas, the provincial university. The remaining four days of the week were devoted mainly to emotion.

## Choosing the children

The ethnographer who settles in a village perforce sees and comes to study the people of the neighborhood. My strategy was different. I lived in a part of Bukittinggi where there were few Minangkabau children to study in any case, and I deliberately chose the children for the study from a wide area of Bukittinggi and environs. The first step was to find research assistants. In

18  *Visual research projects*

this, as in each step, I had the most incredible luck in finding three middle-aged women, all Minangkabau, all familiar with the area. They in turn located the children, accompanied me on my visits, helped me transcribe the Minangkabau and translate it into Indonesian (this was especially important during the first months as I was learning Minangkabau), and finally they helped me make sense of what was going on.

The size of the sample was a matter of compromise. There had to be few enough children so that I could make my rounds fairly often and get good data on each child, but there had to be enough children to assure some reasonably broad representation and so that the study would not be crippled if one child were to withdraw. Minangkabau are famous for temporary out-migration—*merantau*—especially to other islands, and I had to be concerned about how it might affect the study if a family suddenly decided to move away. As it happened, one family did move after my first visit and so I replaced their son with another boy. But over the next three years, I did not lose another child. (By 1987, several of the children had moved away from the area, and one had died.)

The model for this study was one which Gregory Bateson and Margaret Mead had carried out between 1936 and 1939 in a remote Balinese village (Bateson and Mead 1942; Mead and MacGregor 1951). Elsewhere, I have commented on this work at length (Heider 2007: 28–31), but here I need to compare their work with where we are now, 80 years later. (For more on the Balinese project, see Sullivan 1999 and Ness 2008.)

The Bateson and Mead Bali project is the first major landmark in what we now call visual anthropology research. A central feature of this project was a study of Balinese children as they grew into their own culture. The data were collected by the two principals, who had separately carried out notable fieldwork in Samoa and New Guinea. Mead (and their Balinese assistant) wrote down copious notes which were complemented by Bateson's 25,000 still photos and 22,000 feet of 16-mm movie footage. The main results were published in the 1940s and 1950s in two lavishly illustrated books and in four short edited films. Unfortunately, the reporting of the research ran into difficulties. By the time they were back in the US, they had begun to go their separate ways and World War II disrupted this further. Bateson was involved in the first book, but not in the second, and he apparently had little to do with editing the footage. As I began to put together my own project, I had the tremendous advantage of using a totally new generation of equipment. In the 1930s, Bateson had to use 16-mm film without sound, presumably in 100' reels running for three minutes. Fifty years later, I could shoot my videotapes for one hour, reload with a clean tape and shoot for a second hour. But most importantly, I was making records that were both visual and audial. This was not possible in the 1930s, certainly not in an isolated mountainside village in Bali. And it is clear how important it is to know precisely what is being said.

Bateson and Mead lived in the village and followed seven children born in 1936, just before or just after their arrival. An eighth child, the younger sister of one of the first, was born in 1938 and added after their main research in the village was finished. Of the seven, five were boys, two girls, and in fact the bulk of observations (as well as their four films) seem to have been made mainly on just one boy, Karba. There is an obvious danger in relying too much on a single informant, and subsequently there have been suggestions that Karba may have had an unusual personality for a Balinese. Since I lived not in a village, but in the relatively neutral center of the city, I had more freedom in choosing my children. I determined to begin with one-year olds and four-year olds, half of them boys, half girls.

I had planned two years of fieldwork, split in the middle by a year back in the US reviewing the data from the first year. So, I would be able to follow the one-year olds until they were four, and the four-year olds until they were seven, thus getting some coverage for the ages from one to seven. Having gender balance seemed particularly important for Minangkabau because of its gender complications: it is a matrilineal society with a particularly patriarchal religion, Islam. And prior to the Second World War and the Japanese occupation of Sumatra, gender differences were undoubtedly intensified by the mosque dormitory system, where the boys lived in relative isolation from females for several years before marriage.

For more details about the children, and the research schedule, please see the addendum at the end of this chapter.

## The goal of naturalistic observation

Naturalistic observation is limited to what spontaneously happens, and there is no way to assure the spontaneous occurrence of comparable events, especially if one is looking for emotion behavior. So, in the end, we are looking for significant anecdotes.

A major problem with presenting this analysis in print is confidentiality. The parents of the children were well informed about my goals and knew that I planned to publish the results of my research. At the end of each week, I brought the videotapes back to their houses to let them review what I had shot and to give them a chance to delete anything. In fact, people soon got bored with looking at themselves. No one watched a full two-hour tape, and there were no requests to erase anything. Yet, descriptions and analyses of emotion behavior could be embarrassing. This is especially true of behavior which exposes cultural norms by violating them. And, I knew that by the time these words would be in print, some of the children would be college students, reading English and perhaps studying anthropology. In fact, some years later, one of the children did enroll my own class on Antropologi Psikologi at Universitas Andalas.

With these concerns in mind, I have used pseudonyms (lifted from my class lists at Andalas). I have tried to omit identifying details and to stay away from the most sensitive events. The result is a flattened-out account drained of much specific flavor.

So, this is not claimed to be an account of randomly selected incidents in the lives of 16 randomly selected Minangkabau children. Here, we shall consider only five of the 16 children, drawing on video-taped events which illuminate particular aspects of their emotion behavior.

## Return to Eva, the first girl

The videotape records of two hours in the life of a child provide good data on the nature of interpersonal engagement. My presence, with camera and with my research assistants, certainly changed the flow of behavior. But this effect, so obvious in the first part of many of the tapes, diminished rapidly. The fact is, it is hard to maintain performance for very long, especially if the intrusive observers are determinedly neutral and low key, as we always tried to be.

The tape of Eva, made in 1986, the second year of the study, is especially good in showing this. Two years after the contest with her aunt, analyzed at the beginning of this chapter, Eva is now six, again hanging around her aunt's house. She is mainly playing with Derwita, another six-year-old girl in the neighborhood. Her brother Budi is not in evidence, but we see her with a new one-year-old sibling.

I have brought Eva a present, a set of plastic tea things. She spends a lot of the time sitting on the floor, totally absorbed in the new toys. She lays out the cups and saucers, pours imaginary tea from the pot, and serves imaginary guests.

Her interactions with real people are less engaged. When Derwita arrives, the aunt urges them to sing for me. They do try some school songs together, in an abstracted way, and Eva returns to her tea set, but Derwita is not included in this play. Four boys, also about six years old, drift in, spot the tea set, and take it over. There is no conflict. Eva simply slides away as the boys move in. They are more energetic. They pour drinks and several times toast each other (saying "tos!"). Minangkabau are quite Muslim, and such a toasting has no place in any Minangkabau interaction. I assume that the boys saw it in an American program on television.

The boys tussle with each other, rolling around on the floor, and do martial arts jabs at each other. There is a lot of body contact and touching, but no touching of the girls, and the two girls almost never touch each other.

When Eva's mother and baby appear, Eva has several brief rough interactions with the baby as her mother looks passively on. In each of these, Eva approaches, touches, then the baby begins to cry and Eva retreats. Once she harshly wipes the baby's nose and he cries; later she picks him up in such a way that he cries. And once, even though she pinches his cheeks, he doesn't react.

## Eva's emotion world

Eva at school was an entirely different person. There she sat silently in her seat, interacting with no one, not even those other little girls with whom she played so much after school. In the first year, she was in a village kindergarten, which was extraordinarily unruly compared to the other Minangkabau schools I visited. The two teachers were very young and inexperienced women and they were faced with a roving group of boys who specialized in disruption. But Eva, who at the same period, was so lively and even naughty at home, sat still and silent through the school day.

Eva's emotional world, seen in the three major sessions—an eight-hour observation plus the two videotaping sessions—can be characterized as one of brief engagements, low intensity, and much indirection. Eva at home was always on the move, flitting from activity to activity, often making contact with someone else, but except for the periods of solo involvement with the plastic tea set, or when singing the songs from school, Eva is never focused.

## The second older girl: Reni

Reni is another girl in the older group. Like Eva, she had a younger brother (named Nasrul) and another boy who was born just at the beginning of my study. Reni's father was often away from West Sumatra working, but her mother's brother lived nearby and often dropped in. So in that sense, she had a more traditional Minangkabau family life, ordered by her matrilineal clansmen.

## Nasrul, a naughty boy

In each of my visits to this house, ostensibly to see Reni, the action was completely dominated by her little brother Nasrul, by far the most obstreperous Minangkabau child I saw. Nasrul was constantly on the go, constantly being disruptive. Although he was not on my list of targets, I saw much of him. To give some feeling for his behavior, here are some of his acts in the first videotape session, when he was just two years old:

- He sticks out his buttocks at his mother
- He shoots at everyone in sight with a coat hanger saying

"I've shot everyone, they've had it!"
*Temback sadonyo, abih!*

- He threatens to drop a cloth out of the window
- He and Reni hit each other
- Reni accuses Nasrul (probably accurately) of farting
- Their mother tells him not to wave the stick around
- He uses scatological language
- He fights with Reni
- He comments disparagingly about one of my research assistants
- He shoots his mother's buttocks
- She accuses him (correctly) of farting

That is just 20 minutes of Nasrul at two. Two years later, he was even more disruptive and because of his greater strength, somewhat more dangerous. His behavior differs greatly from Eva, just described. Where Eva was always active, she played by Minangkabau rules and in fact, I began this analysis with her for that reason, that she so dramatically exemplified Minangkabau patterns. Nasrul broke Minangkabau rules in 1) his generous use of obscenities, mainly scatological/anatomical, both verbal and nonverbal; 2) his chaotic vandalism; and 3) his feints and direct physical attacks on everyone else, child and adult.

The others respond to Nasrul as people did to Eva, through indirection ("you are going to hit the baby") or directly ("come sit here"). Occasionally, people, especially his mother or Reni, made direct evaluatory comments on Nasrul. The most common phrase was "*akua jahe*," "you are naughty," or "*bodoh*," "stupid." The videotape record two years later shows the same pattern: Nasrul, the terror of the household, is barely controlled by others.

Of course, it was Reni whom I was really focused on. In the second videotaping session, when Reni was six, I brought her a plastic tea set like the one that I had given to Eva. But predictably, little Nasrul fought for the tea set from the moment of its appearance. Another girl, a classmate of Reni, came to play but they could not get the tea set away from Nasrul and eventually gave it up and went outside to play in the yard.

## Reni's emotion world

Even when Reni was four, her household was shaped by the need to manage Nasrul, her younger brother. So, we see Reni already as manager, more or less modeling on her mother.

## Summary after two children: naughty stupid children

Much indirection is used in interactions. Especially when an older person wants to instruct, chastise, or reform a younger person, there are two words which recur so frequently and seem so directly abrupt that they are worth special consideration.

**JAHE** occurs usually in a phrase like *akau jahe*, you are *jahe*. *Jahe* is perhaps best glossed in English as "naughty." It is usually used by a parent for a child, or by an older sibling to a younger sibling, although once in the second family, Nasrul used it to describe his older sister Reni. It is particularly interesting because of its relationship to its cognate: in Indonesian, the cognate *jahat* refers to more serious transgressions, and suggests real evil or sin. But the best translation equivalent of the Minangkabau *jahe* is the Indonesian *nakal*, a comparatively mild term used for children. Like the English word naughty, *nakal* and *jahe* could be used for more serious adult transgressions but more as consciously colorful speech.

There are other examples of this same phenomenon, which I have called a blue shift (Heider 1991a: 96). *Nafsu*, a word from Arabic, which in Indonesian (and especially in Acenese [see Seigel 1966]) is a very strongly negative "animal lust," in Minangkabau is a quite mild sort of "like," and in fact the translation equivalent of the Minangkabau *nafsu* is not the obvious choice, the Indonesian *nafsu*, but the milder Indonesian *ingin*.

The recurring pattern in this blue shift, then, is where the Minangkabau word A is not equivalent in strength to its Indonesian cognate A, but rather to a weaker Indonesian word B. Of course, Minangkabau precedes Indonesian. Historically, Indonesian is a recent language, coming into its own in the 1920s and developed out of traditional languages in the general Sumatra/Singapore area, where Minangkabau live. Individuals learn Minangkabau first and later through Minangkabau, they learn Indonesian. So it might seem more accurate to assume a "red shift." That is, people using these relatively mild Minangkabau words learn to use them with much more power when speaking Indonesian. Further pursuit of this phenomenon takes us too far afield. For the moment, let us just note that the word *jahe*, mildly naughty, is frequently thrown at these children.

The second word **BODOH**, is also used for and to these children. It has more interesting reverberations. At first glance, it just means "stupid," and is a mildly scolding word used for younger children who have violated some norm, for example:

The naughty two-year old Nasrul (Reni's little brother) is sitting with his feet too close to the plate which Reni is eating, and the mother says to Nasrul:

*Bodoh, awak uni kamakan!*
*Bodoh,* your sister wants to eat!

But this is not simply an abusive term. The implication is not so much of stupidity as of one who had not yet learned. The literature from elsewhere in Indonesia is suggestive. Hildred Geertz (1959) discussed the Javanese expression "*durung Jawa,*" not yet Javanese, and "*durung mengerti,*" not yet understanding. These phrases are used for children with the expectation that they will achieve Javanese understanding (the phrases are also used for adults who violate norms of respect toward others and for "mentally unbalanced persons.") But Geertz also stresses how careful Javanese are not to upset children by pushing them too fast. These Minangkabau children, on the other hand, are constantly being accused and corrected. "*Bodoh*" and "*jahe*" are not just Minangkabau understandings. They are epithets thrown at children. Ward Keeler, in his description of Javanese family dynamics does describe "thunderbolts of warning" hurled at children by their parents. But Keeler also mentions the "crude epithet, '*goblog*' (idiot)" (Keeler 1987: 65) hurled at children who do not use the refined linguistic forms of Javanese appropriately. Home's Javanese dictionary (Home 1974: 212) defines goblog simply as a coarse term meaning stupid.

But it is now clear from the context how *bodoh/goblog* are culturally charged. They refer to people, especially children, behaving inappropriately in important areas of culture involved with interpersonal respect expectations. In a similar vein, Benedict Anderson writes (Anderson 1966/1990: 145) that *bodoh* is applied to those who are not yet skilled in the nuances of political discourse. He says that appropriate use of language demands a special discipline, and is an indication of idealism and sophistication. But in an aside, Anderson raises two other issues somewhat more debatable:

> In the West stupidity is determined, and is a trait of fixed personality. We never talk of people "still" being "stupid." For the Javanese "stupidity" is the reverse of being "educated" or "awakened." It is therefore a failing that can, in theory, always be remedied (Anderson 1990: 145 fn8).

It is important to distinguish between *bodoh* or stupid as 1) a stage of personality development versus 2) a permanent personality trait versus 3) a characteristic of an act. But East cannot be distinguished from West on these grounds as absolutely as Anderson suggests. (I can say "that was stupid" of an act, or even "that was stupid of me," without implying that I am irremediably stupid). It is important not simply to translate *bodoh* as stupid, but perhaps more as "immature in social graces" in order to capture the development aspect which Indonesians so clearly understand.

Secondly, Anderson suggests that on the political stage, "stupidity" is the reverse of being educated or awakened. But certainly here, the opposite of bodoh for these children is "santiang," which I have translated in the past as "clever." Now, I would translate it as "mature." It is used for children who are not necessarily assumed to have reached that stage (and not for adults, who certainly should have).

### Older girl #3: Derwita

We have already met Derwita, another of the older girls, playing with Eva. Derwita has had serious health problems. When I saw her first at four years, she had just recovered from a serious illness and had been given a new name to symbolize and announce her recovery. She led a normal life, playing indoors and out with other children and going to kindergarten in the village. At school, she was silent and totally passive, but at home, she was cranky and contrary, alternately aggressive and sulking. The next year, she underwent a serious operation and when I saw her again as a six-year old, she had become very subdued and quite unresponsive even at home, and she never showed the same sparkle as the other children.

During the first videotaping session, in 1984, Derwita was constantly active. Her mother and another older woman often called "*bodoh*" at her. As we now expect, "bodoh" was used not for all misdeeds, but in instances when she violated the rules of respect:

- When Derwita bites the older woman's hand
- When Derwita slaps her mother
- When Derwita spits on her mother's face
- Again, when Derwita both slaps and spits at her mother

But two years later, after her operation, she is no longer active and is not chided. She sits on the floor, legs spread wide, which is not proper for a six-year-old girl. But no one reacts or corrects her. Eva's bossy aunt drops by for a social call, perhaps to check up on my progress and chat with my research assistants, and as Derwita runs across the muddy yard, the aunt scolds her mildly:

*Oi! Jatuah beko!*
Oh! You'll fall down!

Now, Derwita is slow and clumsy. As she is playing with the plastic tea set that I brought her, the naughty little Nasrul wanders in, watches her spill some water, and shouts:

*Mati lah, Derwita!*
Drop dead, Derwita!

Much of the time other children take over Derwita's tea set and as they play alternately quietly or raucously, Derwita sits in silence to the side, not participating. The only time during the second video session when anyone used the term "*bodoh*" was when Derwita, after numerous urgings by her mother, still refused to sing (a school-type performance, but here intended for my video camera). Then, Derwita's mother said:

*Bodoh tu, maleh hana!*
Bodoh, you're lazy!

This seemed an unusually mild breach of manners to draw the word "*bodoh*." In her one act of aggression, she accidentally on purpose bumps her mother in passing. This was the sort of act which two years earlier brought down a "*bodoh*" on her head, but now the mother ignored it. Derwita's unusual, even traumatic, history has removed her from any sort of typical Minangkabau pattern.

## The fourth older girl: Murni

Of the girls in the older set, Murni was the dazzler, doted on by her mother and showered with gifts by her mother's parents. Murni's mother is a strong, self-confident entrepreneur. Like several other mothers of these children she has gone into business working out of her home, but she is by far the most innovative and successful. More than most of the children, Murni was on display, prompted by her mother or her visiting grandmother.

When I first visited Murni, she hid in the back room of her house. Her mother called her repeatedly, saying she was "*bodoh.*" At this time, I was puzzled by this usage, but somehow relieved when her mother told me that she was "*malu*" (shy, ashamed). As we have seen in the analysis of *bodoh*, the mother was excusing Murni's shyness to me, but to Murni she was saying "you are impolite, breaking the rules of good behavior." Eventually, Murni did come out and soon became very comfortable with me. In fact, she was one of the most sophisticated of the children. During my second visit, the eight-hour stay, I brought Murni a piece of cloth as a present. She took it silently and her mother said "*eh, bodoh*" at her lack of acknowledgment.

Even Murni, certainly the most proper of the four older girls, shows a bit of aggression as she hits her grandmother in the face with the paper that wrapped the gift cloth. And later, Murni clambers all over a small metal swing, ignoring her mother's call to sit down in it. Later, she and another girl amuse themselves while grownups talk and she interjects an occasional word into the conversation. Once, as she walks around the adults, an old woman grabs at Murni's skirt as she goes by, then pulls it off in a sort of offhanded bawdy move. Murni turns around and hits at the old woman a couple of times, but no one reacts. One of my research assistants comments to me that Murni is "*lincah,*" energetic, compared with Derwita, who is "*diam,*" quiet.

During the first video session, Murni is nearly five. Her mother frequently calls Murni "*bodoh*":

- When she won't sing
- When she won't read the Koran for me
- When she won't answer (in contrast to Reni, who was "*rencak,*" good, and then the mother uses *rencak* when Murni does obey)
- When she picks her nose
- When she won't come back

Conversely, once the mother calls Murni *santiang*, smart, but Murni replies "*indak 'anti,*" not smart. The mother says that the girls are *pandai* at singing; the mother says that Murni is *santiang*; the mother says that Murni is *pandai* at jumping; and the mother twice says that Murni is *pandai* at holding her doll.

Two features stand out in this session with Murni. First, there is more talk in general going on than there was with the other three older girls. Second, although Murni is often called *bodoh*, her mother also often uses complimentary words like *rancak, santiang,* and *pandai*. Two of these words have cognates in Indonesian (*rancak, pandai*). These three words are all positive and between them cover an area of good, clever, and knowledgeable. In meaning, they are not quite antonyms, although they function as positive alternatives to the negative *bodoh* and *jahe*. But where *bodoh* refers to children who are not yet following the norms of politeness, these others refer to the skill with which a child does the right things. So, if Murni refuses to sing, she is impolite, if she sings she is skillful.

In the videotaped session two years later, when Murni was six, there was little of this close monitoring. Her mother was not present much of the time and when she was, her new baby absorbed her attention. Murni played actively with the other children. They developed elaborate fantasy games with the tea set I had bought, they sang, and they acted out episodes from a children's television series called Si Unyil. And Murni now was a disciplinarian, several times calling out *jahe* (naughty) at the other children for minor transgressions.

## The first older boy: Indra

Indra, whom we met at Eva's house, seems at first glance to be the most extraordinarily proper little boy, quiet, well-behaved, with perfect manners. The whole family: Indra, his mother, his younger sister, and (by the second year) his new little brother are always impeccably dressed. Even Indra's school uniform is cleaner and less wrinkled than those of his peers. The house is large, featuring a large common room with bedrooms and kitchen opening off it. There is the usual lounge set, a dining table, and in one area there are mats and a mattress spread out on the floor. This is where most interactions take place. On my arrival, we usually would sit first in the lounge set by the front door for a period of formalized greeting and then retire to the mats to talk more casually as the children's play swirled around us. The room seems especially cavernous because it is open to the bare metal roofing. During the frequent heavy rain storms, conversation is virtually impossible because of the drumming on the roof. The walls have the usual decorations: religious pictures, a clock, family photographs, and by 1985, a small television set appeared (but it was never turned on while I was present). Unlike many other homes, there were no toys in evidence. When children played, they adapted other things: pencils, ruler, even furniture to their play.

When I would arrive, Indra would be told to perform, not just to sing songs, as the girls had done, but to be grilled on words and numbers by his mother and my research assistants. A great show of approval and applause greeted his correct answers to the extent that even when he farted he was applauded by the women.

At first, it seemed that he was an angel at home, a devil at school. His home impression shaped by his extremely clean and attractive appearance and his command of a few basic acts of politeness like kissing my hand as I entered. But in many other ways, he seemed self-centered and indulged. During several different visits, he wolfed down snacks—usually pieces of cake not shared by his sister or visiting neighbor children. A distant contrast with the usual meticulous sharing which adults force on children.

There was little or no adult reaction when:

- He sat systematically destroying a candle
- He locked his sister out of the house, much to her displeasure
- He knocked over a radio more or less intentionally

Once when he was four, Eva's bossy aunt dropped by, perhaps to see what I was doing, perhaps to check on Eva, who was also visiting. The aunt gave Indra an intensive lesson in the choice of second person pronouns:

*Jan baa kau aka utu*
Don't call people *akau*
*Urana ba, aka utu, urana uriah*
People who say *akau* like that are people from upstream (upstream/downstream is a common dichotomy—upstream people are crude, unsophisticated, distant from the center)

It will be recalled that when the aunt remonstrated with Eva she spoke Indonesian, presumably for my benefit. Here, she instructs Indra in Minangkabau. Whatever the long-term effect of this on Indra may be, he immediately shouts at Eva a very crude epithet (*kanciang ko!*) and Indra's mother chides Eva:

*Jan di kadua juo Si Indra*
Don't disturb Indra!

Indra's pampering seemed to be summed up by a scene when he was still four: he ate alone, sitting on the mats, as his mother knelt beside him, serving his meal. Despite the strong matrilineal aspects of Minangkabau social and economic organization, many husbands are catered to in this manner by their wives. But here was four-year-old Indra, taking his father's place as a male to be deferred to.

Two years later, Indra had a 15-month-old little brother and Indra's behavior had changed. He spent much time looking after the little boy, including him in play, carrying him about, straightening his clothes. Even Indra's speech seemed less coarse. But his school behavior remained wild. There he was a little hellion, one of the gang of rover boys who take advantage of the teachers' youth and inexperience to keep the school in constant turmoil. He races about with his small gang, bumping other children, ignoring teachers' pleas, and challenging the older boys to fight.

## Conclusions

This longitudinal approach, incorporating videotaped records of children's behavior, reveals considerable variation even among these five children. It also tracks changes in their behavior over the three years' duration of the study. The use of video records of behavior and speech allows a fine-tuned description of their emotion talk and actions, and shows how early and thoroughly these children are using Minangkabau cultural patterns.

## Addendum: the subjects and the schedule of visits

My assistants and I selected 16 children—8 of them boys, 8 of them girls, 8 of them one years old, 8 of them four years old. Both parents of each child was Minangkabau, and I had specified that they all be first born (although with extended families and large village play groups, these is probably less of a birth order effect than there is in societies where children are brought up in nuclear families living in detached residences).

Actually, we were not able to locate children of exactly one year and exactly four years of age, and in the end, there was about a ten-month range for each age level.

Ages of the children at the beginning and the end of the study:

The 8 older children:

- At the beginning (September 1983):
  - four years six months to three years six months
- At the end (June 1986):
  - seven years three months to six years three months

The 8 younger children:

- At the beginning (September 1983)
  - one year one month to four months
- At the end (June 1986)
  - three years ten months to three years one month

It is relevant to note that my own three children fell into this same range. In September 1983, they were five years nine months, three years four months, and one year two months. Although they rarely accompanied me to visit the Minangkabau children, everyone knew about them and this awareness certainly eased my access to the Minangkabau families. Also, undoubtedly having an intimate knowledge of three comparable children affected my observations of the Minangkabau children.

Thus, the characteristics which I established for these children concerned age, gender, birth order, and parents' ethnicity. A fifth constant emerged as the result of asking for children who lived neither in the center of the city nor in isolated rural villages. Each of these children lived on the fringes of the city, in semirural areas within a ten- or twenty-minute bus ride from the center of the city, and so for their families marketing and jobs in the city were accessible and common.

I did not try to control variables related to status. This is a complex matter, especially among Minangkabau, who are ideologically egalitarian. (Mochtar Naim, the sociologist, has used the Minangkabau as the epitome of egalitarianism to contrast with the extremely hierarchical Javanese [1983].) But like that other ideologically egalitarian culture, the USA, Minangkabau society is actually stratified, or at least differentiated in a subtle manner. Generally speaking, families have a high status if they own much land, or have professional occupations, or are aristocratic (*bangsawan*) or a combination of two or three of these. Families have low status if they own no land and have low income manual labor occupations. By these criteria, the families of the 16 children varied widely and covered most possibilities. But it is my impression that the distance between the highest and the lowest in my sample, as in Minangkabau generally, is relatively slight. Certainly, there is neither the very rich nor the very poor whom one sees so obviously in Jakarta and in other areas of Indonesia.

Another social indicator, the education of the parents, also showed considerable range.

Of the 16 mothers:

- 25% had attended primary school but did not graduate
- 25% had graduated from primary school but did not go further
- Half had some secondary education, and one had attended a (religious) college

Of the 16 fathers:

- Two had only primary education
- Most had attended secondary schools
- Three had attended universities

The parents had their first born children relatively late in life. The mothers at ages 17 to 32, for an average age of 24.8; the fathers at ages 25 to 37, for an average age of 30.3.

Anecdotes about these matrilineal Minangkabau families, supported by anecdotes about patrilineal American families, suggested that the importance of having a girl to continue the (matrilineal) clan was so great that families who had only boys would be more likely to keep trying until they got a girl. There was only the slightest hint of this factor in the reproductive histories of the 16 families. Eight couples, after having only boys, had another child; 6 couples, after having only girls, tried again. Incidentally, although each of the 16 children was a first born, by the end of the third year of the study, all but three had at least one younger sibling.

## The visits

1. First visits in September 1983

Each sort of visit was paid to all 16 children. I never went alone, but always with at least one, and often all three of my research assistants. We were far from invisible. I am, at 6'4", considerably taller than any Minangkabau, and I was of high status as a professor at both the University of South Carolina and at Universitas Andalas, and in addition, of course, a foreign guest. In mitigation, I spoke adequate Indonesian from the beginning (all but one parent and all the children old enough to speak knew Indonesian) and I was learning Minangkabau. I sincerely like children, Minangkabau food, and living in West Sumatra. I did not pay any of the children, but usually brought small gifts; candy and photographs (and duplicates of the videotapes for those who wanted them). The three research assistants were each elegantly educated women. As might be expected, our relations with the families ranged from very warm and even collegial to occasionally strained. We visited only during the day, and usually the mother was around and often so was the father or other male relative.

The basic visits were:

- The introductory visits, September 1983
- Formal interviews with questionnaire, October 1983
- Eight-hour observations, November and December 1983
- Videotaping each child, two hours ten minutes, March to May 1984
  (In June 1984, I left West Sumatra, returning in July 1985)

- Second two hour ten minute videotaping, August 1985 to May 1986
  (In January 1986, I made brief visits to four Javanese children in the Yogakarta area and shot two hour ten minute videotapes of each of them for comparison with these Minangakabau tapes)

- With parent(s), eliciting attributes of the behavior of their children from the videotape records, May 1986

## Microcultural incidents embedded in ethnographic films

It may well be that ethnographic films have comparable nuggets embedded in their footage. For example, one of my own films, *Dani Sweet Potatoes*, is 19 minutes of sweet potato horticulture and food preparation. But I also slipped in footage of Dani child rearing. There are two sequences featuring a two-year-old girl, Hagigake, which are especially revealing. In one, she, her mother, and I are in a sweet potato garden as the mother is harvesting tubers. Hagigake is being a real nuisance, sitting on a mound her mother is digging, getting in the way, and then, when her mother removes her to the side, she quickly intrudes again. Finally, her mother can take it no longer and "inadvertently" slips, hitting Hagigake hard enough to make her cry and to crawl away from that particular mound. This is a wonderful moment, caught on video almost in its entirety, showing how Dani adults simply may not spank children, no matter what the provocation. So, the mother here must create an accidental hit.

A second, related incident, occurs as the sweet potatoes are being cooked in a steam bundle. The bundle has been loaded with heated rocks and tubers, the adults have retired into the houses surrounding the compound yard, and only Hagigake and a little boy are left playing around the coals of the fire that had heated the cooking rocks. The little boy lights a stick in the coals and he and Hagigake run toward a house. He waves the burning stick, seemingly about to light the roof thatch on fire. A men strolls past, takes in the scene, and passes by totally indifferent to the little arsonist. When I show the film to an American audience (and especially if it includes parents of small children), it invariably gets gasps of horror. In fact the man did not intervene, the thatch did not catch on fire, and actually in three years, I never saw any fire begun by careless children. But like the gardening scene described above, this was a realistic picture of typical Dani low-level child discipline. I did not spend narration time in the film discussing these two incidents because I was focusing on sweet potatoes, not children. But I suspect that many ethnographic films contain such telling moment, such microcultural incidents, if we would only look for them.

## 2 *Dead Birds* revisited: rethinking emotion in a New Guinea Dani funeral

This film is a famous example of the representation of the understanding that Gardner gained of a group of Dani in the highlands of West New Guinea in 1961. Gardner was aided by the other members of the Harvard-Peabody Expedition—among them, Jan Broekhuise, Peter Matthiessen, Michael Rockefeller, and myself. Here, I want to analyze ten minutes of the film to say something about the ethnographic enterprise itself.

By now, it is surely obvious that while a camera cannot lie, the use of a camera involves such a complex chain of choices that the resulting film is subject to all manner of subjective influences. In this spirit, I shall analyze a brief scene in a well-known ethnographic film to show how and why we got it wrong.

In 1961, Robert Gardner organized and led the Harvard-Peabody Expedition to Netherlands New Guinea, where he shot the footage for his film *Dead Birds* among the Grand Valley Dani. I was part of the expedition, serving as a back-up cameraman and ethnographic advisor. The expedition lived in the Grand Valley of the Balim for five months and then I stayed on, making several visits for a total of nearly three years, doing ethnographic research for my PhD dissertation and subsequent publications. In 1962, while I was still with the Dani, Gardner returned to New Guinea to screen a preliminary cut of the film (see Gardner 2007). By then, I had learned more about Dani culture and was able to correct some minor errors in the film. But on the whole, I was quite satisfied with it. That was in the 1960s, and much has changed in anthropology and filmmaking since.

A bit of background. Some 50,000 Grand Valley Dani live in the high valley of the Balim River in the western half of the island of New Guinea, what was Netherlands New Guinea until 1963 and is now the Indonesian province of Papua. When the Harvard-Peabody Expedition arrived in April 1961, the Dutch had pacified parts of the Grand Valley, but in some areas, warfare with bows, arrows, and spears continued. Christian missionaries had made some converts. But for the most part the Dani were still animistic, using stone axes and raising sweet potatoes and pigs.

*Dead Birds* follows events that we observed between April and August 1961, omitting much in order to come in at 83 minutes. The sound of the film was all added later for in 1960, when the equipment was bought and shipped to New Guinea, there was no portable synchronous sound equipment available that would withstand the rigors of New Guinea. And as was still the norm in those days, the film was given a heavy explanatory voice-over narration.

The film has been extensively discussed by Gardner himself (Heider 1972, Gardner 2006, 2007) and many others (e.g. Heider 1991b, 1997, 2006, 2007; Barbash and Taylor 2007), but almost exclusively on general cinematic grounds. Some virulent attacks on the film (e.g. Mischler 1985) have been made by people with no first-hand knowledge of the Dani.

What I want to do here is to revisit one sequence in the film in the light of what we think we know about the Dani and emotions six decades later. To repeat, when I had the chance to vet the film after my first full year with the Dani, I had no major reservations about the ethnographic accuracy. I do not know how many times I have watched it since then, but I still find it compelling. However, there is one scene about which I now have second thoughts.

## The boy's funeral

Toward the end of the film, a sacred stone renewal ceremony is interrupted by the killing of a local boy in an enemy ambush. The ceremony is postponed for a few days and the film cuts away to follow the boy's funeral. During the first day of the boy's funeral, the corpse is placed on a special chair erected in the courtyard of the boy's compound. Cowrie shell bands are draped on the corpse, and pigs are slaughtered, butchered, and cooked in steam bundles. Mourners gather from across the alliance area. The cowrie shell bands are redistributed to the appropriate kin. The funeral pyre is prepared and lit. The corpse is smeared with pig grease one last time and laid on the pyre. A grass bundle is held over the pyre, shot with an arrow, and carried out the entrance of the compound to speed the departure of the boy's soul matter.

Throughout, we hear the dirging of the people, hosts, and visitors, sitting on the ground in the courtyard. This was nonsync wild sound recorded by Michael Rockefeller at the ceremony and laid into the film in the editing process. Periodically, a new group arrives bringing pigs (from members of the boy's patrimoiety) or shell bands and nets (from members of the opposite moiety). The newcomers can be heard from a distance dancing and dirging their way through the sweet potato fields toward the cremation site. Stopping outside the compound entrance, the group reforms, makes an entrance, and holds just inside the courtyard. The men of the compound, the hosts of the funeral, who have been sitting at the far end of the courtyard in front of the men's house, rise to greet the visitors. For a few minutes, the hosts and the guests sing an antiphonal dirge, commenting on the death: "Weyakhe has been killed," "Killed by the

Widaia." As they sing, they weep, wiping their tears on their legs. For virtually, the entire ten minutes of the funeral sequence, the sound track carries this penetrating dirging.

It is a powerful moment in the film. I had had little experience with death or funerals and was overwhelmed. I think that the other members of the expedition had similar reactions. The funeral sequence as shot and edited by Gardner and endorsed by me a year later presents the power and poignancy of the event.

But it didn't actually happen that way. Indeed, during the course of the event, each time when a visiting group had taken their places, the hosts rose and the antiphonal dirging began. But it would only last a few minutes until broken off as the two groups met, shook hands, lit cigarettes, and caught up on each other's news. The atmosphere was constantly changing from deep sorrowful mourning to casual everyday chatting and back again. We of the expedition (I think that I remember accurately) were put off, even offended, by this abrupt alternation of deep emotion and banal chat. One man, who was the most dramatic dirger (until he turned it off), we disparagingly dubbed "Willie the Weeper."

Needless to say, this switching on and off was not shown in the finished film. The funeral scene was edited so that the intensity of sorrow appropriate to the event was maintained through the entire ten minutes of the scene.

At this point, the reader might well be appalled at the distortion of Dani emotion behavior that we created. But the purpose of this paper is to explain what happened in our creation of the ethnography of this ethnographic film. Some background is useful here:

Gardner and I had been trained during the 1950s in anthropology at Harvard by distinguished scholars like Clyde Kluckhohn and Cora Du Bois. I think that it is fair to say that thanks to our preparation we got most things about the Dani right. Those aspects of culture that were on the anthropological agenda of the 1950s such as kinship, symbolism, social structure, and exchange were what we had looked for and re-presented in the film and in our written works. But emotion was not yet an anthropological concern. I do not remember Kluckhohn or Du Bois or any others talking about emotion. Indeed, in the late 1950s, especially at Harvard, we were excited about ethnoscience, an early formulation of cognitive anthropology. We explored the ways in which different cultures organized their world in categories—categories of kinship terms, categories of firewood, and any other sets of categories significant or banal. It was nearly ten years later that Jean Briggs published her book, *Never in Anger* (Briggs 1970). Briggs, a student of Du Bois, had gone to the Arctic to study Inuit shamanism but her hosts had become Christians and denied knowing about shamans. So, marooned there for the winter, she invented the anthropological study of emotion.

My own route to the study of emotion was slower. My dissertation research with the Dani began with a study of their material culture. In the summer of 1960, I had done archeology for the University of Pennsylvania at the classic Maya site of Tikal in Guatemala, excavating a thousand-year-old house mound and working on the artifacts we recovered. When Robert Gardner invited me to join his expedition to New Guinea, I accepted. It was an easy transition from thousand-year-old Mayan stone axes to the very similar stone axes being used by the Dani in the 20$^{th}$ century.

Gradually, I expanded my research into a broad ethnographic account of the Dani culture. By my third year in the Grand Valley, I was just beginning to study Dani psychology, including emotion behavior. By the 1980s, I had narrowed my entire focus of research to emotions and I began research in West Sumatra, home of the Minangkabau, where I spent nearly three years. As I became more and more involved with emotion research among the Minangkabau, I continued to think, write, and teach about the Dani, and wondered what I had missed by my inattention to Dani emotions. Gradually, I began to see the significance of what we had left out of the boy's funeral.

Clifford Geertz, in a much-quoted passage, wrote:

> "The Western conception of a person as a bounded, unique, more or less integrated motivational and cognitive universe, a center of awareness, emotion, judgment, and action organized into a distinctive whole and set contrastively against other such wholes and against its social and natural background, is, however incorrigible it may seem to us, a rather peculiar idea within the context of the world's cultures."
>
> (Geertz 1983: 59)

Similarly, I had written that:

> "Indonesian cultures on the whole place more emphasis on social interaction, Western cultures on the whole place more emphasis on inner states of autonomous individuals."
>
> (Heider 1991b: 9)

Like any generalization, this inner state versus interaction distinction must be used cautiously, but it does suggest some insights (see, for example, my use of it in analyzing Indonesian cinema, Heider 1991b: 28–34). Applied to emotion behavior, we can suggest that for emotions at a funeral, some cultures will use a more interactional script, while others emphasize a more inner state script.

I have already claimed that Gardner and I used our own anthropological training to understand those aspects of Dani behavior that had been subjects of anthropological attention in the 1950s. Now, I take this a step further to suggest that when it came to emotion, which had been neglected by anthropologists at the time, we intuitively fell back on our own folk models. And for both of us, these folk models were very much toward the autonomous, inner state individual end of the spectrum. Specifically for funeral behavior, one should feel, or at least display, an inner state of sadness throughout the event. And that is why we reacted to what we considered an inappropriate, even callous or hypocritical switching on and off a display of sadness. And that is why the film presents what we could term a New England, not a Dani, stream of emotion behavior. (More recently, I have spent decades in South Carolina embedded in a wide social network, and this experience has broadened my ideas of possible appropriate funeral behaviors considerably.) On the other hand, the Dani follow an interactive scenario, which stipulates times for display of intense grief and other times of relaxed collegiality. The emphasis is on the correct display, and not nearly so much on deeply felt emotion.

But this raises the question of audience reaction. How would one edit the funeral showing the interactive scenario in such a way that a New England audience would appreciate it? One could consider a little didactic lecture in voice-over narration, but that would create its own problems.

In an earlier scene in *Dead Birds*, a battle between our friends and the enemy Widaia is broken off when a heavy rain begins. We see warriors ducking into a garden shelter away from the battlefield and the narration says "many are worried that the rain will spoil their hair or feathers." This is true, but American audiences sometimes snicker at it and get the idea that Dani warfare is merely frivolous play.

Recently, I have often thought of trying to re-edit ten minutes of the funeral, to create a different account, assuming that Gardner had kept his camera running during the different phases of the interactive scenario. At least as a thought experiment, it leads us into some important issues in ethnographic filmmaking that lie beyond the scope of this book.

It helps to think of the origins of a ten-minute film on a funeral. This is the result of extensive choices. The day of the funeral had perhaps 12 hours of events. The camera was shooting for perhaps two hours of that time and even then its lens was directed to only a tiny slice of the action. Then, from that two hours of footage, the editor chose only ten minutes to include in the final version. We see an extraordinarily brief fraction of the total possible. So the question is, how was the selection accomplished?

But meanwhile this story illustrates what I have called The Rashomon Effect (Heider 1988), named after Kurosawa's famous film in which four different witnesses give four different accounts of an encounter in the forests of Medieval Japan. In ethnography, also, what the investigators see and choose to tell us is influenced by their culture of origin and their particular anthropological training, the intellectual baggage that they bring to the enterprise, to mention only two important factors.

Thus, an ethnographic film or, in this case, a sequence in an ethnographic film is not simply a privileged account of some cultural behavior. This sequence of a Dani funeral is a cultural construct and can be analyzed in its own cultural terms even as the filmmaker, through his shooting and editing, is analyzing the funeral itself.

# 3 Comparing styles of teaching and learning in some South Carolina and West Sumatra kindergartens: video-cued multivocalic ethnography (by Karl G. Heider and Louise Jennings)

## Introduction

This research had its origins in the mid-1980s, when Heider spent two years in Indonesia studying the cultural construction of emotions among the Minangkabau of West Sumatra. Since the 19th century, Minangkabau have been committed to formal European-style education (in addition to Koranic training) and they enthusiastically support their schools.

As described in Chapter 1, one of the projects in my emotion research during the 1980s was the close observation of 16 Minangkabau children, hoping to catch them in the act of learning and expressing appropriate Minangkabau emotion behavior. (That project was patterned after the study that Gregory Bateson and Margaret Mead made of Balinese children 50 years earlier [Bateson and Mead 1942].) Toward the end of my research, I was following the older children to their first grade classrooms, where I watched them interact with their classmates and their teachers. Thus, I began with focusing on individual children and backed into classroom ethnography almost by accident. The three schools I had come to know made a dramatic contrast set.

One of these schools served a village on the outskirts of the city of Bukittinggi. It was at best a makeshift operation, run and taught by two teen-age women who did their best to control an unruly group of children. The second school had been organized by a talented dancer who ran a very tight ship. The third school, sponsored by a Muslim foundation, was organized along strict lines by an imposing Minangkabau woman with a doctorate in Education from an American university, and the curriculum had a strong Muslim component.

But in the mid-eighties, I was not thinking in terms of schoolroom ethnography and so was not prepared to appreciate the possibilities of these schools except in the relatively narrow sense as a venue for emotion behavior. However, when I returned to the US, and was working up the data, I read *Preschool in Three Cultures* (Tobin et al. 1989) and suddenly realized the potential of schoolroom data.

## Tobin et al.

Joseph Tobin and his colleagues had developed a powerful methodology. They observed preschools in three cultures: the US, China, and Japan, making video records of one day in each school (Tobin et al. 1989). They first showed selections from the videos of preschool teachers in the same country, asking if the target school was reasonably typical of that country. Then, they showed the videos to teachers and parents in the other two countries to elicit their impressions: how were these other schools different or the same as their own, and how did they evaluate the differences? In 2002, Tobin did a new study, doubling the number of schools to two in each country, working with a new set of collaborators, and published a new report, *Preschool in Three Cultures Revisited* (Tobin et al. 2009). They now term the multivocalic research method "video-cued multivocalic ethnography."

The great advantage of this research design is that it draws on local expertise—the teachers themselves—to identify and evaluate important differences between preschool styles. It adds tremendous analytical power to the investigation. I think that it is fair to say that even the most experienced scholars would miss things that would be obvious to a teacher looking at video records of schoolroom behavior in another culture.

## The research schedule

### The year 2000

With the Tobin model in mind, I included some kindergarten classroom observations in my research plan for the second round of emotion research when I returned to West Sumatra for another eight months, split between early 2000 and late 2001. It turned out that in the intervening 14 years since my previous research, the schools had been reorganized. Now kindergartens were all run by Muslim foundations, and followed a national curriculum with a strong Muslim component. I arranged to visit three kindergartens in the city of Bukittinggi once a week in a three-week cycle. So, each Wednesday morning for 12 weeks, I spent a couple of hours in a kindergarten. I was accompanied by my two Minangkabau research assistants, women in their late 60s who had helped me in the 1980s and now again arranged interviews and generally served as chaperones. (Minangkabau are not, relatively speaking, strict Muslims, but I always visited women informants with my research assistants, to make everyone more comfortable.) A University of South Carolina anthropology graduate student, David Lyon, ran the video camera as I took notes. The two women sometimes joined us in the classroom, and sometimes sat chatting outside.

In my notes, I paid special attention to evidence of emotion behavior, and the teacher's instruction in and control of such behavior. The standard video camera use was to first establish the schoolroom context with some wide sweeping pans. Then, since the camera lens could not include the entire classroom in a single frame, most of the time was spent concentrating on one section of the room. The camera zoomed in only occasionally to pick up details of events, but never to follow a single individual for a long period of time. This is difficult. The temptation to use the zoom capability of the lens is hard to overcome, for close-ups seem important and revealing. But the tighter the camera is in on one person, the less chance there is to catch interaction. (In 2001, the second year of this project, I had no camera assistant, so I would set the camera up on its tripod and let it run for an hour, thus resisting zooms.)

But this raises the first crucial problem: when filming something like classroom interaction, is it more effective to zoom or not to zoom. I chose not to zoom in, and so missed close-up views of significant behavior. Tobin carefully selected prime subjects whom he thought would provide the best data and focused on them and so missed what may have been happening out of frame. Bringing in a second (or third?) camera is another strategy, but it greatly increases the intrusiveness of the research team and introduces the problems of coordinating and synchronizing the multiple video records. I have no ideal solution, but it is well to be aware of the dilemma.

As I was leaving West Sumatra in 2000, I showed clips from the videotapes to two focus groups, each made up of three kindergarten teachers in Padang, the provincial capital. I wanted to get reactions to these tapes from Minangkabau teachers, and since Padang is 100 kilometers from Bukittinggi, I could assume that these teachers would not know the schools that I had been observing. I also asked these women some general questions about education.

## *The year 2000–2001*

Between the two field research periods, I spent a year back at the University of South Carolina, where I had a chance to work over the data, rethink my research plans, and talk with colleagues about it all. Louise Jennings, then on our School of Education faculty, had been doing similar classroom ethnography in the US, and we decided to collaborate on this project. Through her contacts, we visited kindergarten classes in Columbia, South Carolina, closely replicating the procedure in Bukittinggi. In a second session, we showed clips from the Bukittinggi tapes to the two South Carolina teachers for their reactions.

Jennings and I each took the opportunity to show video clips from the first set of Bukittinggi tapes to our graduate seminars at the University of South Carolina, asking the students to analyze the classroom behavior and comment on whatever struck them. This added voices to the multivocalic approach.

## The year 2001

In July 2001, I returned for the second four-month research period in Bukittinggi. I had promised the Bukittinggi principals and teachers that I would return to spend more time with their schools, and that I would show them tapes from the US kindergartens. Jennings received funding to come to West Sumatra, and I now explained that in October, she, a real education expert, would visit each of the Bukittinggi schools for a week each, and would talk with the staffs at length. But my research, visa process was more complicated than usual. I was given a three-month visa instead of the six-month one, I had requested, and was told to reapply in October for a month extension. So, Jennings' travel plans were on hold. By early October, when I was granted a month extension, the aftershocks from the September 11 terrorist attacks in the US were being felt, and in the end, Jennings did not come to Indonesia at all. So, I finished up the research on my own, showing the US videotapes to the Bukittinggi teachers and to the two Padang focus groups. This time I had spent 4-, 3-, or 2-hour recording at each school. Despite the unforeseen problems, we did gather those various sorts of data that provide a "multivocalic analysis" of the teaching and learning in South Carolina and West Sumatra.

## Multivocalic analysis: comparing US and Indonesian kindergartens

### The researchers' view

There are many quite obvious differences between these South Carolina and West Sumatra kindergartens. The South Carolina kindergartens are attached to a neighborhood primary school and students drift in to their classrooms as they arrive on foot, dropped off by a parent, or by a school bus. In West Sumatra, the students of each school live more scattered around the entire city area, are delivered by parents or more usually by minibuses, and mill about in a front yard waiting for the formal opening of the school day.

The American students are dressed informally and with great variation. The Minangkabau students wear the uniform of the day. (There is one national uniform for each level—primary, middle school, and high school—but each kindergarten is free to design their own uniforms and these three schools had a different uniform for each of the six school days.)

As the American students entered their classrooms, they were greeted by the teacher and the teacher's assistant and slowly the class was organized. In the Indonesian school, the teachers and students of all classes met together in the yard during the first 15 or 20 minutes for opening exercises. The students were grouped by classroom in military-like rows and files, they did stretching exercises, were lead in songs and prayers and special announcements. I was formally introduced both years and asked to make a speech. I told the students about my family and how, when I lived in Bukittinggi in the 1980s, two of my children attended kindergartens like theirs.

American parents who dropped off their children left them at the front door of the school building and vanished; there were always a few Indonesian parents who hung around at the fringes of the yard watching until the students went inside to their rooms.

Indonesian students had individual cubbies for their shoes in many classes, but not all. In some they wore only stockings, in others they did wear shoes. And they did have drawers for work materials. American students each had hooks for their outer wear and cubbies for their work materials.

In both cities, the classrooms were laid out with one or two carpeted areas where the students could sit together for group instruction. There were also work tables with chairs for doing special tasks. The walls were covered with decorative and/or didactic posters or other materials. The American classroom decorations were more individualized, featuring names and accomplishments of the children, their birthdays, and records of their new teeth. The Indonesian classrooms had posters featuring membership in the "100 Club" (both Arabic- and European-derived), numbers (also, both Arabic and European style), fruits and vegetables, and prayer instructions, but no students' names.

The American classes had about 15 students each, with one teacher and one teacher's assistant; the Indonesian classes had about 30 students each, with one teacher and one teacher's assistant.

*From Heider, the anthropologist*

One of the underlying cultural themes that I had paid most attention to in my emotion research was the greater Indonesian emphasis on groupism compared to the American emphasis on individualism. But it turned out to be far from the extreme difference that I had expected, either in the realm of emotions or here, in classrooms. Some descriptions of the classrooms of American Indians, who are presumably more group-oriented than the US population as a whole, have claimed that students are unwilling to put themselves forward, to stand out in any way from their classmates. Although in many respects, from uniforms to wall decorations, Minangkabau tend toward the groupist end of the spectrum, there is much individualism evident in classroom behavior. Even in these kindergarten classes, when the teacher would ask questions, hand would shoot up, offering to answer. Most students were eager to be called up to perform individually in front of the class.

## From Jennings, the school ethnographer

Whereas Heider's impressions relate more to culture, not surprisingly, my impressions refer to pedagogical similarities and differences. I have been researching how learning activities can be structured to give children opportunities to take initiative, develop responsibility, and solve problems. Such opportunities continue to be more the exception than the rule in American classrooms, and I found this to be the case in the Indonesian classrooms as well. Kindergarten in the US, and in much of the world, is very much geared toward socializing children to perform well in the role of student for the next 12–16 years. Such socialization usually involves helping children learn interactions including: following instructions, remaining silent until you are addressed, sitting still through much of the day, waiting to be asked a question, raising your hand when wishing to answer a question or have one of your own, learning how to write on prepared lesson sheets, playing well with other children during designated play time, and learning how to share materials and cooperate with your peers and teachers. Even with a growing number of children attending preschool in the US, kindergarten is seen as the launching ground for socializing children into acceptable and productive school behaviors, as well as a place for gaining basic skills in reading, writing, and math. Although there were variations between the Indonesian classrooms and the US classrooms that I had experienced as a student, teacher, and researcher, it appeared that the general purposes were strikingly similar. Given my interests as a researcher, I was hoping to see greater differences, as I continue to look for classroom and school cultures that socialize children to become active, thoughtful, critical agents in their local and larger communities.

## The University of South Carolina students react to the Indonesian tapes

### Department of Anthropology

The 13 participants in my Psychological Anthropology seminar were anthropology undergraduate and graduate students. Two had taught at the secondary school level but none had had any recent experience in kindergarten classrooms. They had read *Preschool in Three Cultures* (Tobin et al. 1989) and had seen the videotape that accompanies that book. They were primed to think in terms of individualism versus groupism. But overwhelmingly, they were impressed with how similar the Indonesian classrooms were to American kindergartens. They identified examples of group conformity—the uniforms of both students and teachers, the military-style formations of the opening exercises, and such. But they were also struck by the times when the Minangkabau children were free to play or work on their own. Many wrote about how happy these children seemed. Several noted instances of gender separation when the girls played with housekeeping toys as the boys did reading or writing exercises.

## School of Education

Jennings was teaching qualitative research method classes that involve 18–25 graduate students, the majority of whom were experienced teachers and educators. She gave her students in two different classes copies of segments from the Indonesian videotapes and asked them to use the data analysis technique they had been learning to analyze the tapes. Of course, they had to focus on the nonverbal interactions since all but one student knew no Indonesian. Like Heider, Jennings was surprised that most students saw more similarities than differences between Indonesian and US classrooms. Many teachers commented that there were virtually no distinctions, except for language, the use of prayer, and uniforms. Many also noted that there were fewer materials in the Indonesian classrooms. Otherwise, they found that activities were similar, with classroom instruction where students were seated on the rug and/or at their tables, "center time," where children moved in small groups from one activity (e.g. blocks) to another (e.g. working on an art project). Many students commented on the smooth transitions from one center to the next in one tape, and the higher tolerance for noise in another segment than would be found in most US classrooms. A variety of teachers found the use of a tambourine by one teacher to be a very effective tool for managing transitions.

## The two American kindergarten teachers react to the Indonesian tapes

In South Carolina, we were referred by a colleague to two kindergarten teachers, whom we call Mary and Denise. These two teachers were recommended because they taught in a school in a small southern city, rather than suburban school, and because they were viewed as strong teachers who were familiar with video cameras in their classroom due to their collaboration with other university researchers on literacy education. They are two European American women who have taught for almost 30 years and 15 years respectively. They were both in their first year of teaching at a school that served students who were mostly African American (about 85%) as well as European (about 10%), and in a working class neighborhood.

Mary and Denise were struggling with what they viewed as issues of classroom management; several students in each class could be uncooperative and might have outbursts that landed them in the principal's office. Mary and Denise commented that their experiences at other schools presented some of those challenges, but not to the extent that they faced in this school. They found the principal supportive, but at the end of the school year, they remained frustrated with some students' behavior. When we showed them tapes of very effective lessons in their own classrooms, Mary and Denise expressed some surprise at how well the students were engaging in the classroom activities. They realize that they expend much of their energy on trying to keep the class running smoothly and they hadn't realized how much the children had learned various reading, writing, and math skills. They commented that the principal had often remarked on how well their students were doing academically, but they admitted that it was hard for them to see that progress when they felt the children could have learned much more if they have fewer behavioral problems in the classroom.

This is an important context to consider as we outline some of the impressions that these two teachers had of Indonesian classrooms. Like the graduate students, the teachers felt that, in many ways, the classrooms looked "just like us!" Children worked in small groups as well as engaging in whole class lessons, they moved to different "centers," and the classrooms were brightly decorated. They also remarked on the practicality of the school uniforms, which they wished they had, and noticed that there were fewer materials in the Indonesian classrooms compared to theirs.

Several times, Denise and Mary commented on how well behaved the Indonesian children were. Denise remarked, "they transition well (from one activity to the next), they aren't aggressive toward each other at all." They discussed one of the school's morning exercises and commented that they would not be able to keep their children standing in such neat rows. They also noticed that it seemed permissible for individual children to disengage from a learning activity, to go off and "do his own thing." Denise commented on her experience teaching children who were learning English as a second language, noting that some children, especially boys, from other countries also had a tendency to "wander off and do their own little thing." "It takes them about a month to realize that they need to move along with the rest of the class. You can't just get up and go to the playground," she said. Denise noticed that, like their classes, the Indonesian classes would move from a whole class, collaborative activity to individual activities (when the children were playing the musical instruments that they had made). While many American observers commented on the high noise level, Denise was not uncomfortable with it. "That's what I call working noise. I don't really mind working noise." In sum, the two teachers found the Indonesian classes very orderly and productive.

Academically, these two teachers saw more differences between the Indonesian classrooms and their own classrooms compared to the graduate students in Jennings' class, who mentioned few academic differences. Mary and Denise were surprised that the Indonesian children were not engaged in more higher level literacy activities; they did not seem to be reading or writing much. The teachers commented that at the end of the school year, they would expect children to be beyond naming items, such as a paintbrush and pencil, as the children were doing in one of the tapes, and to be reading and writing at a beginning level. They saw little evidence of literacy engagement in the Indonesian classrooms. This is not surprising, given these two teachers' recent involvement in a professional development opportunity to improve literacy education. We asked how these classrooms compared to most kindergartens in the US. Mary and Denise agreed that the Indonesian classrooms were more akin to what American classrooms looked like 10–20 years ago with an emphasis on "learning letters and numbers." Denise noted that the children individually worked on phonics through computer lessons now in her classroom, allowing her to engage children more in reading books. (Neither teacher remarked on the lack of computers in the Indonesian classrooms). Upon further reflection, the teachers did think that many US teachers probably continue to focus on phonics and less in holistic reading experiences, as that was their own experience in school. Although there was a shift away from phonics and toward more authentic reading experiences. Denise noted that more materials are available to help teachers engage children in reading, such as "Big Books," with large print and corresponding illustrations that are designed to help children learn to read. "Children started coming to school knowing their letters and numbers from watching Sesame Street—if they already have those skills, then they can move on to other skills in kindergarten." Both teachers also noted that some groups of children come to school at a disadvantage if they don't possess basic literacy skills when entering kindergarten, yet children were tested with an expectation that they would have those skills, and if not, they would be enrolled in special literacy programs, sometimes struggle to keep up, and perhaps not succeed in school. In other words, some inequities grew when expectations for kindergarten children grew over the past few decades.

The two teachers also realized that they are more apt to help children "figure things out" than their Indonesian counterparts. For example, after watching several centers where children drew, and perhaps wrote, in uniform booklets and put together small art projects, Mary commented that she knows a lot of teachers who do that. "I know that's one thing we're trying to get away from—crafts and worksheets," she added. When asked what they would do similarly or differently in one of the activities on the tape, Denise saw a missed opportunity to help children figure out the number of materials that they needed rather than simply tell them.

Mary and Denise reflected on their own growth as teachers throughout the interview. They realized how their involvement in the professional development program to improve literacy education has helped them to improve as teachers. For example, they noticed that they integrated the content areas more (teaching math through reading), were more likely to help kids figure things out instead of telling them, engaged them much more in rich literacy experiences, such as reading out of "Big Books," writing journals, etc. They also now structure opportunities for children to learn from play. "When activities are structured so that children think 'I don't have time to think, I just have to do what you told me to do,' they never learn to be autonomous—if we are going to regiment, that's a problem."

### Indonesian teachers from each of the three schools react to the American tapes

We had planned for Jennings to spend time in October 2001 with each school, observing the classrooms through an entire week's cycle (for two years, I had only visited on Wednesdays) and doing extensive interviews with teachers and principals. Because of the September 11 attacks on the US, she did not come to West Sumatra, and in the end, I did only a single exit interview at each school, showing the teachers clips from the US classroom tapes and trying to elicit their thoughts about the American kindergartens. Each session was scheduled for an after-school hour, when the teachers were tired and distracted by their own children. And in any case, they were more interested in cross-questioning me about how US kindergartens were run. Unfortunately, that is not my area of expertise and I felt considerable embarrassment at my unsatisfactory answers. I told them that the American teachers were positively impressed with the opening exercises, with the school uniforms, with the good behavior of the students, and with the brightly colored tables.

They were surprised to see that the US teachers sometimes sat as they presented their lessons, for Indonesian teachers are not allowed to sit. They all said that the US schools seemed to have much more in the way of educational materials available. The Indonesian teachers frequently used the word *bebas*—free—to describe the American students' behavior, their ability to choose their own tasks, as well as the clothing of both teachers and students.

### The two focus groups of Indonesian kindergarten teachers from Padang react to the Indonesian tapes

In the first meetings with the two Padang focus groups, in May 2000, I began by asking them some very general questions about Indonesian education. (I had in mind what Elizabeth Colson once wrote (Colson 1974) about John Ogbu's research: as an outsider from Nigeria, Ogbu got away with asking some questions in a California city—questions that would be so ridiculously simple-minded that they would not be taken seriously had they been asked by an American.) Thus, I could ask "why do children go to kindergarten, why not learn at home?" The answers revealed fairly low opinions of home life as compared with the experiences offered by the kindergartens.

These teachers said that home learning is haphazard and informal, and children learn only from family, are exposed to coarse language and substandard manners, and have few toys to stimulate creativity and thinking.

At kindergartens, on the other hand, the teachers provide formal lessons, teaching the children good values (*adat-istiadat*), independence (*mandiri*) in things like eating, patterns of belief (*akidah*), and, with the toys and other objects found at the school, the children develop their thinking skills and creativity. And they learn amongst children of their own age, making friends. In Ronald Lukens-Bull's study of an Islamic boarding school for college-age students in Java, he found a similar emphasis, especially on the importance of *mandiri*, self-sufficiency (Lukens-Bull 2001: 364–365).

I asked about the differences between kindergarten and first grade: the teachers see the kindergartens as a time for basic remedial work on manners and self-sufficiency, taught in an atmosphere of nurturance (*kasih-sayang*), as the students learn by "CBSA" (*cara belajar siswa aktif*—active learning). But when they enter first grade, it's all study, no play, and in a harsher atmosphere.

As a left-hander, I have long been interested in the strongly negative meanings attached to the left hand, and the strict restrictions on the use of the left hand found especially across Southern Asian. And so I have been surprised to see a small number of left-handers using their left hands among youngsters of five and six, as well as among Minangkabau college students. I asked how the teachers dealt with left-handedness.

The teachers said that they would try to influence the left-handed child (*anak yang kidal*) to change. Sometimes they would even wrap the left hand in a handkerchief so the child could not write with it. But they would not force the child to change. "A long time ago, if the child wrote with the left hand, for sure it would have been forced by the teacher to write with its right hand, but now we are pretty open."

I asked about having boys and girls together in class but all the teachers said that there was no problem anymore. I asked about the students who just roam around by themselves when others are engaged in tasks. The teachers said that it was up to the teacher to try and persuade the child to join in the assigned tasks. Two teachers think that such lone behavior is a sign that the child doesn't get enough attention at home and is using this to ask the teacher for attention.

I asked about the noise level, which seemed to me to be quite high in the Bukittinggi classrooms, but is generally ignored by the Bukittinggi teachers. They said that teachers try to control the noise—"the goal of the teacher is to create peaceful children (*menciptakan anak itu damai*)" and if the class is too noisy (*ribut, ramai*) it means that the teacher doesn't have enough control over the children.

When I asked if there are any male kindergarten teachers (I hadn't seen any at all), one teacher explained the absence of men: "women are more patient and men are less patient, women have a high sense of motherhood while males feel that it is trivial (*remeh*) or they feel that it is inconsequential (*anteng*) to teach kindergarten children, it's really a woman's job."

I asked about the role of creativity in the tasks. One focus group interpreted this to refer to the way that children create what the teacher has done—in folding paper, for example, by following instructions precisely. The other focus recognized this imitation and memorization as a problem and said that "hopefully, for the future, if we get the opportunity, we'll change."

As for the ideal teacher–student ratio, one group said that 18 or more, but less than 30 per teacher was ideal. The other group said that 10–15 students per teacher is ideal and more than 15 is too much.

What is the most difficult thing in a teacher's work?

- "As for me, as a teacher in kindergarten, there's nothing difficult. Because the work in school, that's the work of a teacher, and we already know how to do that work—sincerity coming out from the heart (*ikhlas keluar dari hati sanubari*)—that's the job of education."
- "In my experience, the most difficult thing is to teach the children what we give them. It has to be compatible with the education that is given at home, but often the parents are inadequately compatible with what we teach. For example, too often the students get whiney (*cengeng*) because, for example, they are the youngest or only child. When they come to us, they have been spoiled or pampered. You have to tell them to feed themselves, they have to dress themselves, and sometimes the parents are very agreeable in front of us but behind our backs, they spoil the child again."
- "For sure, because we love each child, so the work at school—if our work wasn't compatible with the environment, we would be creating difficulties but the social environment, the environment at home—for example, we are not allowed to recognize that they have done anything wrong. For example, saying in front of the child, 'this child is a baldy (*kepala botak*)—We're not allowed to call them "Baldy." But at home, the neighbors call him Baldy."

I then showed each focus group video clips from the Bukittinggi kindergartens. The Padang teachers were concerned with the problem of managing the children doing their tasks. The students had been divided into three groups of about ten each, and sat at one of the brightly colored tables. Each table had the materials for one of the three tasks. After ten minutes or so, the children would be lined up and marched around to the next table and its task. The problems came when some child had finished a task and had to kill time waiting for the slower ones to finish so that the entire class could rotate tables at once. With only one teacher and one teacher's assistant to help the slower ones, confusion was inevitable.

One focus group blamed the large class size, the small room, and poor equipment, and the system of teaching. The focus groups liked the outdoor exercise learning about traffic lights and signs that had been set up in the front yard of one school. The group recognized that it was all rote learning, but the children seemed to be happy and well-disciplined: "good relations and leadership between students and teachers." The teachers obviously had enthusiasm (*semangat*) and the children were at least active.

*The American tapes*

I met again with the two Padang focus groups in October 2001 to show them the video clips from the two South Carolina kindergartens. They noticed minor details: that the South Carolina teachers were able to sit down while explaining the lessons, and that the South Carolina classrooms had much more equipment and materials than do the West Sumatra ones. But their main interest was in how the South Carolina classrooms were run. Both focus groups commented at length about the freedom (*bebas*), or relative lack of rigid structure in the South Carolina classrooms, where children had much more choice of activities much of the time.

## Discussion

We were struck most by the similar responses by all teachers in all cultural groups to the tapes. We had expected this multivocalic approach to accentuate different cultural expectations yet we could not ignore what was being said over and over by members of both cultural groups—as well as what was not being said. By combining the insights of our participants with our own interpretations, we gain a more complex view of cultural expectations regarding childhood socialization into schooling specifically and society in general. These cultural expectations both relate to the nature of classroom interaction.

First, Jennings entered this research project to examine how teachers in two different countries respond to state-enforced academic standards even in grades as young as kindergarten. Although she saw vast differences between the academic activities of schools in both cultures, she could not ignore the fact that all respondents focused almost entirely on the behavior and classroom management aspects of the classrooms and discussed academic activity only when pressed. This uniformity of response speaks volumes about cultural expectations in both countries for viewing kindergarten as a space for socializing children into "school" behaviors. Although in the US, there is a strong push for children leaving kindergarten to be able to read, and for preparing children with basic literacy skills even before they reach kindergarten through programs such as Head Start, the fact that dozens of University of South Carolina students and South Carolina educators focused on classroom management and behavior suggests that it is still a deeply embedded cultural norm that American kindergarten is a place for learning how to be a student in a classroom setting more than learning the alphabet and math.

52  *Visual research projects*

Had Jennings in fact been able to join me in Indonesia, she might have missed this point, for she would have focused her questions on the academic system. She'd learned over the years to provide space and time to hear informants' perspectives without guiding or leading them in a great deal (e.g. Briggs 1986; Patton 2001). As she did with the South Carolina teachers, she would have started the Indonesian focus groups with open questions about their reactions to the US and Indonesian classroom tapes. However, eventually she would have asked the Indonesian teachers, as she did the teachers in South Carolina, dozens of questions about academic expectations and activities, and this no doubt would have become the focus of her analysis. Such an analysis could have provided worthwhile insights regarding cultural norms for academic preparation in kindergarten; it would have also led us away from the stronger reactions that focused on classroom management.

By combining the reactions of the teachers and the USC students with the researcher perspective, we are offered a more complex perspective of socialization that either view could offer alone. As Tobin and his colleagues found in their preschools, kindergarten in both Indonesia and the US is a site for both socialization and academic preparation. Indeed, our participants pointed out that the classrooms in both countries included academic activities such as whole-class instruction (e.g. reading aloud a text, developing a list of words on the white board), activities at different tables or "centers," and "free play" (e.g. playing with blocks, toy trucks). Although these activities appear similar at first glance, upon closer examination, some clear differences become evident, and these differences point to shifts in educational thinking in both countries. The Indonesian focus groups suggested that at least some of the Indonesian educators were in flux between an emphasis on imitation and memorization and a view toward developing a curriculum that offered more opportunities for students to be creative and to engage in more meaning-making activity. As Denise suggested in our interview, in the US, debate continues about the value of socializing children into learning through rote activities versus immersing them in meaning-making activities. Although there has been some movement toward the latter, many kindergarten classrooms continue to be organized around the former. While the academic activities appear similar on the surface, these differences between rote learning and learning that engages children in authentic meaning-making activities can have large academic consequences for children throughout their school lives (Comber and Simpson 2001). In the US, often the difference occurs along the lines of class and ethnicity, which raises important questions of equality of opportunity. Those questions of equity are not as readily applied to Indonesia, where it appears that the current curriculum is consistent across schools and class lines.

With respect to the participants' focus on classroom interaction and classroom management, a second theme became evident through this multivocalic method:

## Individualism and groupism

From the beginning, it has seemed reasonable to expect strong evidence for an American individualism contrasting with an Indonesian groupism. Anthropologists have long found this individualism–groupism distinction a useful frame in comparative cultural studies, even when it has been conceptualized as a continuum rather than an absolute dichotomy. (As, for example, in my comparison of Indonesian and American cinema [Heider, 1991b: 30ff].) Indeed, a casual first view of the Bukittinggi kindergartners wearing their school uniforms and lined up in military formation for their group calisthenics reinforces this expectation of Indonesian groupism suppressing individualistic behavior. But as we have seen, the situation is considerably more complex, evident from the Indonesian and US participant views that there was little difference between the two cultures with respect to individuality and groupism. This complexity is also revealed in classroom responses to "loner" children. In the Indonesian schools, when a single child wandered away from the opening assembly or a classroom work table, no teacher took steps to bring the child back into the group; wandering American children were immediately returned to the group. On the other hand, the usual punishment for disruptive uncooperative American children was banishment from the group for a period of solitary "time out." (There was no observable punishment in the Indonesian schools). And, where the American teachers envied the school uniforms of the Indonesians, the Indonesian teachers appreciated the freedom that they saw in the American videotapes.

Tobin and his colleagues had also found somewhat unexpected responses. All three of their groups—American, Chinese, and Japanese—said that self-reliance and independence were important goals, even as the American informants thought of independence as being "characteristically Asian" (Tobin et al. 1989: 139). The Tobin group concluded that the three cultures' "approaches to balancing groupism with individualism and equality differ more in theory than in practice" (Tobin et al. 1989: 148). And they did distinguish between Chinese and Japanese behavior:

> In Japanese preschools, where groupism is closely associated with egalitarianism, talk of individual differences in children's ability is virtually taboo. In Chinese preschools, where groupism is associated with a shared acceptance of order and responsibility, individual differences in aptitude and performance are less threatening (Tobin et al. 1989: 107).

It appears that these Indonesian preschools resemble the Chinese model more closely than the Japanese model but this is certainly a question that needs more research.

Finally, a methodological note: we are strong proponents of this "multivocalic" approach, of listening to what the local experts say about the videotaped behavior of classroom behavior in other cultures. However, we would point out that this approach is a sort of indirect, or second-hand classroom ethnography. The main data come from the teachers, and the research time needs to be allocated accordingly. One hour of in-school recording must be supported by many hours of discussion with the teachers.

# 4 Three styles of play: New Guinea Dani, Central Java, and Micronesia

Having the possibility to videotape means that it is possible to store data which has no immediate research use. I did this, taping a children's game of the New Guinea Dani which I saw for the first time in 1970. I had not seen it in the 1960s, and I had no particular research goal in mind. I used it for classroom exercises in the US, asking my students to work out the rules of the game on the basis of a 15-minute take. Later, I taped the same game in Java, in 1986, and found a film of the same game from Micronesia. Taken together, the three versions of the game, from three different cultures at three different times, offered an interesting research puzzle.

Although I began studying the Dani in April 1961, I first saw this play in 1970. I was staying in a house on a mission station and after school a gang of Dani children would take over an abandoned sweet potato field, playing noisily, disturbing my writing. I tried to ignore them but after a few days of noise, I stopped to watch, and stayed to analyze. At first, I saw only random motion, but slowly I was able to work out repetitive patterns of behavior. It then occurred to me that this would provide a good exercise for introductory cultural anthropology courses: look at this behavior, figure out the rules (that is, the cultural models, or schemas, that these Dani children had in their heads.) I chose a 15-minute sequence that included all the major events and have presented it as a challenge to a wide range of people. American schoolchildren are the quickest to solve the problem. College undergraduates do well. Anthropology graduate students are reluctant to even try, perhaps feeling that this is a career-threatening trick. But despite the poor quality of the video, most groups can work it out with only a few hints from me. For example, I would point out the short stick, the long stick, and the shallow hole. I would recommend they not try to translate the action into American baseball terms. And I urged them to observe closely, make a hypothesis about the action, test its predictive value with further observation and then, if it failed, to revise the hypothesis and try again. This little exercise would simulate important aspects of ethnographic fieldwork, illustrate the concept of schema (the cultural scenario), and make the point of the utility of visual records in ethnographic analysis.

This footage is also useful in other visual anthropology courses, introducing the idea of the close reading of visual records. There are two other kinds of information that can be gleaned from this footage, despite the low quality of sound and image. First, with all the children milling about, there is plenty of nonverbal communication to note: the way these Dani children hold their bodies, their gestures when they fail to win an encounter, their brief arguments, and the ways in which they use and contest space in the playing field.

As play is a part of culture, we can expect that when a game is introduced from one culture to another, it will to some extent be altered to "fit" the second culture. So, a third set of questions arises from the anthropology of play: in what sort of culture do children learn to play in this particular style? What might you predict about adult Dani culture from watching the style of Dani children's play? When you were that age, did you play this way?

And the point here is that the video record provides data that no purely textual description could. Now, let me cite passages from the article that I wrote about the Dani play before seeing the comparative material (Heider 1977):

> "Roberts and his colleagues have made a useful definition of games that specifies one part of the total realm of play. They define games as: Recreational activity characterized by
>
> 1) Organized play
> 2) Competition
> 3) Two or more sides
> 4) Criteria for determining the winner, and
> 5) Agreed-upon rules
>
> (Roberts et al. 1959: 597)

They point out that play is pancultural and that nearly all societies know games of some sort:

> "... games are found in most tribal and national cultures, but in some interesting cultures they are either absent or very restricted in kind and number"
>
> (Roberts and Sutton-Smith 1962: 167).

The Dani are one of those interesting cultures that have no games. Previously, in describing Dani play, I had remarked that "there is almost complete lack of competition in play" and "there are no games in which score is kept or in which there is even a winner" (Heider 1970: 193).

In terms of the crucial criteria of the Roberts definition, the Dani lacked games. Then, about 1969, a true game was introduced to the Dani, and in 1970, I frequently saw it played. (Also, I made two 20-minute videotape records of it, and one of which I have had printed out on 16-mm film for purposes of close analysis.)

But according to our definition of games, what I saw was play and no longer a true game. It was the feeble shadow of a formerly robust Asian game which the Dani schoolchildren had already managed to strip of most of its game attributes.

I call the play Flip-the-Stick. (I could discover no Dani name for it in 1970.) It is fairly simple, although at first glance it does seem complex. There are two sides, a batter, and one or two outfielders. (It is hard to avoid at least some baseball terms.) The batter stands at the goal (a small depression in the ground made by rotating a heel in the soft earth) and uses a two-foot long reed bat to flip or hit a short reed stick toward the outfield. The outfielder catches the stick in the air or, if she has missed it, picks it up and throws it back, trying to do something which will allow her to take over as batter. The batter tries to stay at bat, racking up points. There are three different ways to hit and score, which the batter goes through in turn and, if not put out, begins again.

This is the way the game should be played, and the way it is played elsewhere. The game is known from Pakistan to Korea (according to various people from South and East Asia who have seen the Dani footage and recognized the game) and East into the Pacific as far as the Gilberts (according to Kushel's Bellonese informants, who said that their version "originally came from the Gilbert Islands") (Kushel 1975).

Apparently, the game was introduced to the Dani schoolchildren as a recess game by Javanese schoolteachers. But I have no information about the precise circumstances of the introduction. (It is clear from the Maccoby et al. [1964] account of introducing a game to a Mexican village how important such data can be.) At any rate, I did not see it played by Dani in 1968 or between 1961 and 1963. So, it is possible to say with fair confidence that the game was introduced about 1969 by Indonesian (and probably Javanese) schoolteachers; that the Dani children took it up and transformed it; and that in 1970, it was being played spontaneously by Dani boys and girls both at school (during recess) and at home.

Unfortunately, until 1986, I had no firsthand account of the Asian form of the game. But I made certain assumptions about that form based on comments by Asians who had seen my Dani footage and drawn by logical inference from the structure of the game as played by the Dani. For example, when the batter measures out a distance with the long stick and shouts out Indonesian number words (otherwise the game is carried on in the Dani language), I conclude that in Java this was to reckon the score.

## The rules of the game: a formal description

We can examine the changes which the Dani made on a Javanese game and describe how, in important ways, the game was made Dani. But first, I shall describe the basic rules or procedure of the game which can be discovered from watching the Dani children play it. This formal description on which this chapter is based, is of course, much more elegant than the complex activity which I observed and filmed in the Grand Valley. Although the formal description is in some respects and for some purposes adequate, it is obviously a stripped-down account, and it totally neglects those behavioral aspects of the game which figure in this analysis. The methodological implications of this are important. These formal descriptions would not identify the various significant differences in the way the game is played which show up in the video record and so would not allow the sort of cultural analysis which I attempt here.

The formal description, then, of an unnamed game observed and recorded on videotape among the Grand Valley Dani of West New Guinea, Indonesia in 1970, is as follows:

**Players:** 1 batter, 1 or 2 (rarely more) fielders, played by boys and girls, ages about 6 to 14, usually with children of their own gender.

**Equipment:** One reed, about 1 cm in diameter, and about a meter long ("the bat"); one shorter reed, about 10 cm long ("the stick").

**Place:** A reasonably level field extending out at least 10 or 15 meters from the goal; a shallow depression ("the goal") a few centimeters deep, dug out by rotating a heel in the earth; there are no boundaries—the goal is the only ground mark.

**Rules:** The game proceeds through each of three variations and then begins again until a fielder is able to replace the batter. In each variation, the batter sends the stick to the outfield; the fielder tries to catch it in the air and if successful, becomes the batter.

*Variation 1*

**The Hit:** The short stick rests across the goal depression, perpendicular to the batter–fielder axis. The batter puts the end of the bat under the stick and flips it out toward the outfield.

**The Return:** If the outfielder fails to catch the stick, she picks it up and throws it at the bat, which the batter either holds upright in the goal or lays across the goal (these alternatives are apparently in free variation). If the fielder hits the bat with the stick, she takes over as batter; if not, they proceed to Variation 2.

*Variation 2*

**The Hit:** The batter holds the stick upright in the goal with one hand and, wielding the bat in the other, hits the stick toward the outfield.

**The Return:** If the outfielder fails to catch the stick, she picks it up and throws it as close to the goal as possible. The batter now defending the goal with her bat, tries to hit the stick away. From wherever the stick lands, whether hit away by the batter or not, the batter measures out the distance to the goal in bat lengths, shouting out the numbers as she goes. If the distance is less than one-bat length, they exchange positions; if not, they proceed to Variation 3.

### Variation 3

**The Hit:** The stick now rests with one end protruding out over the goal depression. The batter hits that end with her bat to send the stick spinning up into the air, and then hits the air-borne stick toward the outfield.

If she succeeds in both, and if the stick is not caught in the air by the outfielder, the batter measures the distance from the stick to the goal, again in bat lengths, shouting out the numbers. If the distance is more than one-bat length, they return to Variation 1 and so forth.

## The translation

The basic assumption of this analysis is that play is part of culture, to some extent consistent with the rest of the culture. Without taking the assumption of consistency to a ridiculous extreme, it does make sense that a game which was totally inconsistent with other aspects of a culture would have a hard time. If it did not actually alter the culture, it would be rejected or itself altered.

The great model for this approach is *The Chrysanthemum and the Bat*, by Robert Whiting (1977). Whiting is not an anthropologist, but has shown in great detail how baseball, that quintessential American game, has been transformed into a distinctly Japanese game when played in Japan. The rules have not been changed but the strategies emphasize team solidarity over American individualism. As it happens, a visual component complements Whiting's analysis—a Hollywood film, *Mr. Baseball* (1992), was made about an American player on a Japanese team.

This Flip-the-Stick game came to the Dani as part of a whole program of schooling introduced by the Indonesian government, intended to educate—that is, transform—the Dani children into proper Indonesian (i.e. Javanese) children. We have some evidence that in its early years, at least, the program was not at all successful. The schoolrooms were under the control of the teachers, who could maintain the appearance, at least, of Indonesian structure. It turns out that Flip-the-Stick is a sensitive test to what was really happening. It apparently had been given over to the children with no monitoring by the teachers, and it got away from them. The game is still recognizable, but in terms of several major aspects it has undergone change. In each of these aspects, the game was brought closer to other Dani play forms and to Dani culture in general.

## Competition

An important criterion in the definition of games quoted above is competition. In Dani life as a whole, there is strikingly little competition. An obvious place to look for competition would be in the maneuvering for various statuses, or ranks, in a society. But Dani society is quite egalitarian. There are leaders, of course, but they are Big Men who lead by consensus, rather than Chiefs who rule by virtue of coercive authority. And although there are some differences in wealth, these differences are not displayed. Houses, attire, and even the sizes of pig herds are not overt signs of importance (cf. Heider 1970: 88).

Also, Dani engage in little competitive confrontation in their interpersonal relations within the group. The Dani version of the game does retain the two sides of the Javanese version. And one might say that when one player replaces the other at bat, a winner of sorts has been determined. But the idea of counting an overall score and ending up with the winner of the game has been lost. The play itself is relaxed and non-competitive.

## Quantification

Dani culture has little concern with quantification (Heider 1970: 170). The scorekeeping, which is so essential to the form of the original game, has been dropped from the Dani version. And that scorekeeping was, of course, not merely competition, but it was quantified competition, and so was inconsistent with Dani culture on two counts.

Interestingly, the Dani children retain a vestige of scorekeeping in their version of the game. Although when playing, they speak their own language, at appropriate moments, they do shout out Indonesian number words (there are no Dani number words beyond three or four). However, these number words are not being used for counting and, indeed, are not always spoken in any particular order.

## Casualness

The Dani children show a remarkable degree of casualness in the playing of the game. Several games go on in overlapping spaces with only the slightly signs of defense of space. Sometimes, a single player will be an outfielder for two games at once. There are clearly rules as described in the formal account above, but they are not strictly observed. There is a great deal of what I would call fudging or even cheating. For example, outfielders, instead of playing the stick from where it has landed, would usually kick it forward into a more advantageous position (improving its lie). And only rarely, in the most blatant situations, does one child challenge another for breaking a rule.

This casualness, or flexibility, has often been mentioned in accounts of New Guinea Highland societies and the Dani are no exception. Elsewhere, I have discussed how difficult it can be to use such terms to characterize an entire culture (Heider 1970: 5–7). But on the whole, Dani behavior does often seem to exhibit casualness. And this play, which is so far from the strict insistence on rules and procedures, is a good example.

## Discussion

Not only do the Dani lack true games, but certainly as late as 1970, their traditional culture was strong enough to resist games by altering one introduced game into a more compatible form of play. This is a strong conclusion which raises questions about the nature of a society which lacks and even rejects games. But before pursuing this, we should take a look at the definition of game.

One might hold that the five criteria quoted above are absolute attributes, present or absent, according to which we can say that the Dani are one of the few cultures in the world that lack games. However, it seems more realistic to treat the boundary that marks off games from the rest of play as a fuzzy one, or rather, a zone of transition, and consider the criteria as relative, not absolute. Then, we can accurately say that when the Dani play Flip-the-Stick, they have tremendously de-emphasized competition, winning, and scorekeeping, thus moving the game away from that end of the play spectrum in which are found true games.

Elsewhere, I have interpreted the general Grand Valley Dani resistance to change in terms of their basic conservatism (Heider 1975b). The game of Flip-the-Stick provides a partial exception to this resistance to change, in the sense that it is one of the few traits which the Dani did accept from the outside, but because of the changes which it underwent, it supports the general principle of Dani conservatism.

The functional approach to the study of games (in contrast to mere description or historical/diffusionist studies) focuses on the ways in which the games fulfill certain basic needs, whether they be practice at skills important in the culture, "the psychoanalytic notion that games are exercises in mastery" (Roberts et al. 1959: 604) or working out of cultural conflicts arising from the socialization process (Roberts and Sutton-Smith 1962). Since the Dani do not have games to perform these functions, they presumably have other means. Certainly, many of the less formal amusements of the children are means of learning and practicing skills (see Heider 1970: 193–199).

But there is a final tantalizing suggestion: if, following Roberts and Sutton-Smith's line of thought, we suggest that games function to resolve various sorts of conflicts, and further, if games are in some respects especially good ways of resolving some kinds of conflicts and preparing children for adult life, then, might it not be that one would expect to find an absence of games in those cultures with relatively low conflict? This is all very speculative. But elsewhere, I have developed the case that the Dani culture is resistant to change in part at least because of its remarkably low level of stress (Heider 1975b) and that there is in general little conflict in Dani society. So, the Grand Valley Dani do represent a single case of association between low conflict and absence of games. This I present as a suggestion, not a conclusion.

To those who have known the Dani mainly through Robert Gardner's film, *Dead Birds*, which is especially memorable for its portrayal of endemic intergroup warfare, it may seem surprising to think of the Dani as a low-stress society. But I am characterizing interpersonal relations within family, compound, and neighborhood as low stress despite the constant warfare between confederations and alliances. A further thought: virtually, this entire description of Dani culture is based on my fieldwork between 1961 and 1970. These children of 1970, who so successfully transformed that Javanese game into Dani play, had barely been touched by outside influences. The Dani children of today are Indonesian-speaking Christians, and in many ways real Indonesians. If they are playing Flip-the-Stick, one would predict that it has now become somewhat more like its Javanese ancestor game. But that is a matter for future research.

In January 2014, I paid a very brief visit to the Dani and was stunned by the changes since my last visit in 1995. The Dani are overwhelmed by tens of thousands of immigrants, non-Papuans from elsewhere in Indonesia. Buzz Maxey, who had grown up as a missionary kid in the Dani area, was still there deeply involved in development projects. One of these was to organize a Dani soccer league for the youth. One direction for future research would be to study Dani soccer in light of what this chapter has shown. It might even be an index of Dani change: to what extent have these Dani youth turned "soccer" into a Dani thing, or to what extent has soccer changed the Dani? Stay tuned.

## The Javanese game

In the 1977 analysis of the Dani play, above, I had made some assumptions about its origin in a much more formal game that had, presumably, been introduced to the Grand Valley by the Javanese schoolteachers. A decade later, in January 1986, I was able to observe and videotape the same game as it was played by boys in Sulaiman, a suburb of Yogyakarta, Central Java.

As is clear from the video clip, this Javanese version in 1986 was as I had assumed. It was very orderly. The boys lined up to take their turns at hitting the stick. The player in the outfield made a careful X in the earth where the small stick had landed, and made his move from that sport. There was none of the opportunistic kicking of the stick forward for a more advantageous position, as the Dani children did. This Javanese version was competitive, with real scores tallied and winners declared.

In short, it is clear that this children's play, or true game, does reflect some general aspects of the adult Javanese culture. It illustrates the carefully ordered Javanese culture, just as the Dani play epitomizes the ad hoc style of much Dani culture.

## The Micronesian game

There is yet another version on film of this game. It was shot in Micronesia by the anthropologist Gerd Koch as part of the Goettingen Film Archive record of world cultures, housed in Germany. Technically, this footage is of much higher quality than that of my own videos from New Guinea and Java. Although his shots are short and continuity is minimal, and one could not reconstruct the rules of the game from the visuals alone, Koch's accompanying pamphlet tells us much about it. There are some significant formal differences between the Micronesian and the Indonesian versions. Here, instead of measuring out distances on the ground, as we see in both the Dani and the Javanese versions, the boy who has won in a cycle then scores his points by hitting the short stick into the air again and again.

Micronesian cultures resemble Java in their emphasis on a feudal hierarchy and, not surprisingly, the formal style of the Micronesian game looks much like the Javanese style. And both differ from the free-for-all of the Dani play. Much of this analysis of play could only be done with visual records. It would be difficult for a purely textual description to show what becomes so obvious from the visuals.

# 5 Nonverbal studies of Dani anger and sexual expression: experimental method in videotape ethnography

## The expression of anger

During the course of a two-year ethnographic study of the Grand Valley Dani of West New Guinea (now Papua, Indonesia), I had come to the conclusion that the Dani rarely express anger or aggression, and tend to resolve conflict by early withdrawal rather than direct confrontation. This was duly reported in my first monograph on Dani culture (cf. Heider 1970: 92, 101–102, 128, et passim). The basis for these statements, like so many comparable judgments, was the cumulative impressions and observations of countless encounters. It was in the tradition of ethnographic description that such statements made by (presumably) competent observers are accepted as valid and sufficient.

Here, I want to go beyond such ethnographic impressionism to examine Dani expression of anger more systematically and to complement naturalistic observation and interpretation with controlled experimentation. The broader purpose of this is not to debunk ethnography, but to show how the two approaches may be combined.

The proposition "the Grand Valley Dani express little anger" will be investigated by developing a specific measure for the expression of anger, and using it to compare the Grand Valley Dani with their neighbors, the Western Dani of the Konda Valley.

Following my general ethnographic work on Dani culture during 1961–1963, Eleanor Rosch and I carried out basic research on Dani facial expressions in 1968 and 1970. This work was inspired by Paul Ekman's psychological research, which had found that there are pancultural facial expressions for the basic emotions of happiness, sadness, anger, fear, disgust, and surprise (cf. Ekman 1973). In 1970, we replicated Ekman's work and found strong confirmation for his theory.

In our first research on Dani facial expressions, some interesting anomalies appeared (cf. Ekman 1972:273). On the whole, the Dani performed well in a variety of experiments in which they had to recognize facial expressions. For example, in one of the experimental tasks, the subject was shown two photographs of different facial expressions of emotion, was read a brief descriptive phrase, and was then asked which of the two expressions went with that story. Thirty-four Dani subjects were accurate at a significant level ($p < 0.01$) on all discriminations except one; when told an anger story and asked to choose between anger and disgust faces, they tended to choose disgust faces. On the other hand, they were accurate in discriminating the anger face from the happy, sad, and fear faces using the anger story. This suggests that for the Dani, it seems appropriate that a person in an anger situation will show anger rather than happiness, sadness, or fear, but that in the same anger-producing situation, it seems more appropriate that a person shows disgust rather than anger.

This experimental finding is not at all surprising in light of various ethnographic statements which I had made about the Dugum Dani. For example, I had written that "The Dani simply do not live in the tense, aggressive atmosphere that Read and many others since have reported from the Highlands of New Guinea" (Heider 1970:92).

Speaking of Bromley's account of the Southern Valley Dani, I wrote "... we may both be right and the Southern Valley Dani are significantly more aggressive than the Dugum Dani." (Heider 1970:128) And I described the Dugum Dani reaction to interpersonal conflict as a pattern of withdrawal, rather than confrontation. (cf. Heider 1970:101–102).

Ekman made an important qualification to his theory of pancultural facial expressions. His evidence suggests that while the basic facial expressions associated with emotions are pancultural, each culture may have some culture-specific rules for their use, which he calls "display rules." They pertain to performance: whether a person is supposed or allowed to show his true emotion, or whether he must follow the display rule and conceal it, "masking" it with the facial expression of another emotion.

Now, we have seen that the one Dani "error" in recognizing basic expressions is consistent with a previously stated ethnographic generalization. In fact, it is at least partially predictable from the generalization as a Dani—specific display rule. Briefly stated, these Dani mask anger by disgust. The withdrawal pattern which I had described could conceivably also utilize fear or even sadness as a mask, but the experimental evidence suggests that it is disgust, a conclusion which also seems most likely on intuitive grounds. (If it were not for the ethnographic generalization, one might suspect that the Dani "error" was "an artifact of the research procedure," as Ekman suggested (Ekman 1972:273).

Thus, the first facial expression research provided interesting support of the ethnography. But the ethnographic possibilities of this finding lead us further. During our 1970 work in West Irian, we conducted a comparative study between the Grand Valley Dani, whom I had been studying since 1961, and the Western Dani, best known from the writings of D. O'Brien and A. Ploeg. It seemed that the Western Dani expressed anger more readily than did the Grand Valley Dani. Because the Western Dani are in other respects so similar to the Grand Valley Dani, they are an ideal group to use for comparison on the expression of anger dimension.

In 1970, I elicited facial expressions from both Grand Valley and Western Dani. The videotape records of these facial displays provided raw data for the comparative examination of Dani expressions of anger. For each culture, a set of six eliciting phrases was devised, one phrase for each of six basic emotions (sad, happy, fear, anger, surprise, and disgust) (Appendix 1). For the Grand Valley Dani, I devised the phrases, consulting with informants and referring to previous eliciting experiments. The Western Dani phrases were worked out by the Reverend David Martin, a Christian and Missionary Alliance missionary at Karubaga, in the Konda Valley.

Both men and boys in the two Dani cultures participated, although in this experiment only the boys' elicitations were used. The boys ranged in age from about 12 to about 18, and were all attending schools taught by non-Dani.

## The elicitations

Each subject stood or sat in front of the videotape camera. I read the eliciting phrases and worked the camera, keeping the subject's face in full screen. All tests were conducted in the Dani language, although an occasional word of Indonesian crept in. My command of the Grand Valley Dani language was then quite adequate to this task, and Western Dani is close enough to Grand Valley Dani so that I was able to read off the phrases in that language fairly well. The Grand Valley Dani boys were taped alone in the privacy of my house, but the Western Dani boys were taped in a large schoolroom at Karubaga, in the presence of other students and teachers.

An edited videotape was made of the anger and disgust elicitations of all 15 Western Dani boys and all 23 Grand Valley Dani boys. The 76 displays were randomized for affect and culture. I assumed that no American observers would be able to distinguish the two cultures on the basis of cue differences such as background, language, and attire. In any case, the observers were not told that the tape included subjects from two cultures.

The main interest lay, of course, in possible differences between the anger expressions (modified by display rules) of the two cultures. Disgust expressions were included as a control, with the expectation that if both cultures were judged equally successful in showing disgust, possible differences in gross cultural expressive ability could be ruled out.

The hypothesis was that the Grand Valley Dani subjects would follow the display rules and show more disgust expressions, especially withdrawal elements, when asked for anger. A preliminary inspection of the tapes by Ekman, Friesen, and myself suggested that this was true. However, it seemed desirable to have independent ratings done.

Ratings were done by 14 members of my seminar on nonverbal behavior at UCLA, who were unaware of the purpose of the study. They were shown the edited videotape with the 76 expressions after being told:

"You will be shown 76 different attempts to pose an emotion in response to verbal instruction. You should make your judgments on that behavior which is the attempt to pose the emotion—the peak moment. Make three judgments on each attempt:

Head HT—head thrusts forward or sideways
HA—Head turns away, downwards, or sideways
N—Neither
Lips LS ~ Lips sucked or pressed or bit
ULR—Upper lip raised
IM—Lips pursed (no lip raise, no lip back and forth)
Nose—NW—nose wrinkled
A—nose wrinkle absent."

The ratings were done at the same time in a small classroom. The edited tape was viewed once on a single large monitor, I read out the number of each display as it began, and the raters had a few seconds between displays to write down their own ratings. Because of the unfamiliarity of the task, the quality of the tape, and the briefness of the intervals, nearly 10% of the possible 3192 ratings were not made. As the tape progressed, the percentage of possible ratings improved, but the level of rater agreement remained fairly constant.

The raters were asked to make determinations of elements or components of each facial expression, and not direct judgments of emotion per se. The elements were chosen on the grounds that they are relatively easy to detect and occurred with fairly great frequency in the Dani expressions.

## The results

Not all the possible ratings are diagnostic of anger or disgust, of course. Some merely note absence of movement; others, like pursed lips, are ambiguous and could be associated with either anger or disgust. The following elements are considered diagnostic:

    For disgust: head aversion (HA)
     Upper lip raised (ULR)
     Nose wrinkle (NW)
    For anger: head thrust (HT)
     Lip suck, bite, or press (LS)

For each of the 76 displays, there were up to 14 ratings on the 3 different aspects, head, nose, and mouth. The modal choice, that which reflected agreement of the most raters, was taken as the description of the display. Traditionally, ethnographic description is based on the observation of one expert observer. That method uses welcome expertise, and is of course unanimous, but is also very subject to observer bias. The approach used

68  Visual research projects

Table 5.1 Responses by Grand Valley Dani and Western Dani to anger and disgust elicitations, according to the presence of disgust components (HA, ULR, NW) and anger components (HT, LS)

|  | Displays w only disgust components |  | Displays w both anger and disgust components |  | Displays w only anger components |  | Displays w neither anger nor disgust components |  |
|---|---|---|---|---|---|---|---|---|
|  | No. | % | No. | % | No. | % | No. | % |
| GVD disgust elicitations | 22 | 96% | 1 | 4% | 0 | 0 | 0 | 0 |
| WD disgust elicitations | 8 | 53% | 2 | 13% | 1 | 7% | 4 | 27% |
| GVD anger elicitations | 12 | 52% | 1 | 4% | 5 | 22% | 5 | 22% |
| WD anger elicitations | 3 | 20% | 2 | 13% | 9 | 60% | 1 | 7% |

here, based on consensus of naive untrained observers, has weaknesses, but was chosen for its greater strength: it avoids the obvious bias of observations made with the hypothesis in mind.

We can first analyze the 76 displays in terms of how much each cultural group used appropriate emotion-indicating components in response to elicitations for that emotion (Table 5.1).

The Grand Valley Dani did strikingly well at disgust displays, but very poorly at anger displays. The Western Dani did less well on both displays than did the Grand Valley Dani on anger. But the crucial comparison is between the two cultures' anger displays. Sixty percent of Western Dani displays had only anger components compared with 22% for the Grand Valley Dani. Seventy-three percent of Western Dani displays showed some anger components, compared to 26% for Grand Valley Dani. On the other hand, 52% of Grand Valley displays to the anger stimulus were pure disgust displays, compared to only 20% for Western Dani.

Turning to displays for disgust elicitations, we find that 20% of Western Dani displays showed some anger elements (compared to 4% for Grand Valley Dani.

The results can also be analyzed in terms of frequency of disgust or anger components used by each culture (Table 5.2). From this, we can calculate the mean number of anger or disgust components per display used in each situation. Since there are three possible components for disgust, but only two for anger, the two sets are not directly comparable.

Again, we see that Western Dani used more anger elements than Grand Valley Dani for anger elicitations (means of .80 versus .30) and used strikingly more anger elements in disgust elicitations.

Table 5.2 Frequency of disgust and anger components in Grand Valley Dani and Western Dani display responses (table reflects all data that was recovered from the original study)

| Number of displays | Observed components | Disgust points | Anger points |
|---|---|---|---|
| *Grand Valley Dani—Disgust* | | | |
| 2 | WAU | 6 | 0 |
| 8 | WA | 16 | |
| 10 | W | 10 | |
| 2 | A | 2 | |
| 1 | WAS | 2 | 1 |
| Totals 23 displays | | Means: 1.57 | |
| *Grand Valley Dani—Anger* | | | |
| 1 | AW | 2 | |
| 2 | | | |
| 9 | A | 9 | |
| 2 | U | 2 | |
| 1 | UT | 1 | |
| 1 | | | |
| 1 | T | | |
| 1 | | | |
| 3 | S | | |
| 3 | | | |
| 1 | TS | | |
| 2 | | | |
| 1 | SW | 1 | 1 |
| 1 | SA | 1 | 1 |
| 2 | WU | 4 | |
| 1 | WAU | 3 | |
| 1 | none | | |
| 13 | | 9 | 12 |
| | means | .60 | .80 |
| *Western Dani—Disgust* | | | |
| 4 | UW | 8 | |
| 4 | W | 4 | |
| 1 | WS | 1 | |
| 1 | | | |
| 1 | ST | | 2 |
| 1 | WT | 1 | |
| 4 | none | | |
| Totals:15 | | 14 | 4 |
| | Means: | .93 | .27 |
| *Western Dani—Anger* | | | |
| 1 | TS | | 2 |
| 7 | S | | 7 |
| 1 | T | | 1 |
| | Means: | .93 | .27 |
| | | Disgust points | Anger points |

(Continued)

70  *Visual research projects*

*Table 5.2* (Continued)

| Number of displays | Observed components | Disgust points | Anger points |
|---|---|---|---|
| \IN |  |  |  |
| ible 2) |  |  |  |
| .04 |  |  |  |
| .27 |  |  |  |
| −.30 |  |  |  |
| .80 |  |  |  |

By this measure, Western Dani use disgust as much for anger displays as do Grand Valley Dani.

But there is a significant difference in which of the "erroneous" elements each culture uses. The Grand Valley Dani anger elicitations produced 14 disgust elements of which 10 were the head aversion and only 1 the nose wrinkle; the Western Dani elicitations produced 9 disgust elements, of which 4 were nose wrinkle, and 2 the head aversion. This suggests support of the ethnographic statement that the customary Grand Valley Dani reaction to conflict is not angry confrontation but withdrawal. (Also, Grand Valley Dani showed no reaction to the anger elicitations more often than did the Western Dani [21.7% versus 6.7%].)

The results support the original hypothesis that the Western Dani would express anger better than the Grand Valley Dani. Not only is this true of the attempt to pose anger, but some Western Dani even display anger features for disgust elicitations. The original ethnographic finding that Grand Valley Dani show withdrawal behavior in an anger situation is also supported.

The findings of the experimental approach to Dani expressions of anger support the ethnographic impressions. It is worth spelling out the assumptions and weaknesses underlying the experiment. First, I assume that the Dani phrases which were used to elicit Dani reactions did indeed suggest to them the emotions which we term anger and disgust. I assume that there are pancultural emotions such as anger and disgust and that I can recognize them in others, whether they are of my own culture or of another which I have studied; and that the first question which research had to settle was whether or not there are pancultural regularities linking certain facial expressions to certain internal emotional states. In crude terms, I assume that I can know what is going on inside a Dani, and can describe it in English. (Of course, assumptions of this sort are the basis of all ethnography, and indeed, much of human interactions, but only in experiments like this are they actually made explicit.)

Second, I assume that two groups of Dani school boys were responding in a Dani style and not in an American style or a style which they had recently developed for interacting with Americans (or Euro-Americans or non-Dani). The experiments were conducted in the Dani language (Grand Valley or Western) and presumably the facial expressions were also Dani. Of course, the same experimenter performed both sets of elicitations.

But both sets of Dani were attending schools and had been interacting in the Dani language with non-Dani for several years, and so could have learned and were using appropriate North American/European facial expressions. (One could hypothesize that they used a nonverbal code switching when interacting with the American experimenter.) I do not see how to rule out this possibility. But it is worth noting that the Western Dani were all Christian converts while none of the Grand Valley Dani subjects had been converted to Christianity, and one might expect therefore to find less, not more, aggression and anger expressed by the Western Dani.

Third, I assume that the components which were used in the rating tasks are indeed indicative of emotion expressions: e.g., head thrust and lip suck for anger; head aversion and nose wrinkle for disgust.

The use of untrained raters probably weakened the results. The final tape shown for the rating task had interference in some cases making it quite difficult to see the faces (it had been shot in Sony CV, transferred to the Sony AV mode, and transferred again in editing.) This also lessened the accuracy of the observations. There is no question that if experienced raters had worked with a clean tape record, the results would have been even more positive. But despite all these problems, the experiment was able to confirm with systematic, explicit, and replicable methods a pattern of Dani behavior which had been more casually observed and described by the more traditional ethnographic approach.

## The expression of sexual anxiety

Previously, in writing about the Dugum Dani, I claimed that:

1) The Dani observe a four- to six-year postpartum sexual abstinence, and that
2) "the Dani show no overt signs of sexual anxiety during this period of sexual abstinence" (Heider 1970:74)

and I concluded that the Dani have a remarkably low level of interest in sex. And elsewhere, I developed the idea that the Dani can be generally characterized as a low-energy culture.

The first claim, which is not the subject of this chapter, concerns a matter of fact that is difficult to verify. The Dani certainly say that they observe a long postpartum sexual abstinence, but this is an ideal statement that does not in itself establish a pattern of behavior. I had gathered extensive genealogies from Grand Valley Dani and found no evidence children resulting from breaches of the sexual abstinence, but it is as difficult to determine the details of possible contraception, abortion, and infanticide as it is to learn the facts about sexual intercourse itself. Despite these qualifications, everything that I know about the Dani supports the claim that when the Dani report a four- to six-year postpartum sexual abstinence, they are describing their actual behavior. Significantly, a similarly long period of postpartum sexual abstinence was reported quite independently from the Jale, a neighboring Dani-speaking group.

It is the second claim that Dani men do not exhibit anxiety, stress, or discomfort as a result of the long abstinence, which is the subject of this investigation. At first glance, the claim is unbelievable. Of course, anthropologists are familiar with the wide range of possible ways in which the cultures of the world pattern their sexual behavior. But even anthropologists seem to have a belief in a fairly high basic level of sexual energy which must be directed in some way. Thus, a four- to six-year postpartum sexual abstinence, universally observed by a society, is unusual, but not impossible.

However, even anthropologists would assume that it would have to be maintained by a fairly strong (and visible) system of social control, and at a fairly high (and visible) cost to the personalities of the individuals involved.

Now, my claims of Dani indifference might be taken to mean only that I perceived no sexual concern. If this is so, it would only be, perhaps, a sad comment on a botched job of research, and would be of little interest either ethnographically or theoretically. It is difficult to dispose of this possibility totally, but I can note that my research with the Dani lasted for some two and a half years during four different trips to West Irian between 1961 and 1970, that I was comfortable with the Dani language (although by no means fluent in it) and that I often discussed the postpartum sexual abstinence directly with Dani men (but not women). However I should also mention that a Roman Catholic priest, a missionary with the Dani, has challenged my claim, and reports that some of his catechists have told him of their great distress at the long abstinence forced on them (Camps 1972:90). Although I lived at Camps' mission station for seven months in 1970, I assume that these conversations took place after I left. For the purposes of this paper, I shall reject the possibility that these data refute my own. This is not a cavalier rejection of conflicting data, but is based on several points. First, I am confident about my own data; second, there are the special circumstances of a missionary priest talking with young' catechists; and third, there is a remote possibility that after August 1970, under increasing acculturation pressure from missionaries and government agents, the Dani youth did begin to change.

Let us assume that the claim of Dani unconcern about sexual abstinence is not due to faulty fieldwork, but rather is a conclusion which any reasonable investigator would come to after the usual sort of ethnographic observations and interviews. We would still be left with a generalization about Dani sexual attitudes which is quite broad and rather ambiguous. Is it possible to determine more definitively whether or not "sexual anxiety" exists?

It will help to be more precise about my second claim. We know that for those Dani parents of young children, the Dani cultural system dictates a certain behavior, namely, abstinence from sexual intercourse with each other. My claim was that this abstinence has no discernable short-term personality correlates, based on the fact that when a Dani is subjected to this period of abstinence, I could neither see nor elicit overt signs of unhappiness, anxiety, or other sorts of concern. In short, this suggests that sexual activity is psychologically of little importance to the Dani.

As stated, the proposition is a negative, which is impossible to prove. However, if reversed, it becomes a positive proposition which would at least be subject to proof (although still not subject to disproof.) Reversed, then, the proposition reads: Dani men who are long into their period of abstinence are more anxious or concerned about sex than men who have sexual access to their wives.

An obvious way to test this new proposition is to look for differences between men in the two states. I decided not to attempt this through systematic naturalistic observation of two sets of men, since that seemed to promise little more in the way of results than my previous observations and interviews. An obvious approach was experimental, where tests would be administered to provide possible indications of differences.

I used neither the stimuli nor the procedures of the projective test approach for two main reasons. First, I was concerned with the specific problem of sexual anxiety, and not with broad-spectrum analysis of Dani personality, attitudes, or motivations. Therefore, it seemed more economical to use stimuli directed toward this problem. It might have been possible to use drawings or posed photographs of Dani in neutral and erotic situations, but planning, making, and verifying these visual stimuli would have been quite time consuming, without any real expectation of success. By selecting verbal stimuli from the Dani repertory, it was possible to construct a natural and familiar task for the Dani subjects.

Second, customarily, only verbal responses to projective tests are recorded and analyzed. The major innovation of the present method is not the nature of the stimuli but the use of both verbal and nonverbal behavior as data for analysis. I knew from much previous experience with the Dani that if I were to rely on their verbal reactions alone, the data would be meager indeed. The basic research on facial expression plus the availability of videotape opened up the possibility of using Dani facial expressions as data.

## The Facial Expression Reaction Test

The Facial Expression Reaction Test was designed as a Dani-specific elicitation device. The stimuli were Dani songs, words, phrases, and gestures. The subjects were 11 Dani men, 6 celibate, and 5 noncelibate. The subjects' reactions, verbal and nonverbal, were recorded on videotape. Twenty judges, who were unfamiliar with the Dani and their language, were asked to view the videotape record and rate each subject as "celibate" or "noncelibate" on the basis of observed anxiety.

## The stimuli

Four kinds of stimuli were used: 1) short secular songs, called silon, which are generally sung casually by boys and youths and so are well-known to men; 2) common Dani gestures; 3) verb phrases; and 4) short questions (see Appendix 2 for the stimuli and their translations).

Each kind of stimulus was represented in each of the three groups: one group contained only stimuli with sexual references (the "erotic group") and two groups contained only sexually neutral stimuli (the "neutral groups"). I made the selections of stimuli and the judgments as to which were erotic and which were neutral on the basis of my two years' experience with Dani language and culture.

The erotic stimuli contain explicit sexual references; the neutral stimuli do not.

Although I am fairly confident that the neutral stimuli actually are neutral, I cannot completely rule out the possibility that some may contain covert Dani metaphors of allusions relating to sexuality which I did not recognize.

## The subjects

Eleven adult Dani men were selected more or less opportunistically from among those whom I knew, and who, during the period when I was giving the test, happened to come by my house alone at times convenient to me. Of these 11 men, it turned out that five claimed to be noncelibate (had sexual access to one or two of their wives) and six claimed to be celibate because of the postpartum sexual absence period. I was not able to verify their statements about their sexual status, but I have no reason to doubt them.

## The test administration

Each test was administered in my house at the edge of the Roman Catholic mission station at Jiwika. The subject and I were alone in the room. But occasionally, a test was interrupted when a third person wandered by and was asked to leave. The subject sat on a chair against one wall, facing into a Sony 2400 videotape camera. I sat behind the camera. A microphone picked up both our voices. I kept the camera trained on the subject's face most of the time, except for occasional movements to include his hand gestures. Although the subjects were unfamiliar with what the camera was, and what it was doing, it did not seem to bother them unduly. The stimuli were all the sorts of things about which I had been asking for two years, and our roles were familiar and presumably comfortable to all the subjects. Each session took about five or six minutes. At the end of the session, the subject was rewarded with a steel machete or shovel blade. This was an unusually generous reward, but one which each subject accepted with characteristic indifference.

The three sets of stimuli were read in the order: neutral, erotic, neutral. The neutrals were alternated for every other subject. I read each stimulus item to the subject as a question and gave him time to answer. If he did not respond—a frequent reaction at the beginning of each tests—I would repeat the item.

Since I read the stimuli anew for each Dani subject, and since I learned at the end of the erotic set (Question 3) whether or not the subject was celibate, I may have unconsciously revealed information through my voice during the second neutral series, although I tried to maintain a constant voice. The entire experiment was carried out in the Dani language.

The hypothesis was that celibate men had more sexual anxiety and would display more of this during the erotic stimuli presentations. The first set of neutral stimuli was intended to provide a baseline of reaction for each subject. The neutral stimuli following the erotic set were intended as insurance: it is conceivable that the celibate men would unsuccessfully conceal the anxiety created during the erotic stimuli, but then show it during the following neutral stimuli.

## Analysis of the videotape record

There are two possible approaches to the analysis. One would be to define anxiety in terms of a behavioral element or set of elements such as response time, eye movement, head movement, or facial expression, and systematically measure their occurrence in each subject. Although I have not attempted this measurement, it could be done.

Instead, I asked 20 judges in the US to judge each of the 11 Dani subjects as celibate or noncelibate on the basis of whether or not they showed an increase of anxiety during the test. This approach relied on gross intuitive judgments rather than on finer measurements. There was the danger that the US judges might not read Dani expressions correctly—that Dani paralinguistic signals would be as incomprehensible to them as were Dani words. However, the previous research, described above, indicated that Dani expressions could be read by non-Dani. Now, the state of anxiety, or discomfort, which I asked my judges to look for, is a fairly complex one, and is harder to isolate than the more basic states. Also, while the facial expressions for more basic states are pancultural, the circumstances under which affect is expressed (the display rules) vary from culture to culture. Despite these potential problems, it seemed worthwhile to run the judgment task.

The judges were 20 adult US natives, graduate students, and PhDs in anthropology and psychology, of varying cultural backgrounds. Three had done fieldwork in New Guinea with groups generally similar to the Dani, but the judgments of these three were nearly random with regard to the judge group as a whole. The judges were all participants in the Summer Institute for Visual Anthropology at Santa Fe, New Mexico, in the Summer of 1972. The judgment task was performed at the end of the first week of the institute, before they had been massively exposed to microanalysis of film. However, some had had previous experience with such analysis, and in fact one judge had been a collaborator of Ekman's.

The video recordings of the tests had been transferred onto two films, and were played back with the sound track on to the judges, who viewed them on a large video monitor. Judgments were done in two sessions, with ten judges in each session. I explained the purpose of the task and ran the tapes, announcing the start of the first neutral, the erotic, and the second neutral sections, and pausing between each test to allow the judges to write down their judgments. The judges were not told in advance how many tests they would see, nor were they told what the actual celibate to noncelibate ratio was. The task was long and difficult, and most of the judges became somewhat exasperated by it.

## The results

There was considerable variation in the accuracy with which the 11 Dani subjects were judged (from 17 of 20 correct to only 2 of 20 correct). There was also considerable variation in the accuracy of the 20 judges (from 9 of 11 correct to only 2 of 11 judgments correct).

The judges tended to overjudge subjects as celibate. Thus, they were slightly more accurate for the celibate men than for the noncelibate men: for all judges, 59% accuracy versus 56% accuracy. This suggests that the judges were perceiving a general level of anxiety which was independent of the sexual status of the subject.

The small $n$ and the fact that there were 6 celibate subjects and only 5 noncelibate subjects somewhat lessens the overall significance of the judging accuracy. However, of the 3 subjects judged with least accurate, 2 were noncelibate, and 1 was celibate, although 18 of the 20 judges judged him noncelibate.

There was some order effect, since the judges tended to make alternating celibate and noncelibate judgments; also, they tended to have a final balance between total celibate and noncelibate judgments. While there is some evidence that the judges were more accurate than pure chance would predict, the results are not strongly significant. If they had been, the experiment would have shown that there was stress at a level too subtle for gross ethnographic observation, but strong enough to be picked up by this method. As it is, we can only say that it is possible, but by no means certain, that the videotape interviews contain information which permits non-Dani speakers to distinguish between celibate and noncelibate men.

But what can we conclude from this experiment? By any laboratory standards, this experiment is fairly nonrigorous. The major defects were these:

1) the small *n* (11) and the nonrandom selection of subjects;
2) the use of "live" experimenter's voice instead of tape-recorded standard stimuli (thus, the judges may have been correct because of what they got from my voice, rather than what they got from the Dani voices and faces, or I might have differentially affected the subjects);
3) the vagueness of instructions to the judges—perhaps "anxiety" meant different things to different judges;
4) the uncertainty of just where the judges made their judgments: was it on the erotic sections? On the second neutral sections? The first neutral sections? Or on overall changes? Were the clues in the voice track or the visual record? Were they in the "normal" state of the subjects—i.e. do celibate men normally show more anxiety than noncelibate men, which would be revealed as early as the first neutral stimuli? Or were signs of anxiety actually elicited in the celibate men by the erotic stimuli? And, if so, when did these signs appear? If they appeared in the second or third sets, and the judges really react to a change in in anxiety from the first set, or were they actually judging from an external non-Dani baseline? These questions could be resolved by a greatly expanded judgment task, in which different sets of judges were asked to judge different conditions: only visual, only audio, both; and first neutral, erotic, second neutral, entire test. This would necessitate 12 different judging groups, and I have not undertaken it.

We must also consider these results in terms of the distinction between expressions of pancultural emotions and the culture-specific display rules. If the judges accurately perceived anxiety in the celibate subjects, does this mean that the inner states of the celibate subjects were anxiety? Or might the Dani use an expression of anxiety to cover a different emotional state?

The Dani expressions were, of course, spontaneous, in the sense that the subjects were not being asked to demonstrate emotions. On the other hand, we cannot exclude the possibility that the anxiety which the judges perceived was a Dani mask for a different inner state. I tend to doubt that the Dani were acting "in public" even though my camera and I were there. My previous experience made it clear that the Dani men were unusually indifferent to my presence in a wide range of events. (However, in videotapes of Dani mother–infant interaction, there is a fair amount of obvious camera consciousness.)

But despite the defects of the experiment, I suggest that it demonstrates that when Dani men undergo their long period of postpartum sexual abstinence, although their level of sexual anxiety increases, the increase is so slight that it is of little concern to the Dani themselves, and probably, in fact, they are not aware of it.

The importance of this experiment lies not in the fact that it has made a correction to the ethnographic account of a New Guinea Highland society. Rather, that it has attempted to develop a systematic visual experimental method of establishing verifiable ethnographic generalizations. With the use

78   *Visual research projects*

of the Dani-specific Facial Expression Reaction Test, nonverbal behavior was recorded on a videotape, and evaluated by a panel of judges, enabling us to discover facts about sexual expression which were beyond the reach of ordinary ethnography.

This sort of approach will not solve all ethnographic problems. There are many kinds of data for which it is inadequate. Also, there are some areas in which its use would be unethical because it endangered the people. But used with discretion, it promises to be a fruitful new visual anthropological tool.

Finally, although there are great differences between them, the experimental videotape approach and naturalistic observation should be complementary. I have emphasized how, in the case of the Dani, the experiments were used only after I had made ethnographic observations for two years. It was these observations which allowed the problems to be pinpointed and which directed the design of the experiment.

## Appendix 1. Eliciting phrases for six basic emotions in Grand Valley and Western Dani

**Eliciting phrases (Grand Valley Dani)**
Happy: hami-nen jetak wokokhemo, Edo watioko.
  Your mother's brother gave you a shell band, you are smiling.
Sad: Hakoja wadlaikhemo, dleatioko.
  Your mother died, you are crying.
Surprise: 0 bugasinem, hakmagen lan.
  There is thunder, you are surprised.
Fear: Hibango-ne mogat wetek, hai juk-en.
  In the night, there is a ghost, you are afraid.
Anger: Elege-nenhijum igiabusak, wene mu modok.
  A boy stole your clothing, you are very angry.
Disgust: al obasi wejakama.
  The feces smell bad.

**Eliciting phrases (Western Dani)**
Happy: ali'enken, e'ende ari.
  You are happy, you are smiling.
Sad: Ogoba kambekerakrne, leju.
  His father died, you cry.
Surprise: Ogut makerak.
  You are surprised.
Fear: Wimwoko rne, agabiti bakhe.
  Because the enemy comes, he is afraid.
Anger: Anini dukui pukut.
  He's angry, hitting someone with a stick.
Disgust: Obari genok.
  There is a bad smell.

## Appendix 2. The Facial Expression Reaction Test stimuli. (N = neutral, E = erotic. The neutral A set alternated with the neutral B set in first and third positions in the testing.)

Part 1. Songs
1. (NA) sisi eleoi iligik lakako I | He goes through the grass
wusakaik lakaoi | He comes down
Ge Wesakkaput lioksek lokolekma | The path to Wesakaput
Janenat woklakhelo | Is good
2. (E) Dukhe hakin adi abi gen diluk ati | Dukhe, your husband has lots of fleas

Niaige hakun adi alomusi hunik | Niaige, your husband has lots of anal hair.
3. (NA) Dlogop o Jipiga | The reeds at Jiwika
dlogop damirni damomo | The reeds are twisted and turned
4. (E) Dlokolik dlokolikhe girnusi dlukuakhe | Pubic hair looks like moss
dlokolik dlokolikhe dakernusi dlukuakhe | Pubic hair looks like moss
5. (NB) Akali jugunmaijuk sile oe akali | The twigs are plucked for firewood
gegaduk sileoe | The twigs are plucked for firewood
6. (E) Bubukhe almusi dlek dlegat hike oe | Pupukhe's anal hair is raised by the wind

Andok alomusi makat dikhe oe | Andok's anal hair droops down
7. (NB) Gean hakatekhe huniatik sani oe? | Who's singing along the path?
Part 2.
1. Phatet akotorni wusa luokoluk | The Father's boys are going to church
2. Phatet akotomi sokhola luokoluk | The Father's boys are going to school.

## Part 2. Gestures

1. (NA) hunger (Holding the sucked—in stomach with one hand.)
2. (E) copulation (Running the index finger of one hand back and forth between the base of the thumb and the base of the fingers of the other hand.)
3. (NB) smoking (sudden stopped intake of breath)
4. (E) tap penis gourd with flicking motion of index finger. (In fact, I doubt that this has erotic connotations—it is more a gesture of surprise, or

## Part 3. Phrases

1. (E) He itu bpekhatek. (They commit incest.)
2. (NA) Wen lupulkhatek. (They break garden soil with digging sticks.)
3. (E) Humi hakakhatek (They have intercourse with women.)
4. (NA) Hanom dlakhatek. (They roll and mat tobacco leaves into plugs.)
5. (E) Aben humi ilatutu hakat dlekhatekma. (Men seduce women.)
6. (NB) Helegit ikhatek. (They heat rocks.)
7. (NB) Hali ukhatek. (They gather firewood.)

## Part 4. Questions

1. (NA) Hopaije edake gi? (What is the name of your father?)
2. (E) Hake edake gi? (What is the name of your wife?)
3. (E) Hat hake oati bpekhep a? (Do you have intercourse with your wife?)
4. (NB) Hat wam ena wakankhatek a? (Do you raise pigs?)

## Notes

This chapter is based on fieldwork which was carried out during 1970 in West Irian (now Papua) Indonesia, among the Grand Valley Dani at Jiwika in the Grand Valley of the Balim, and among the Western Dani at Karubaga in the Konda (Swart) Valley. The experiments were completed in 1972 and 1973. The 1970 research (including the expense of the videotape equipment) was generously supported by a grant from the Foundations' Fund for Research in Psychiatry. I am most grateful to Eleanor Rosch (then Heider) for her collaboration and encouragement in many phases of this research. Father Jules Camps O.F.M. of Jiwika and the Reverend David Martin of Karubaga were our generous hosts. Paul Ekman, Wallace V. Friesen, and Harold G. Johnson have also made extensive contributions to the development of this research. Dr. Janet Elashoff, Chief Statistician at the Center for Advanced Study in the Behavioral Sciences, was kind enough to do a statistical analysis of the results of the sexual anxiety experiment. I especially appreciate the cooperation of the Dani subjects and the raters and judges who participated in this project. The final version of this paper was written while the author was a Fellow at the Center for Advanced Studies in the Behavioral Science.

# Part II
# Exploring Indonesian cinema

# 6 National cinema, national culture[1]

Ethnographies usually result from long-term involvement of the anthropologist in some cultural setting, usually among tribal or other isolated people. But in the following six chapters, I treat scripted, acted, and directed feature films as ethnographic data. And further, I treat Indonesian films as literal manifestations of an "Indonesian culture." No matter that Indonesia is a huge country containing many quite different cultures. Elsewhere, I carefully teased out differences between Central Javanese and West Sumatrans (Heider 1991a and 2011). Here, I unashamedly generalize about "Indonesian" culture. But these "Indonesian" films are mainly produced in central Java and claim to be Indonesian even when they make glancing references to Bali or West Sumatra. So, with this disclaimer, I proceed to mine these feature films for details and nuances of Indonesian culture.

It is important to emphasize that this approach to feature films was carried out in the 1970s and 1980s. The sorts of general claims about a general Indonesian culture seemed a fruitful approach for an anthropologist thinking about Indonesian films. My book, *Indonesian Cinema*, was published in 1991. But immediately the changing political winds in Indonesia of the 1990s focused attention on the rapid emergence of Islam as the dominant force in Indonesian politics. Where Islam had been an inescapable but background factor in Indonesian life previously, in the 1990s, Islam became—and still is—the important factor in Indonesian public life, including Indonesian cinema.

The English version of *Salim Said's Shadows on the Silver Screen—A Social History of Indonesian Cinema – National Culture on Screen*, and my own *Indonesian Cinema—National Culture on Screen*, both dated 1991, mention Islam, of course, but neither has any entries on Islam in their tables of contents.

Since then, the role of Islam in Indonesian cinema has boomed. To mention just a few recent books that have emphasized the importance of Islam in thinking about Indonesian cinema: Krishna Sen's *Indonesian Cinema, Framing the New Order* (1994), Timothy P. Daniels' edited volume, *Performance, Popular Culture, and Piety in Muslim Southeast Asia* (2013), Ariel Heryanto's *Identity and Pleasure. The Politics of Indonesian*

84  *Exploring Indonesian cinema*

*Screen Culture* (2014), and, most importantly, David Hanan's *Culture Specificity in Indonesian Film* (2017).

And, during the last decade, in another huge step toward the study of Moslam Indonesia, there has been increasing attention paid to the new technology of social media. For example, in the papers collected in *Introduction: Piety, Celebrity, Sociality* (edited by Carla Jones and Martin Slama 2017). For example, Ismail Fajrie Alatas mentions the Islamic Mystic Habib Luthfi bin Yahya, in Java, whose "website is accessed by 100–300,000 visitors each month. His official Facebook fan-page and Twitter accounts have more than 1.9 million and 61,000 followers" (Alatas 2017). The implications of this go far beyond the visual projects described here.

In the following chapters, we see examples of what an ethnographer with a camera and fieldwork experience in New Guinea villages and Sumatran towns brings to an ethnographic appreciation of (older) Indonesian movies.

Although, here, I want to consider only Indonesian cinema, it is in fact just one part of the whole. Even when taking seriously, the notion of constructing a national culture on screen eventually demands that we look at the entire range of images which bombard Indonesians, including the various Indonesian-produced dramas made for the national television channel, and besides the films made in Indonesia, those films imported from abroad and shown in theaters, on television, and rented through video-cassette shops. There are few Indonesians, no matter how isolated or how poor, who are not at least occasionally within sight of some of this visual onslaught.

Eventually, we must pull it all together–movies, television, and the still-lively varieties of more traditional Indonesian theater and dance forms. Ulf Hannerz, the Norwegian anthropologist, has used the term "macro-anthropology" for a conceptual position which looks at cultural phenomena, the sharing of meanings, and cutting across community lines. Hannerz offers this analogy to "the linguistic of contact" described by Mary Louise Pratt. He is trying to go beyond simple center-periphery thinking, whether it be the Wallenstein world system theory and imperial models in which the center controls but allows cultural diversity in the periphery, or a "radical diffusionism" in which "the center mostly speaks, and the periphery mostly listens without talking back" (Hannerz 1989:206). This seems to be similar to the understanding which Pico Iyer develops in his picaresque travelogue "Video Nights in Kathmandu: (Iyer 1988). The central question then focuses not so much on the economic or political relations of periphery as on the cultural question: what sort of emergent cultural form is being created and purveyed to the people? And, of course, here the concern is with an emergent national, not world, culture.

In his influential essay on nationalism, Benedict Anderson talks about nations as "imagined communities." By this, he means to focus on the fact that a nation's commonality is not the result of face-to-face interaction but is in important ways an imagined construction. And he discusses in some detail the impact of the printing press, and how "print-capitalism made it possible for rapidly growing numbers of people to think about themselves, and to relate themselves to others, in profoundly new ways" (Anderson 1983:40).

But the effects of widely available printed materials in vernacular languages since the 15th century are very similar to the effects of widely screened movies in national languages since the 1920s. We can profitably reword Anderson's claim thus: image-capitalism, or commercial movies, make it possible for people to think about themselves, and relate themselves to others, in profoundly new ways.

Indeed, Anderson elsewhere has written about the importance of post-revolutionary monuments in Indonesia as a type of communication. The most important of these material symbols of nationhood stand in public places in Jakarta and are not experienced by most Indonesians except as their images are projected across the nation. As important as books, magazines, and newspapers are in this highly literate society of Indonesia, it is the cinema which has played a major role in the imagining, or constructing, of an Indonesian culture. By virtue of its immense popularity, cinema is important, for those imagined communities are to an important degree *imagined* communities. And, as Anderson, the political scientist, spoke anthropologically about nationalism, here an anthropologist addresses emergent nationalism as an imaging and imagining of national culture.

The ethnic diversity of Indonesia is well-known, for it has been witnessed, even exaggerated, in the anthropological literature. Virtually, all anthropological writing on the area has examined specific, unique, local phenomena. There is a tremendous gap between our focused tribe, village, and ethnic group studies and the ways in which political scientists and others comfortably think on the national level as they discuss things "Indonesian." As early as 1963, Hildred Geertz had begun to talk about an emerging Indonesian metropolitan superculture." However, Edward Bruner, at the same period, flatly stated that "no distinctive national Indonesian culture or society has yet developed" (Bruner 1961:520). And two decades later, Bruner still insisted that "we are deluding ourselves is we believe that there is a fixed thing floating over the archipelago labeled "modern Indonesian culture" just waiting to be discovered and described, with the implication that it is everywhere the same "thing," interpreted the same way by members of the various regional cultures" (Bruner 1979:300). But surprisingly, when one thinks about it, Indonesian films come closer to fitting Bruner's description! For each film is a "fixed thing," a finished product, its duplicated copies sent out to bioscopes across the country offering identical images of this national culture to all audiences. But of course, Bruner raises the crucial question: how the different audiences understand and transform this message for their own uses. This is surely one of the most important next steps in the study of Indonesian cinema.

Of all cultural phenomena on the national level, it is language which is most obviously "Indonesian" in the sense that the national language has been recognized, politicized, debated, and analyzed. No one could possibly doubt that there is an "Indonesian language." But the rest of culture is more problematic. Even when the nationalistic students swore their famous Youth Pledge on October 28, 1928 (today a national holiday), they proclaimed one land, one people, and one language, but not "one culture."

So, despite the great emphasis on language as a unifying common element, there has been much more ambivalence about the rest of culture. The status of regional culture in Indonesian thought is complex. On the one hand, it is celebrated with regional cultural institutes—of Javanologi, Baliologi, etc., but I think that this is a sort of folklorization, for it serves to push regional cultures out of ordinary life and to mummify and trivialize these cultures in museums, tourist performances, souvenir dolls, special regional gift shops, and, as the embodiment supreme, there is a Beautiful Indonesia Mini Park near Jakarta, a sort of Disneyland with samples of traditional *adat* houses from each major Indonesian region. But in another sense, there is an overall formal denial of ethnicity. For example, in conversation, there is often mention that an acquaintance or a public figure is of a particular ethnic group—Orang Batak, Orang Java, etc., but in published biographical sketches, this is almost never done and people are, in this formal context, defined by their place of birth. But of course, this can be misleading, since for all sorts of reasons, a person born in Padang may not be an Orang Padang.

And even using the name of the city, Padang, to designate the ethnic group, Minangkabau, embodies this denial of ethnicity, for Padang is the new capital of West Sumatra, a coastal city lying outside the traditional Minangkabau heartland. After the unsuccessful war of secession in the late 1950s, the Jakarta government moved the capital of the province from Bukittinggi, in the heartland, to the coast, the *rantau*, or the outside. Now, there are Minangkabau living throughout Indonesia, and Minangkabau restaurants flourish everywhere (even in Wamena, among the Grand Valley Dani of Irian Jaya!) But it is now the custom to call the people Padang people (Orang Padang). I have a feeling that this submerging of ethnicity has progressed farther with the Minangkabau than with most other groups, but it is symptomatic of the general trend.

Let us turn to the movies. The first Indonesian film was made in (about) 1926 (see the social history of Indonesian cinema by Salim Said (1991). Through the 1930s, the growing local film industry turned out films based on Indonesian oral traditions—legends, myths, etc., and it also drew on other local theater traditions. The films were all in the Indonesian language but were produced and directed by Europeans or Chinese, with Indonesian or Eurasian performers.

After an almost complete hiatus in the 1940s, during the Japanese occupation and the Struggle for Independence, filmmaking resumed with a flourish: 1950, the first year of peace, saw 23 Indonesian feature films (only 1 of which survives). Production waxed and waned after that, but more recently, it seems to have settled into a steady 60 or 70 feature films per year. This is modest compared with other Southeast Asian countries, and accounts for less than half the films shown in Indonesian bioscops or available in videocassette rental shops across the nation. Imports from the Chinese-speaking countries, the USA, India, and Europe make up the majority of films available in Indonesia.

James Peacock, in his study (Peacock 1987) of the *ludruk* proletarian drama in the Surabaya region of East Java in the early 1960s, argued that these stories functioned to show people from rural areas how to adjust to urban modernity. Embedded in coarse humorous formulaic were models for their new behavior. (It may be that Nigerian television performs a similar function of satirical familiarization—see Hannerz 1989.) Indonesian movies also perform that function, both by what they show and what they do not show; they provide a model for modern, pan-Indonesian culture.

From the beginning, Indonesian movies have been made in the Indonesian language. There are no regional language movies, not even Javanese (although the population of Javanese speakers alone is larger—100 million people—than that of any other Southeast Asian country.) A few distinctive words in a regional language may be tossed into the script, and the Indonesian may be spoken with a regional accent but even when scenes are set in remote villages, the people speak to each other in good Indonesian, not in the local language which would be appropriate to the setting. There are few exceptions, such as comedies which use Jakarta slang. The most celebrated film of 1988, *Djyut Nya Dien*, about the Acenese heroine of the resistance against the Dutch, was the most striking exception—much of its dialogue was actually in Acenese with Indonesian subtitles. But it does not seem to have started a trend toward regionalization.

Many films are set outside Jakarta, but only a few aspects of a locality are depicted: famous views of landscapes, distinctive regional house forms, and ceremonies. The extensive genre of sentimental films specializes in ceremonies: wedding ceremonies especially but also ceremonies for circumcision, funerals, harvests, and bridge openings. These are shown with ethnographic fidelity. One could make quite an acceptable compilation film on Javanese rituals or weddings of Indonesia by assembling clips from these feature films. But the authentic nuggets are found edited into stories which otherwise show no sign of regional culture. They are used indexically to say "these people are truly Batak, or Minangkabau, or Javanese" while at the same time, the entire weight of the film is saying "these Batak, or Minangkabau, or Javanese act, even dress like Indonesians everywhere."

## *Salah Asuhan*: the Minangkabau who are not Minangkabau

*Salah Asuhan* is a movie which was made in 1973 from one of the first, and still one of the most famous, Indonesian novels, a Dutch period melodrama, published in 1928 (de Queljoe 1974). Both the author of the book and the director of the film were Minangkabau and the story is mainly about

Minangkabau. Much of the film was shot on location in West Sumatra, home of the Minangkabau and we see Minangkabau great houses, pony carts, and famous landscapes. The first wedding scene looks completely authentic and was probably done entirely by local experts, and the final shots of the Tabut ceremony on the beach at Pariaman were surely shot at the ceremony itself.

But although Minangkabau has a famously matrilineal clan organization (see Kato 1981), what is presented in the film could just as well be cognatic Java or even a strongly patrilineal society. We see the hero, his mother, his mother's brother, and his mother's brother's daughter, whom he marries, but no sign at all of any other members of either clan involved. It is especially unlikely that no clanmates of the mother's brother's daughter support her when the hero abuses her and deserts her.

When I raised this issue with the director, he objected to my reading, saying that it was typically Minangkabau to send the young man abroad for schooling. But it would have been done by the boy's clan and his uncle would have been only the manager and agent of the clan. Stretching matters, one could contend that the film allows such Minangkabau-ness to be inferred, but in fact, nothing in the film makes any of it explicit, and the boy's obligation is clearly shown to be to the uncle, not to the clan.

## *Putri Giok:* The Chinese Indonesian who are not Chinese

Another more elaborate example of this flattening of ethnicity is *Putri Giok*, one of the only Indonesian films to deal in any way with social tension between Indonesians and Indonesian Chinese. This film is vaguely reminiscent of *Romeo and Juliet*: an Indonesian Chinese brother and sister (she is Putri Giok, The Jade Princess) are both dating pribumi Indonesians. Their father, an authoritarian real estate developer, breaks up both relationships, egged on by his wily business partner, who is worried about the effects of ethnic mixing on the business. (Interestingly enough, this partner, the agent of disorder in the film, is cast as and played by, a South Asian, not an Indonesian of any sort.)

The entire film is an argument for harmony through assimilation to the pan-Indonesian culture. None of the Indonesians have any recognizable ethnicity and the main activity of the youth centers around a girls' softball team—softball being a decidedly un-Indonesian sort. The film's message is that Indonesian Chinese are to be accepted as Indonesian, not as Chinese. The Chinese–Indonesians are, in fact, already quite Indonesian. Only a few signs point to their Chinese origin: their names, their faces, and a single Chinese wall scroll.

It is especially interesting how the film handles religion. It could have ignored religion, as do most Indonesian films. But it could not have generalized—there is no common national religion as there is a national language which cuts across parochial boundaries. So, improbably, the mother is Buddhist, the daughter Catholic, and the son Moslem.

## National cinema, national culture  89

Yet in another sense, there is a national religion. The appeals to understanding and acceptance of the Chinese as Indonesians are formulated in a particularly religious sense but in the symbols of the republic: through the national anthem, through an Independence Day speech by the wife of the Vice President, and especially by the large wall ornament of the Garuda holding the symbols of the Pancasila, the Five Principals of the Republic. At the moment of sudden conversion of the agent of disorder, the South Asian, he turns to the Garuda hanging on the wall above him and stands at attention as voices of reason echo in his mind and a heavenly choir sings. No Indonesian would suggest that patriotism is a substitute for religion, glossed as "belief in One God," but that is certainly how it appears in the film's setting.

At the end of the movie, the father and his partner have the sudden conversion typical of Indonesian melodramas, the two couples are reunited with blessings all around, and the different gene pools are united in a single national culture. (There is a very curious twist at the very end of the film. Giok, now reunited with her Herman, is applauded by the guests at the party, as she wears a Chinese silk dress. This is a little subversive touch which denies the assimilation message of the rest of the film.)

But it is actually the long opening scene of the film which is the most elegant statement of assimilation into the national culture. There is a great chorus of youths singing Indonesia Raya, the very European-style national anthem, accompanied by a European-style brass band (no traditional tune, no gamelan orchestra here). The camera pans first across rows of singers wearing black and white school uniforms, those obligatory pan-Indonesian costumes which are literally uniform for school children through high school and whose uniformity is especially striking in this country which has—or recently had—the world's richest variety of local textiles. Soon, the camera moves to more singers, now each in a different, readily recognizable regional ceremonial costume. And of course, they are singing the patriotic hymn in unison. One thinks, again, of Benedict Anderson's words:

> there is a special kind of contemporaneous community which language alone suggests—above all in the forms of poetry and songs. Take national anthems, for example, sung on national holidays. No matter how banal the words and mediocre the tunes, there is in this singing an experience of simultancy. At precisely such moments, people wholly unknown to each other utter the same verses to the same melody. The image unisonance.
>
> (Anderson 1983:132)

Again, we have regionalism used indexically to say that we are all one. Regional differences are toned down and regional cultural distinctiveness is reduced to a few standard motifs which are used to deny regionalism.

The sorts of settings, behaviors, and social relations which are presented constitute a generalized national culture. And this is a generalized successful middle-class culture. Lower class life, even generalized poverty, is rarely shown. (Krishna Sen 1988 and 1989 has discussed some films which do deal with poverty but these are rare exceptions.) And social conflict—that is, problems arising from intrinsic structural incompatibilities such as race, ethnicity, economic differences, or especially political positions—is rare indeed on film.

Of course, from the standpoint of the economics of the film industry, each film should have as wide an audience as possible. One way to appeal to audiences across the archipelago is to make films of overwhelming spectacle. Here, Indonesian filmmakers draw on the Central Javanese 15th century kingdom of Madjapahit. I was surprised to see the most successful (and expensive) of these, *Saur Sepuh*, playing in Irian Jaya in 1988. Is it possible that in addition to the common Indonesian culture which films are creating for present and future, the historical spectaculars are delivering a specific (*Majapahit*) past to all Indonesians? (Relatively few Americans were ever actually engaged in pushing forward or resisting the Western frontier, yet thanks in part to Hollywood, the Western dominated our shared history.) To some extent, this reanimation of past *Majapahit* glories through cinema does function to provide a common past in the way that archeology does in many countries.

By discovering the traces of forgotten, prehistoric cultures and by establishing continuity between these past cultures and the present, archeologists provided an added prestigious depth to the claims of nationalism. This was true for European powers as well as for minority, third world, or colonial peoples. Bruce G. Trigger describes the close relationship between archeology and nationalism since the mid-19th century:

> Like nationalist history, to which it is usually closely linked, the cultural–historical approach can be used to bolster the pride and morale of nations or other groups. It is most often used for this purpose among peoples who feet thwarted, threatened, or deprived of their collective rights by more powerful nations or in countries where appeals are being made to counteract serious internal divisions. Nationalist archeology tends to emphasize the more recent past rather than the Paleolithic period and draws attention to the political and cultural achievements of indigenous ancient civilizations.
>
> (Trigger 1989:174)

This describes nicely the *Majapahit* movies. With perhaps the difference that while the historical *Majapahit* was mainly limited to Java, the movie *Majapahit* implicitly becomes the ancestral state for all Indonesians. It would be instructive to examine Indonesian archeology in this light. Although the central government has been active in restoring the great Hindu and Buddhist temples of a millennium ago (Borobudur is the most famous), I suspect that on the whole, Indonesian archeology is not as effective in this way as archeology in other, comparable countries, and that cinema has taken on the burden of providing an imagined past.

But most Indonesian films construct a pan-Indonesian culture in modern form. These plots and settings are probably driven more by economics than by some central political planning of the Jakarta government. The government interest in encouraging, censoring, and occasionally sponsoring films seems to focus more on protecting and enhancing the images of specific events or individuals, and not on broader social planning (see Sen's discussion of censorship [1988]). *Desa di Kaki Bukit* (The Village at the Foot of the Hills [1980]) by Asrul Sani, is a rare exception: its unacknowledged sponsor was the national family planning program, and its plot shows how conservative village resistance to family planning and other sorts of modernization is overcome by determined patriotism and love (see Heider 1991b:81–86). Similarly, Lutze attributes the "catholicity" or "all-Indianness" of Hindi films primarily to economic motivation. (Lutze 1985:5).

Many Indonesians, while acknowledging the absence of regional ethnographic verisimilitude, feel that Indonesian films have become Americanized under the impact of all the Hollywood imports. I would agree that in a few rather superficial ways, particularly concerning sexuality. This is true: kissing, handholding, and form-revealing clothing have become almost routine in the films of the last decade. The artifacts of upper class Westernized Jakarta Indonesians, from dining tables to automobiles, are shown constantly. And in this respect, these dramas and melodramatic films do present a model for Western style domestic life. They show people how to live a middle-class, unethnic life in Indonesia today. It would be interesting to learn just how the imports, especially American domestic dramas, fit into this picture. I suspect that the American contributions are generally seen as totally unrealistic models for any Indonesian behavior (indeed, many Americans feel the same way), while the Indonesian versions are the more accessible models, presenting a possible future, giving instructions in the new national culture. In this sense, the Indonesian films really do convey a strong Americanization of world culture.

But if one goes beyond the settings to consideration of the actors and the central conflicts of the plots, it appears that these Indonesian films have become more Indonesian, not less. I would identify the two most important features of Indonesian-ness as: 1) emphasis on social groups rather than autonomous individuals; and 2) emphasis on conflict between order and disorder rather than between good and evil. Films of the 1950s, made by men trained in Western cinema, are more Western, less Indonesian, in these particulars, than are films made in the 1970s and 1980s (see the extended argument to this effect in Heider 1991b). Asrul Sani, one of the grand older men of Indonesian cinema, who began his career in the 1950s, exemplified this shift in the landmark films of his own career.

Finally, I would like to look briefly at those who were responsible for making Indonesian films, those who were the constructors of this national culture on the screen. We find an irony: they were at first, overwhelmingly from abroad—from Europe and from China, but later they were Indonesian (especially Minangkabau). In various respects, then, they were from the outside or the periphery, and certainly not the core, of Indonesian society. People who could not be players in the classic wayang of Java found opportunities in the new niche of cinema. And, in many respects like the Jews who invented Hollywood (to use Neal Gabler's phrase), these outsiders were responsible for creating the image of the common Indonesian culture.

Gabler also suggests that the Jews of Hollywood had a special compatibility with the industry, one that gave them certain advantages over their competitors. For one thing, having come primarily from fashion and retail, they understood public taste and were masters at gauging market swings, at merchandising, at pirating away customers and beating the competition (Gabler 1988:5). Again, this suggests the Minangkabau, famous for their small business skills across the country and even more the Chinese Indonesians, who had long concentrated in business (Peacock 1973:46).

And the parallel goes further: in America, by the late 1930s, virulent anti-Semitism allied with rabid anticommunism found the cinema industry Jews an irresistible target. Ironically, this was in the name of the very all-American culture which these men had done so much to create (Gabler 1988:311–86).

In Indonesia, there have been sharp but cryptic attacks on "non-Indonesian" influences within the film industry which subverted the true Indonesian cinema. It is specifically "Indonesian Chinese filmmakers who are being attacked ... the non-native producers who still dominate the domestic film industry..." (Said 1982:10, 1991:9). Even the appearance of Eurasian actors has been criticized:

> Any domination, if it could be called that, of Eurasian faces in Indonesia occurs only in films. And it was this relatively frequent appearance of Eurasian films that gave rise sometime ago to controversy among observers of the world of film.
>
> (Depari 1990:78)

But for all that critics may deplore the commercialization and the "non-native" influences on Indonesian films, it is just these two factors which have been most influential in producing national culture in a national cinema which can be sold and viewed across the archipelago. There is an emergent national Indonesian culture. It is not localized—there are no "Indonesian villages"—but it is being imagined and modeled and developed in the national cinema.

## Note

1 Reprinted from Dissanayake, Wimal (Ed.) 1994. *Colonialism and Nationalism in Asian Cinema*. Bloomington: Indiana University Press, pp. 162–173.

# 7 Analyzing emotion in scenes from Indonesian cinema

In the past century or more, many thousands of acted feature films exploring human behavior have been produced by natives in countless countries and cultures. What a potential treasure trove of cultural data! Yet even now only a few dozen of these films have been analyzed by anthropologists. And much of that research began and ended during the Second World War. Ruth Benedict's contribution, *The Chrysanthemum and the Sword*, published in 1946, used Japanese films to study Japanese culture, and a collection of essays by many other contributors was published under the title *The Study of Culture at a Distance* (Mead and Metraux 1953). Two of the groups then collaborated on a 1950 book, *Movies. A Psychological Study* (Wolfenstein and Leites 1950) whose second edition (1970) updates the first. And one of the group, John H. Weakland, contributed a chapter on *Feature Films as Cultural Documents* for the 1974 *Principles of Visual Anthropology* and then updated that essay for Hockings' second edition in 1995.

To the extent that anthropologists have looked at cinema for cultural insights, they have mainly considered overall plotlines looking for cultural patterns writ large in these films. Here, we mined Indonesian fiction films for brief interactions which reveal details of Indonesian emotion behavior. I carried out this work during my second year in West Sumatra, showing ten scenes from Indonesian movies on videotape and asking Minang informants to closely analyze the emotion talk.

My own interest in fiction films came about almost by accident as I was carrying out ethnographic research on emotion in West Sumatra, Indonesia (see Chapter 2). I lived with my family in a small highland city, Bukittinggi. I had brought video equipment for my research, and began to rent Indonesian feature films from various shops in the city. At first it was for casual entertainment and Indonesian language practice, but slowly I came to see these films as cultural documents. When I returned to the University of South Carolina, I began to offer a course in Indonesian Cinema Through Film. This turned into a book titled *Indonesian Cinema. National Culture on Screen* (Heider 1991b).

In this chapter, I describe a pseudonaturalistic experiment, using short clips of emotion-packed scenes from Indonesian movies to elicit attributions

94   *Exploring Indonesian cinema*

of emotion from some Minangkabau respondents. The results indicate how Minangkabau understand emotion behavior as it was then depicted in national Indonesian cinema.

What better place to look for emotion behavior than in movies? The very features which make movies untrustworthy sources of ethnographic data in some respects work to provide revealing enactments of emotions. Movies are false: they are scripted, rehearsed, staged, and acted. But all this is done by natives for natives. The demands of commercial success mean that movies must be understandable to their audiences.

Movies are exaggerated: but this means that a 90-minute movie will include economically described scenarios of the flow of emotion, including the preliminary antecedents, the peak moments, and the outcomes. Real life is rarely so compact: emotion events are rare, and when they do occur, they have long prehistories and reverberate long after the climax. A movie, in contrast, must describe all this in a few succinct moments.

But, however, much movies exaggerate, this cannot be a random exaggeration. When they are made in a culture for that culture, they must be transformations based on the realities of that culture. Anthropologists have made surprisingly little use of the cinema of a culture for understanding the culture. In part this is due to our bias toward small—scale tribal societies which produce no cinema. And then, in Indonesia, the very blaring intrusiveness of cinema, the garishness of the advertisements, the prominence of the American imports of the Rocky/Rambo sort, and the scorn of Indonesian intellectuals have tended to blind us to the possibilities of Indonesian cinema. Indonesia has a strong intellectual tradition. At the time I was studying Indonesian cinema, there were several Indonesian social scientists who were prominent to the national discourse, whose writings were found regularly in *Tempo* and *Kompas*. Whatever else one might have said about the Indonesian press, it could certainly match the Western press in using the talents of intellectuals. But most of these same intellectuals shunned—even scorned—Indonesian cinema as a subject of concern.

In contrast, the West has a long and fruitful tradition of serious film scholarship, much of which is at least potentially useful for anthropologists. Perhaps also, cinema was "popular culture," until recently (with the exception of the activity noted at the beginning of this chapter) neglected by anthropologists. The anthropological neglect is especially curious because there have been influential and widely read exceptions, books like James Peacock's *Rites of Modernization* (Peacock 1968) on the popular Javanese theater genre ludruk.

## The ethnography of emotion

My own research has been based on the assumption that while much emotion behavior is pancultural, a significant part is culture-specific. The goal is to sort out the mixture of pancultural and culture-specific behavior, and to relate it to other aspects of the cultures, Minangkabau or Javanese.

Here, I describe one task pulled out of the total context: how clips of emotion scenarios from commercial Indonesian movies can be used to solicit attributions and judgments of emotions from Minangkabau informants. I had not included this task in my original research design—in fact, I had no idea that Indonesian films would be at all useful in the research. It was serendipitous, although my previous work with ethnographic film and casual acquaintance with film theory in general undoubtedly helped me to take advantage of the opportunity.

In my emotion work with the Minangkabau, described in Chapter 2, I tried to use videotapes of children as stimuli to elicit reactions. There were two problems with the design: while the videotape records of the children were ethnographically rich, they rarely captured much good emotion behavior and what they did capture was mainly anger. Random moments in lives do not easily provide a satisfactory range of overt emotion behavior.

Also, people made few comments when they viewed the tapes. In part, perhaps, this was because people generally have little perspective on pictures of themselves and their children. (However, other researchers have found that that still photographs of people in familiar settings are good elicitors—see Collier and Collier's book, *Visual Anthropology* 1987). More important, I believe, was the reluctance of Minangkabau to analyze and thus possibly criticize their own children in front of outsiders.

But the Indonesian films offered a solution to both these problems: they contain many scenes of emotion behavior, but because people know that the scenes are fiction, there is little hesitation to make attributions and even to criticize the behavior of the fictional characters.

## Methodology

After viewing several dozen Indonesian films on videotape, I selected eleven for careful study and for use in teaching. These were chosen to cover a wide range of genres, rather than for their cinematographic excellence. Then, I had bilingual (Indonesian and English) scripts prepared for each film and viewed each film several times. I picked out what seemed to me to be the best representation of the widest range of emotion behavior. This amounted to some 80 scenes, which I edited onto a single master tape. In my second year of fieldwork, I went through each scene with my three Minangkabau research assistants, working in the Indonesian language (the films are all in Indonesian). I asked them to describe the emotion or emotions in the scene: first, for each actor, an overall judgments for the entire scene. Then, in a second viewing, I stopped the tape at crucial moments and asked for the emotions of an actor at that moment. It is worth noting that the Indonesian term I used for emotion was perasaan hati. And in Indonesian, there is not the singular/plural distinction which is obligatory in English, so the eliciting questions were conveniently ambiguous as to whether one or more emotions were to be named. This is significant, since one of the research problems concerns the multiplicity of emotions which a person feels at any one moment. The questions at each stop were:

What emotion does X feel?

How do you know this?

What emotion does X show?

How do you know this?

How appropriate is X's emotion behavior?

The task was unworkable: too many scenes, too many questions. It took several hours to complete. I reduced the task to the ten scenes which seemed to promise the best responses, and used only the simplest question: "what emotion(s) does X feel? I then worked through the task six or seven times with informants (singles or pairs, but since the pairs would agree and present me with a consensus opinion, I am considering the responses as coming from seven informants).

Each of the interviews took about an hour. The total results were over a thousand emotion words (7 informants giving 1 or more attributions to 87 instances). These words were then analyzed in terms of a cognitive map of emotion words in Indonesian as used by Minangkabau. Preparing this map had been the first step of the overall emotion project, and it is described in Heider 1991a. It is constructed from synonyms given by 50 Minangkabau who were bilingual (in Minangkabau and Indonesian Minangkabau) for a list of 229 Indonesian emotion words. It is a composite representation of how Minangkabau understand relationships among Indonesian emotion words. (The study also produced comparable maps of emotion words in Minangkabau itself, and in Indonesian, as used by Central Javanese.) The map generated by the 229 emotion words actually shows 300 words grouped into clusters of closely—related terms. The map is used here in the analysis of this task to provide the authority for lumping of responses into similarity clusters.

To use an analogy in English: if a character in a scene is described as "angry, furious, embarrassed, and ashamed," any fluent speaker of English understands that the person has been described as having two different emotions, one is sorts of anger, the other sorts of shame. But what we do intuitively with our native language we need some better authority for in our other languages. Dictionaries may hint at such clusters of related words, but they do not go far enough. The cognitive map I had constructed is intended to be such an authoritative guide to meaning clusters in Indonesian.

## Analysis

Let us turn to the detailed analyses of the results from each of the ten scenes. These results are described actor by actor for the scene overall, and then for each crucial moment in turn. In most cases, all seven interviews produced one or more attributions. The cognitive map is intended to be such an authoritative guide to meaning clusters in Indonesian. References to emotion word clusters use the labels (number, English gloss, Indonesian key word) which are described in Heider (1991a).

FOCUS NUMBER OF CLUSTERS This is the number of clusters used by the respondents to describe any one character in a scene or cut. To anticipate the outcome, this measure showed that several different clusters were used for most of the 78 cases. The mode was four clusters, and up to ten were used. The distribution is:

| Number of instances:     | 4 | 5 | 0 | 18 | 14 | 13 | 12 | 4 | 6 | 2  |
|--------------------------|---|---|---|----|----|----|----|---|---|----|
| Number of clusters used: | 1 | 2 | 3 | 4  | 5  | 6  | 7  | 8 | 9 | 10 |

In the scene—by-scene analysis, special attention will be paid to characters who attracted attributions from very few clusters (one or two) and to those who attracted many (seven to ten).

FOCUS: INFORMANT AGREEMENT The percentage of the seven informants who agreed on any one cluster. Agreement on a given term is less significant (it is certainly more rare) than agreement on a more general emotion cluster. Sometimes the informants do not agree at all, even on the cluster; sometimes there is strong agreement on a single cluster; often there is strong agreement on more than one cluster.

COMPLEXITY The percentage of informants making attributions in more than one cluster. Here, the use of clusters for analysis is essential, for simply measuring raw numbers of different words, counting sad and depressed, that is very different from being sad and fearful).

NUANCED The total number of nonkey words in proportion to the overall total of words used for an actor in a scene.

In the mapping of clusters, nearly all clusters have a single word which has more and closer connections to the other members of that cluster. These key words are the most obvious, best known words for their clusters and the words which are first named in English–Indonesian dictionaries for a general emotion term (e.g. sad—sedih; angry—marah). This measure of nuance indicates the degree to which people pick less obvious emotion terms, and so is a second measure of the emotion complexity which people perceive in an actor at a specific moment.

Again, to anticipate the results, the percentage of nonkey terms runs from 11% to 90%. We shall pay particular attention to values in the highest quartile (67%–90%) and the lowest quartile (38%–11%).

## Choosing the scenes

Ideally, perhaps, one would choose scenes which would exemplify the behavior of each of the 40 emotion clusters or just the 10 most salient clusters. In fact, here I have worked with 11 films which I had studied, and for which I had prepared Indonesian–English scripts. The first selection of 80 scenes was based on my own judgments about which scenes contain strong accounts of emotion and would be likely to evoke interesting comments. After going through all 80 scenes with a group of three informants, I made the final cut to the ten scenes which seemed to offer a good range of behavior: male and female, adult and child; simple and complex; direct and deceptive; and positive and, especially, negative. I tried to include positive emotions. (Intense negative emotions, especially anger, are easy to find in these films, in part because the films permit acting out what otherwise is so masked and dangerous in Indonesian life.) But in fact, the results show that my expectations of the emotional content of a scene were often wrong. I shall describe the rationale for each choice in turn below, but it is important not to claim too much randomness or representativeness for these ten scenes.

In my book on Indonesian Cinema (Heider 1991b), I tried to show how the plots and behaviors in Indonesian movies, although often confusing to Western viewers, could be understood on Indonesian terms by taking into account such cultural factors as Indonesian concepts of morality and traditional Indonesian plot forms. This experiment allows us to take a further step in this direction. We can examine in some detail how some people, who are Minangkabau Indonesians, interpret the emotional complexity of characters in dramas. As we shall see, in some scenes the Minangkabau respondents see quite different emotions than those which seem so obvious to a westerner. And despite the exaggerated fiction of these scenes, they are Indonesian and so tell us something of the dynamics of Indonesian emotion.

## National culture, national emotion?

These films present a sort of behavior which is pan-Indonesian (Heider 1991b). Bits of regional cultures are inserted as local color: words, landscapes, house forms, and rituals (like the Minangkabau wedding of Scene 3). But the language and the behavior generally are nonregional. These films are in fact a major medium for the construction of a national culture. But what, then, about emotions? Are we looking at national emotions? Or a national culture of emotion?

No, I think that we are looking at how people of one ethnic group interpret the emotions offered up in Indonesian movies. In a previous book, I have already shown how differently Minangkabau and Javanese, coming from quite different regional cultures, understand the national language,

Indonesian (Heider 1991a). This experiment now puts a new twist on it. We could repeat the same experiment in Central Java, and most likely those Javanese would respond differently from Minangkabau in predictable ways. To anticipate: Scene 1 is about "bangga," which in Minangkabau is pride, but part of the "happy" cluster. Javanese understand the same word as a "pride" but not part of their idea of "happy." (Both cultures have another sort of pride, sombong, which they see as isolated, isolating, and very negative—a sort of arrogance (Heider 1991a:316). From a cultural standpoint, it seems likely that for proper Javanese, any sort of pride is not acceptable, although for the somewhat more relaxed.

Minangkabau the bangga-pride is acceptable (Heider 1991a:67). Therefore, it seems likely that this bangga-scene would have different meanings for Minangkabau and for Javanese. This emphasizes the fact that although for convenience we may speak of "the" Indonesian language, and although it is undeniable that exactly the same film is screened in theaters in West Sumatra and Central Java, there are differences in how different peoples use and understand language and film. When we study films, we must eventually come to understand their meaning as constructions achieved by particular, culture-bound peoples working with mass-distribution raw materials.

## SCENE 1 The father hears his son praised

As a relatively simple example of this approach, let us begin with a scene from *Desa Di Kaki Bukit* (The Village at the Foot of the Hills). Said, the conservative village head and wealthy tobacco farmer, has tried to block modernization in the village by closing the new health clinic and the school. By the end of the film, he has changed his position, and this key scene shows one of his two moments of sudden conversion. He eavesdrops on a session between the schoolteacher, Rais, and Said's own son, Hasan. When Hasan gives the correct answers to Rais' questions (ignoring the wrong answers which his father whispers to him), Said makes his dramatic exit, crowing with triumph.

I chose this scene because it was so straightforward, lacking the emotional complexity of other scenes. Here, one could focus on only one actor and also embedded in the scene itself is an explicit attribution of emotion which can be compared with the respondents' attributions. Also, this is a rare intense positive emotion.

### The dialogue:

*Rais (the schoolteacher):* What is the most famous thing in Bogor, 'San?
*Said (the father, prompting):* Tobaco, 'San. Yeah, tobacco, 'San.
*Hasan (the son):* Not that.

| | |
|---|---|
| Said: | Why not that? Here people plant tobacco. There people plant tobacco. People plant tobacco everywhere. |
| Hasan: | The Botanical Gardens, Sir. |
| Said: | How do you know that? |
| Hasan: | You often told me about it. |
| Rais: | What else, 'San? |
| Said (prompting again): | Tobacco, 'San! |
| Hasan: | The Presidential Palace, Sir. |
| Rais: | That's right. |
| Said: | Hey, that's what I thought too! Hasan is clever, Teacher! My son! (leaves, laughing). |
| Rais: | Your father is proud of you, 'San. |

**The Indonesian dialog:**
Di Bogor yang terkenal apa, 'San?
Tembakau, 'San. Ayo, tembakau 'San.
Bukan yah.
Kenapa bukan? Di sini orang tanam tembakau
Di sana juga tanam tembakau. Di mana-mana
Orang tanam tembakau.
Kebun Raya, Pak.
Kau tau dari mana?
Ayah sering cerita pada saya.
Apa lagi, San?
Tembakau, 'San!
Istana Presiden, Pak.
Betul.
Hah! Saya maksud juga itu!
Hasan pintar, Guru! Anak saya!
Ayahmu bangga, 'San.

**Analysis:** In this scene, one of the actors, Rais, makes his own judgment of Said's emotional state, saying that he is bangga, happy/proud. The six respondents described Said's state in relatively simple terms, with great agreement among themselves.

**Focus:** (the number of respondents agreeing on a particular cluster): 100% gave gembira, the key word in the happy cluster; 16.7% (one of six) also gave haru (from a sad cluster), or malu (shame) in the lazy cluster, or sombong in the arrogant cluster.

**Complexity:** (number of respondents making attributions in more than one cluster): 33% gave happy, sad, and arrogant or happy and shame. And all offered two or three words, but only two of six made attributions in more than one cluster.

## Analyzing emotion from Indonesian cinema 101

**Nuanced:** (proportion of nonkey words offered): 46% (6 of 13). The respondents agreed strongly on locating Said in the happy cluster and all used the key word in that cluster (gembira) but only two of the six agreed with the school teacher's judgment that Said was bangga (which is also in the happy cluster.)

Incidentally, the standard dictionary definition of bangga as proud, stubborn, misses the meaning of happy/proud which both Rais and these respondents clearly gave for Said's state. In the previous study, also, bangga was firmly located in the happy cluster and the scenarios for bangga indicated a happy pride emotion (Heider 1991a:21–48). There is another set of emotion words in the arrogant/pride cluster, including sombong. Coming from English, it would seem that these two are closely related, but in Indonesian, they are quite unrelated, and far apart in the emotion map. Interestingly, only one respondent offered the word sombong, from the arrogant/pride cluster, to describe Said.

### Rethinking the emotions of the drama

Rais announced that Said was bangga, proud, while the respondents, in an unusual show of unanimity, all said that he was happy, gembira. But since, in Minangkabau Indonesian, bangga and gembira are such closely-positioned members of the happy cluster, there is less discrepancy between bangga and gembira than between the English proud and happy. (See, for example, the hierarchical cluster analysis of English emotion words in Shaver et al. 1987:1067 (reproduced in Heider 1991a:238). While Shaver finds happiness and pride in the same general branch (joy), they are on quite separate sub—branches.)

As for the happy scenario, I wrote: "But when the Minangkabau are speaking Indonesian, 'happiness' is more the result of personal achievement and overt displays such as jumping or smiling are common." (Heider 1991a:68)

This is an accurate description of Said. He is celebrating his son's achievement in a school task, and he responds with unconcealed crowing and flapping of his arms as he struts away.

So, the respondents unanimously produce gembira, the key word of this cluster, which we might well call the happy/proud cluster. As I suggested above, since Javanese do not consider bangga part of the happy cluster, it is unlikely that Javanese while speaking and responding in Indonesian would generalize to gembira, especially after having been prompted by Rais' use of bangga. And it is likely that a Javanese audience would take a dimmer view of Said than did these Minangkabau.

And so, rather than simply repeating Rais' judgment of bangga, each Minangkabau respondent interpreted Said's emotion by going to the key word of the same cluster. There was a comparable shift in an earlier study, when Minangkabau were asked to give the equivalent of a Minangkabau emotion word in Indonesian and vice versa. People had a strong tendency not to match the nuances but to go for the key word of the appropriate cluster as the best equivalent (Heider 1991a:296).

## SCENE 2 The ex-girlfriend confronts the present girlfriend

A second scene from the same film, The Village at the Foot of the Hill, is considerably more complex. Rais, the young man who had come to the village from Jakarta to teach school, has fallen in love with Wati, the traditional village maiden. But Rais' former lover, Santi, a very stylish Jakarta woman, has driven into the countryside to lure Rais back. As this scene begins, Rais and Santi are alone in his house. Rais rejects Santi. When Wati appears, Santi immediately realizes that she has been replaced in Rais' affections. Santi first suggests that Rais is in love (using the word cinta), then asks to be introduced to Wati, then insultingly suggests that Rais is ashamed (malu) of Wati because, as a village girl, her hands smell of mud. Wati gasps, hand to mouth, and runs out. Rais hesitates and then runs after her, leaving Santi alone.

I chose this scene for its rather un-Indonesian intensity of emotional confrontation, and because the script itself has one character making explicit emotional attributions to the other two characters. The respondents were asked for assessments of each of the three characters for the scene as a whole, and then for their assessments of each at the moment when Santi says that Wati's hands' smell of mud.

### The dialogue:

*Cut to Rais' house. Santi arrives, very chic. Rais is reading.*

Rais: Santi!

Santi: I looked all over for you and finally I find you here. You are a lot different. There is one Rais in Jakarta, another here. Like heaven and earth.

Rais: What do you want here?

Santi: Aren't you happy to see me? You disappeared just like that. You aren't the type to meditate in the woods, to leave the world.

Rais: I am not meditating. I'm here in the midst of the village. Why are you here?

Santi: To meet you.

Santi!

Ku cari kau ke mana. Akhirnya kau ketemu juga. Di sini kau tinggal. Berbeda sekali antara Rais di Jakarta dengan Rais di sini. Seorti langit dengan bumi.

Mau apa mau ke mari?

Apakah kau tidak senang melihat ku? Kau menghilang begitu saja. Potonganmu bukan potongan seorang yang suka bertapa, mennjauhi dunia.

Saya tidak betapa. Justra saya berada di tengah kampong. Mengapa kau ke mari?

Menjumpat kau.

| | |
|---|---|
| Rais: I wrote you a letter before I left and explained everything. | Sebekum aku pergi sudah aku tulia surat pada kau semuanya sudah aku terangkan dengan jelas. |
| Santi: You wrote that letter in anger. What's more, no girl wants to be left behind just like that. | Kau tulis surat itu dengan rasa marah. Agi pula, tak seorang gadis pun yang mau ditinggalkan kekasihnya begitu saja. |
| Rais: Ah, no, not in anger, it's just that I suddenly realized something. | Ah, tidak, tidak dengan rasa marah, saya cuma tiba-tiba sadar. |
| Santi: What was wrong between us? Everything was so happy. | Apa yang salah diantara kita? Semua begitu menyenangkan. |
| Rais: Yes. Too much so. You with your false eyelashes and fake hair, me with the wealth my father gave me, we floated on a borrowed dream. | Ya, bahkan terlalu menyenangkan. Kau dengan bulu mata dan rambut kau yang semu, aku dengan kemewahan yang diberikan ayahku. Kita mengabang atas memimpi pimjaman. |
| Santi: So... | Lalu? |
| Rais: So I realized it was all a lie. | lalu, aku sadar semua itu bohong. |
| Santi: A lie? What about our love? | Bohong? bagaimana hubungan cinta antara kita? |
| Rais: There was no love. What we called love was only sex, nothing more. | Tidak ada hubungan cinta di antara kita. Yang kita sebutkan cinta hanyalah sekedar hubungan kelaminan, tak lebih. |
| Santi: And what is there here for you? | dan apa yang kau kemui disini? |
| Rais: I have found the meaning of life again. I feel needed by people here and I live by my own efforts. | Saya telah menemukan arti hidup kembali. Saya merasa diperlukan arti hidup kembali' dari usaha saya sendiri. |
| Santi: It's not possible, not possible you have changed so completely. | Tidak mungkin, tidak mungkin kau berobah begitu rupa. |
| Rais: It's best you accept it, Santi. It's a long way from the kisses and dreams that that infatuated us. | Sebaiknya kau terima kenyetaan ini, Santi. Memang begitu berat sekali dari siuman dari yang begitu memgasyikkan. |
| (Wati enters, sees them.) | |
| Wati: Kak! | Kak! |
| Santi: You not only found life, but love apparently. Won't you introduce me to this village girl, Rais? Or are you ashamed because her hands smell of mud? | Kan tidak hanya menemui hidup tapi juga cinta rupanya. Apakah kau tidak man memperkenalkan ke kasihumi kepada gadis desa ini, Rais, atau kau malu barangkali karena tangannya bau lumpur? |
| (Wati gasps, runs out. Rais runs after her.) | |
| Rais: Wati! Wati! | Wati! Wati! |

104  *Exploring Indonesian cinema*

*The analysis*

*Table 7.1* The degree of focus on clusters. The total number of clusters used and the number of respondents agreeing on a particular cluster, described for the three characters for the scene overall and for the "mud" segment. The agreement figures indicate how many respondents choose a particular cluster, and the cluster is described by the English gloss and the identification number assigned to it.

|  | *The scene as a whole* | | *The "mud" segment* | |
| --- | --- | --- | --- | --- |
|  | Clusters | Agreement | Clusters | Agreement |
| Rais | 10 | 2: love #6<br>2: annoyance #28 | 8 | 2:shame #38<br>2:sad #10 |
| Wati | 10 | 3: annoyance #28<br>3:5urprise #11<br>2:shame #38/9<br>2:sad #10 | 5 | 3:depression #33<br>3:5urprise #11 |
| Santi | 7 | 3 surprise #1<br>3: jealousy #15 | 7 | 4: annoyance #28 |

*Table 7.2* Complexity. The number of respondent attributions with more than one word or from more than one cluster.

|  | *The scene as a whole* | | *The "mud" segment* | |
| --- | --- | --- | --- | --- |
|  | Cluster 1< | Word 1< | Cluster < | Word 1< |
| Rais | 3 of 7 | 3 of 7 | 3 of 6 | 3 of 6 |
| Wati | 4 of 7 | 5 of 7 | 3 of 6 | 5 of 6 |
| Santi | 4 of 7 | 4 of 7 | 3 of 7 | 5 of 7 |

*Table 7.3* Nuances. The number of nonkey (i.e., less salient) words used by respondents for the three characters.

|  | *The scene as a whole* | | *The "mud" segment* | |
| --- | --- | --- | --- | --- |
| Rais | 9/13 | 69% | 5/10 | 50% |
| Wati | 11/18 | 61% | 10/14 | 71% |
| Santi | 13/15 | 86% | 7/13 | 53% |

*Discussion*

The degree of agreement on what emotions are being shown is overall much less for all three characters in this scene than it was for Said in Scene 1. The respondents drew on a total of four clusters for Said, while here they used

*Analyzing emotion from Indonesian cinema* 105

from five to ten clusters. Everyone located Said in the happy cluster, while here there is majority agreement in only one of six instances (Santi in the mud segment.)

Nuances are considerably greater here. The respondents used more key words and only 46 nonkey words to describe Said. In this scene, the percentage of nonkey words runs higher, from 50% to 85%. There is, further, a suggestion in the responses from Scene 2 that some emotion words are gender-specific. Of the total of 23 words in 16 different clusters used for all three characters in this scene

> five words are applied to both women but not to the man;
> five more words are applied to one woman but not to the man;
> four words are applied to the man but not to either woman; and
> five words are applied to the two lovers but not to Santi.

## Rethinking the emotions of the drama

The great amount of disagreement about all three characters in this scene is indicated by the large number of clusters which were drawn on for the attributions, and by the low number of respondents who could agree on any cluster. But looking at what was agreed on, the annoyance cluster with its key word kesal stands out for all three characters. (Surprise, shame, sadness, love/nurture, jealousy, and depression also are agreed on for one instance or another.) But here, of all places, one might expect someone to be angry: Rais, whose past has broken in on his present; Wati, suddenly insulted by a glamorous rival; and Santi, definitively rejected in favor of a simple village girl.

The annoyance cluster is particularly intriguing because it is what I called a way-station emotion (Heider 1991a:273). In the emotion scenarios, annoyance leads to other emotions, especially those in the anger clusters. Annoyance seems on the brink of anger, or has the strong potential for anger, but it is not anger. Although there are plenty of anger words in Indonesian available to these respondents, they did not draw on them to describe the characters. By drawing on annoyance, the way—station emotion, rather than on anger, the end point emotion, the respondents seem to be emphasizing the contained negative intensity of the scene. But here, at least, they do not seem to indicate any masking of anger.

Also we must ask why the respondents should have such a hard time getting a handle on the characters in this scene. I mentioned above that looking at all ten scenes, the distribution of numbers of clusters drawn on for a character falls into a continuous range, following a normal curve, from one cluster to eight clusters. No one used nine Clusters, but ten clusters were used twice, and both times on this scene. Why?

The most obvious characteristic of this scene, compared with the other nine scenes, is that this one involves a quite nontraditional lovers' triangle of three unrelated people. Of the other scenes, seven involve family members, one is an employer-dependent pair, and one has two girls who are best friends and college roommates. All these relationships are relatively common and well understood. Here, although Rais and Wati will eventually marry, their courtship is abruptly interrupted by Rais' former lover, a jarringly untraditional character in every respect.

We cannot expect that people will interpret a scene in a completely unbiased or naive manner. They bring their cultural expectations of particular role interactions to their interpretations. And in those scenes with more traditional interactions, more agreement was reached. But in this scene, with its relatively untraditional modern love triangle, shared cultural patterns were of less relevance and so consensus was lower.

## SCENE 3. The lovers are interrupted by her little brother

In a third scene from *Desa di Kaki Bukit*, Rais is just declaring his love for Wati. Her little brother comes to call her for dinner and catches them in a compromising situation. Rais tries to cover it up by reading from the novel, Max Havelaar, but the little brother slyly points out that the book is upside down. I chose this scene because it shows a light and positive emotion, yet also has undertones of deception and public shaming, complicated by the fact that in this case "the public" is the slyly disrespectful younger brother—cum—student.

The respondents were asked to attribute emotion to Rais and Wati for the scene overall, and then for three moments in the scene: to Wati as her little brother bursts in, to Rais as he pretends to read, and to Wati as her brother points out Rais' subterfuge.

### The dialogue

| | |
|---|---|
| Rais: Wati, from the first time I saw you I had feelings. Didn't you? (He takes her hand.) I love you. Don't you understand yet? I want you to be my wife.<br>",,,,,,,,,,,,,,,,,,,,,,,,,,,,,, | Wati, sejak pertama aku melihat kau, aku sudah merasa? Aku cinta padamu. Apa kau belum juga mengerti? Aku ingin kau jadi isteriku. |
| Brother: (bursts in) Sis!<br>................... | Kak! |
| Rais: (pretends to read) In educating children we have to be patient. The old ways, using force and compulsion, we have to put aside. | Dalam mendidik anak-anak kita harus mengambil sikap yang sabar. Cara-cara dulu seperti mengunakan kekerasa dan paksaan harus kita hindarkan. |
| ...................<br>The Brother: The book is upside down. Can we go home, Sis? | Bukunya terbalik. Pak. Kita pulang, Kaka? |

*Analyzing emotion from Indonesian cinema* 107

*Table 7.4* The degree of focus on clusters: Scene 3. The total number of clusters used and the number of respondents agreeing on a particular cluster.

|  | Number of clusters | Agreement for scene overall |
|---|---|---|
| Rais (6 respondents) | 5 | 4: shame #38 |
|  |  | 3: surprise #1 |
| Wati (6 respondents) | 6 | 4: shame #38 |
|  |  | 2: happy #2 |
| Cut 1. Wati as brother enters | 3 |  |
| Cut 2. Rais pretends to read | 6 |  |
| Cut 3. Wati, as subterfuge discovered | 6 | 6: shame #38 |
|  |  | 3: surprise #1 |
|  |  | 4: pura-pura (pretend) |

*Table 7.5* Complexity and nuance. The number of respondents who make their attributions with words from more than one cluster or with more than one word, and total number of key words used.

|  | Clusters 1< | Words 1< | Nonkey words |
|---|---|---|---|
| The scene as a whole: | Rais 3 | 3 | 81% 9/111 |
|  | Wati 3 | 3 | 70% 7/ 10 |
| Cut 1. Wati | 3 | 4 | 81% 9/11 |
| Cut 2. Rais | 4 | 4 | 90% 10/11 |
| Cut 3. Wati | 3 | 3 | 88% 8/9 |

## Analysis

The respondents used five or six clusters for most of these instances, although there was strong agreement on attributing malu (shame) to both characters. In one cut, four of seven said that Rais was pretending. They used the word pura-pura, a word which is not on the emotion map, yet in the third case, obviously, the four respondents did not hesitate to insert it into this emotion context.

## Rethinking the emotions of the drama

The emotions of the two lovers in this scene are strongly malu, shame. The earlier study was singularly unsuccessful in explaining this emotion and these present results do not help much. It appears that malu covers a wide range of possibilities. Originally, I had expected malu and marah (anger) to be similarly elaborated in Indonesian. In Indonesian, as spoken by Minangkabau, marah was a strong focus for the anger area, which includes about 30 words in four clusters (plus a very closely bound cruel cluster.) (Heider 1991a:225). Malu, on the other hand, was not nearly so central. It had no clusters, but was a peripheral member of a cluster dominated by enggan, lazy (Heider 1991a:302).

Why should the anger area have so many words while the shame area has so few? This is surely an instance where the simple equation of lexical elaboration with cultural salience does not hold. Rather like contemporary American English, where the word "love" is used for attitudes toward ice cream, pets, spouses, and God. It is a case where quite complex, important, and differentiated emotions must be expressed with a relatively impoverished vocabulary.

In this scene, then, malu is used even though the stakes for the characters are low, the tone is humorous, and the "public" is only the mildly impudent little brother/student. Malu is modified by a few benign secondary emotions of surprise and happy. It is a very different malu from what we shall see in later, more intense shaming scenes.

At first glance, the degree of nuanced attributions (as measured by the percentage of nonkey words) looks remarkably high. It is at the extreme end of the distribution, but actually this is an artifact: because malu itself, being peripheral and unaccounted for in the map is automatically a nonkey word and so inflates that measure.

## SCENE 4. The young man rejects his cousin

The fourth scene is taken from *Salah Asuhan* (Wrong Upbringing), a film made of one of the earliest and most famous novels; it was written by Abdoel Moeis, a Minangkabau, and published by a Dutch sponsored publishing house in 1928. Set in West Sumatra, it tells about three young people caught between Indonesian and Western cultures, between the demands of Minangkabau matrilineal tradition and the standards of modernizing Indonesia. Hanafi, the young man, has been given a European education (his "wrong upbringing") financed by his (matrilineal) clan, which is managed by his mother's brother, Sutan Batuah. Now, St. Batuah expects Hanafi to make a traditional marriage to his daughter Raphia. Hanafi's mother (Ibu) is caught between her brother and her son as Hanafi crudely rejects Raphia.

In this scene, St. Batuah has brought Raphia to visit Hanafi and his mother and presumably to plan the wedding. We see the four having a meal together. I chose this scene for the great intensity of public shaming, and the very un-Minangkabau behavior of Hanafi in attacking his own closest relatives. Unlike the tongue-in-cheek tone of the previous scene, this one strikes at the core of Minangkabau tradition.

The respondents were asked to attribute emotions to each of the four characters for the scene as a whole, and then to make attributions to single characters at nine points in the scene: 1) Raphia as she looks up, not able to handle the Western utensils at Hanafi's very Westernized table; 2) Hanafi, watching his cousin's distress; 3) Ibu, Hanafi's mother, gently encouraging her niece to use the fork; 4) Hanafi sneering at Raphia's inept attempt; 5) Raphia flees the table; 6) St. Batuah looks up from his meal at the interaction between Hanafi and Raphia; 7) Hanafi stalks out to have coffee alone in his study; 8) St. Batuah, left at the table; and 9) Ibu, after St. Batuah leaves, sits alone and sighs.

## The dialogue

Scene at Hanafi's house, where he is eating a meal with his mother (Ibu), his uncle (Sutan Batuah), and his cousin, Raphia. Raphia having trouble eating with the Western utensils, looks up (1). Hanafi observes her distress (2).

| | |
|---|---|
| Ibu: Use a fork, child. (3) | Pakai garpu, Nak!! |
| (Hanafi sneers at Raphia's manners. (4) She runs from the table in disgrace (5). St. Batuah looks up from his plate (6). | |
| Ibu: Let her eat with me in the kitchen. | Biar ia makan bersamaku di belakang. |
| Hanafi: Cung! Bring me coffee to my room. (He leaves) (7). St. Batuah alone at the table (8). | |
| Ibu reenters from the kitchen. | |
| St. Batuah: Have the things gotten ready. | Suruh Rapiah menyiapkan berang-berang |
| The train leaves shortly. | Kereta sebentar lagi berangkat. |
| Ibu: Don't you want to stay here a couple of nights longer? | Apa kakak tidak mau di sini duduk barang semalam dua lagi? |
| St. Batuah: Apparently people aren't too happy to have us here. It's been a day and a night we've been here and your son hasn't said ten sentences to me. | Kelihatannya, orang tidak begitu senang menerima kami di sini, sudah sehari semalam kami di sini belum sampai (10) Kalimat yang diucapkan anakmu padaku. |
| (St. Batuah leaves. Ibu sighs (9), | |

## The analysis

*Table 7.6* The degree of focus on clusters. The total number of clusters used and the number of respondents agreeing on a particular cluster, first described for the four characters in the scene as a whole, then for one character in each of nine points in the scene. The agreement figures indicate how many respondents (out of seven, unless otherwise noted) chose a particular cluster, and the cluster is described by the English gloss and the identification number assigned it.

| The scene as a whole | Number of clusters | Agreement |
|---|---|---|
| Ibu (Hanafi's mother) | 7 | 4: sad #10 |
| | | 3: love/nurturance #6 |
| | | 2: disappointed #33 |
| Hanafi | 6 | 5: annoyance #8 |
| | | 2: mocking disapproval #6 |
| | | 2: arrogance #40 |
| Sutan Batuah | 6 | 3: annoyance #28 |
| | | 3: angry #22 |
| | | 2: sad #10 |

(*Continued*)

110  *Exploring Indonesian cinema*

*Table 7.6* (Continued)

| The scene as a whole | Number of clusters | Agreement |
|---|---|---|
| Raphia | 6 | 5: shame #38 |
|  |  | 4: sad #10 |
|  |  | 2: respectful #38 |
| Cut 1. Raphia looks up | 5 | 2: fear #14 |
|  |  | 3: shame #38 |
| Cut 2. Hanafi watches | 4 | 3: annoyance #28 |
|  |  | 2: anger #22 |
|  |  | 3: mocking disapproval #35 |
| Cut 3. Ibu encourages her | 5 | 6: sad #10 |
|  |  | 3: love/nurturance #6 |
| Cut 4. Hanafi sneers | 5 | 4: mocking disapproval #35 |
|  |  | 3: annoyance #28 |
|  |  | 2: anger #22 |
| Cut 5. Raphia flees | 4 | 6: shame #38 |
|  |  | 2: sad #10 |
|  |  | 2: fear #14 |
| Cut 6. St. Batuah looks up | 4 | 4: anger #22 |
| Cut 7. Hanafi leaves | 5 | 3: anger #22 |
|  |  | 3: arrogance #40 |
|  |  | 2: annoyance #28 |
| Cut 8. St. Batuah alone | 6 | 4: annoyance #28 |
|  |  | 3: anger #22 |
|  |  | 2: sad #10 |
| Cut 9. Ibu sighs | 4 | 6: sad #10 |
|  |  | 2: annoyance #28 |
|  |  | 2: shame #38 |

*Table 7.7* Complexities and nuances. The number of respondents who make their attributions with more than one word or with words from more than one cluster, and the total number of nonkey words. (Unless noted, seven respondents.)

|  | Cluster 1< | Word 1< | Nonkey words |  |
|---|---|---|---|---|
| The scene as a whole: |  |  |  |  |
| Ibu | 4 | 6 | 60% | 6/10 |
| Hanafi | 4 | 6 | 50% | 6/10 |
| St. Batuan | 5 | 5 | 42% | 6/14 |
| Raphia | 7 | 7 | 64% | 11/17 |
| Cut 1. Raphia looks up | 2/6 | 3/6 | 67% | 6/9 |
| Cut 2. Hanafi watches | 3/6 | 3/6 | 60% | 6/10 |
| Cut 3. Ibu comforts | 2 | 3 | 72% | 8/11 |
| Cut 4. Hanafi sneers | 5 | 5 | 57% | 8/14 |
| Cut 5. Raphia flees | 4 | 4 | 72% | 6/11 |
| Cut 6. St. Batuah looks up | 2/6 | 2/6 | 50% | 4/8 |
| Cut 7. Hanafi leaves | 3 | 3 | 45% | 5/11 |
| Cut 8. St. Batuah alone | 5 | 5 | 38% | 5/13 |
| Cut 9. Ibu sighs | 5 | 6 | 50% | 6/12 |

*Discussion*

The pattern of emotion attributions shows the great complexity of emotions in this scene, which results in little agreement among the seven respondents about what is happening. If we add the four assessments of the overall scene to the nine separate assessments, between four and seven clusters were drawn on. This, of course could simply indicate the complexity of the scene. But, as an indication of agreement, in 9 of 13 assessments, a majority of respondents agree on 1 cluster. For the most part, there was much less agreement on any cluster.

Of the 162 separate namings of words for this scene, there were 3 words not on the emotion map (kaku and itiku, both meaning clumsy, plus the English loan word groggy; mendengus, not in the dictionary, and two indak senang, meaning "not happy."

*Rethinking the emotions of this scene*

In this scene, we have one of the most familiar of conflicts: the split within a family over conflicting pulls of Minangkabau traditional adat and modern national ideas. And the respondents were in greater agreement on this scene than on the more unfamiliar lovers' triangle of Scene 2, above. Compared with that scene, they here used fewer clusters and more of them agreed on the same cluster. The two women have much sadness and the younger woman also much shame, while the two men show anger and annoyance. This speaks to the nature of malu. It is significant that Raphia, whom Hanafi so mocks, is the only character with much malu. One might have expected that the mother, whose son rejects his family and his culture, or the uncle, whose daughter is so mistreated, might be shamed, but they are not. In the scenario, main results from the person's own shortcoming, especially when it is made public (Heider 1991a:308). And of course the scene focuses on Hanafi's scorn for Raphia's shortcomings. The mother and the uncle are not shamed, but saddened and angered.

## SCENE 5. The bridegroom explodes at the wedding

This is another scene from the film *Salah Asuhan*. Sometime after the events of Scene 1, Hanafi does agree to marry his mother's brother's daughter, Raphia. For the wedding, she wears the traditional Minangkabau costume but he shows up in formal Western tuxedo. Ibu, his mother, asks him to wear traditional Minangkabau attire also, saying she is ashamed (malu) when he wears Dutch clothes. He yields in a surly manner. The confrontation between Hanafi and his mother takes place in front of the wedding guests. I chose this scene because it goes a step beyond Scene 3 in depicting public shaming, because the wedding guests offer an opportunity

112  *Exploring Indonesian cinema*

to assess the emotions of an actual "public," and because in the script, the mother makes an explicit attribution of emotion to herself. The respondents were asked to assess Hanafi, Ibu, and the guests for the scene as a whole and then particular characters at four moments in the scene:

1. Hanafi, hands on hips, angrily resisting his mother;
2. the guests, watching;
3. Ibu, when she says she is ashamed of his behavior; and
4. Hanafi, when he gracelessly yields.

### The dialogue

Preparing for a traditional Minangkabau wedding, Raphia is being dressed in formal attire and ornaments. Hanafi, in tuxedo, is furious (1). The wedding guests look on in silence (2).

| | |
|---|---|
| Hanafi: Have I met all your wishes or are there more? | Semua keinginan Ibu sudah kepenuhi Apa belum, cukup? |
| Ibu: I am ashamed (3) when you wear Dutch clothes. | Ibu malu kalau kau pakai pakian |
| It would be better to adapt yourself to these ways. | Belanda kebon itu. Sebaiknya kita menyesuaikan kita diri. |
| Hanafi: Okay, enough! You don't have to preach the | Ah—sudahlah! Filsafat bermasyarakat |
| local philosophy to me. I can read it in books. | Tidak perlu Ibu ajarkan padaku. Cukupku |
| If you want me to wear the clothes of music | baca buku-buku. Kalau Ibu ingin aku |
| comedians, fine. I understand. I am a | menyewakan pakaian Stambul comedian |
| mortgaged man. | aku tau, aku sudah jadi orang tergadai. |
| (Sneering, he takes off the tuxedo jacket. (4) | |

*Table 7.8* The degree of focus on clusters. The total number of clusters used and the number of respondents (of seven) agreeing on a particular cluster.

| | Number of clusters | Agreement |
|---|---|---|
| The scene as a whole: Hanafi | 5 | 7: anger #22* |
| | *Unanimous choice of key word marah | |
| | | 3: annoyance #28 |

(*Continued*)

*Table 7.8* (Continued)

|  | Number of clusters | Agreement |
|---|---|---|
| Ibu | 6 | 2: depression #33<br>5: sad #10<br>4: shame #38 |
| Onlookers (5 respondents) | 4 | 2: surprise |
| Cut 1. Hanafi, hands on hips | 5 | 7: angry #22 + #24*<br>*6 of 7 use key word marah<br>3: annoyance #28 |
| Cut 2. Onlookers | 6 | 6: surprise #1<br>2: annoyance #28 |
| Cut 3. Ibu, ashamed | 6 | 6: sad #10*<br>*all use key word sedih<br>5. shame #38*<br>*all use malu<br>2. annoyance #38 |
| Cut 4. Hanafi yields | 6 | 5: Angry #22<br>5: annoyance #28<br>3: arrogance #48 |

*Table 7.9* Complexity and nuances. The number of respondents who make their attributions with more than one word or with words from more than one cluster, and the total number of key words used (unless noted, seven respondents).

|  |  | Cluster 1< | Word 1< | Nonkey words |
|---|---|---|---|---|
| The scene as a whole: |  |  |  |  |
|  | Hanafi | 7 | 7 | 29% 5/17 |
|  | Ibu | 5 | 5 | 46% 6/13 |
|  | 5 Resp Onlookers | 1 | 1 | 60% 3/5 |
| Cut 1. | Hanafi | 5 | 5 | 38% 5/13 |
| Cut 2. | Onlookers | 5 | 5 | 25% 3/12 |
| Cut 3. | Ibu | 7 | 7 | 52% 9/17 |
| Cut 4. | Hanafi yields | 7 | 7 | 37% 6/16 |

## Analysis

The results for this scene are remarkable. They show not only great complexity—of the seven sets of judgments, six use five or six clusters—but they also show more agreement than most previous scenes. Not only do we find unanimity or close to it on most of the seven sets of judgments, but in several, we find the second most popular choice is near unanimity also. For example, in Cut 3, assessing Ibu, five respondents link the two words malu and sedih. Also, these responses tend to use key words and not the full potential of the word cluster. (This is somewhat obscured in the nuance figures

114  *Exploring Indonesian cinema*

because malu, although quite seminal in Indonesian, does not happen to be a key word in its cluster—a persisting puzzle—see Heider 1991a:302).

This scene is especially powerful, of course, because Hanafi shows extraordinary and public anger in attacking both his mother and Minangkabau tradition, so it not surprising that the respondents were so focused. It is interesting, though, that especially in Cut 3, they did not accept more readily the mother's own judgment—in the script, she says she is malu, ashamed, yet more respondents judged her to be sad (sedih) than malu. In Scene 1, we noted a similar reading, when the respondents resisted Rais' judgment that Said was bangga (proud).

### Rethinking the emotions of the drama

As with Scene 4, we find malu (shame) strongly qualified. The mother, publicly attacked by her son, is more sad than ashamed. Even though she herself claims to be ashamed. Why should these Minangkabau respondents not agree with her self-assessment more strongly? Remember the scenario from the earlier study: malu is caused by one's own shortcomings. And here it is her son's behavior which is in question, not hers. She is, unanimously for the respondents, sad. The onlookers, who in the West might have been embarrassed by all this, are more surprised.

And Hanafi is strongly angry. The unanimity of judgments that Hanafi is angry is itself unusual. On the whole, anger is not so clearly felt or expressed by Minangkabau. In all ten scenes examined in this chapter, only one other character is ever unanimously judged to be angry and that, as we shall see, is the mother in Scene 10. These are the two most Westernized characters: Hanafi, educated in Europe, scorning Minangkabau custom, and the mother, Indo-European, back from years in Holland, hating life in Jakarta.

In the West, perhaps, onlookers might be more apt to turn away in embarrassment at such public airing of family conflict. But these Minangkabau onlookers take it as their right to observe, however surprised they are. Returning once more to the question of why the respondents did not accept the mother's self-assessment of shame, we can speculate. Although we lack specific hints from the emotion maps (as we had for bangga in Scene l, above), it seems likely that there is a comparable situation: that for these Minangkabau respondents, malu is actually less appropriate than sadness.

## SCENE 6. Raphia and Ibu read Hanafi's letter

This is yet another scene from *Salah Asuhan*. Hanafi reluctantly agreed to marry Raphia, they had a son, but after several tension-filled years, Hanafi went off to Jakarta, where he married his first love, Corrie. Raphia and the son live in the village with Ibu, Hanafi's mother. The two women have grown very close. Now, Hanafi writes a letter to his mother. Since she cannot read, Raphia must read it out loud to her. In it, Hanafi announces that he has discarded Raphia and married Corrie. Both Raphia and Ibu weep.

I chose this scene for its intense sadness, and in hopes that the respondents might differentiate between the sadnesses of the two women. The respondents were asked to describe the emotions of Raphia and Ibu.

## The dialogue

The mailman delivers a letter.

| | |
|---|---|
| Raphia: For you. There's nothing for me. (offers the letter to Ibu.) | Buat Ibu. Buat saya tidak ada. |
| Ibu: Read it. I can't read Latin script. | Bacalah. Ibu tidak pandai membaca huruf Latin. |
| Raphia reads: Dear Mother. Really this letter should be addressed to Raphia but since I got the woman from you, I want to return her to you. I will not follow through with any of the plans or feelings I had while I was married. Therefore allow me to give back all of your gifts to you yourself. | Ibu Yang Tercinta. Sebetulnya surat ini haruskhu alamatkan pada Raphia. Tapi karena perempuan itu keperoleh dari Ibu pulalah ia kendek ku kembalikan. Ananda akan minikah dengan Corrie. Segala rencana dan rasa ananda yang Ananda—Tanggung selarna mengikat kan diri pada seorang istri pemberian Ibu tidak Akan ananda bangkit lagi. Oleh karena itu, Ibu izinkan Ananda untuk mernulangkan barang pemberian Ibu ketangan Ibu sendiri. |
| Ibu: Piah! (The two women embrace, weeping.) | Piah! |

*Table 7.10* The degree of focus on clusters: Scene 6. The total number of clusters used and the number of respondents agreeing on a particular cluster.

| | Clusters | Agreement |
|---|---|---|
| Raphia | 8 | 6: sad #10 |
| | | 3: depression #3 |
| Ibu | 7 | 6: sad #10. |
| | | 3: love/nurturance #6 |
| | | 2: depression #33 |

116  *Exploring Indonesian cinema*

*Table 7.11* Complexity and nuances. The number of respondents who make their attributions with words from more than one cluster or with more than one word, and the total of nonkey words used (seven respondents).

|        | Clusters 1< | Words 1< | Nonkey words |
|--------|-------------|----------|--------------|
| Raphia | 5           | 5        | 62% 10/16    |
| Ibu    | 6           | 6        | 41% 7/17     |

*Analysis*

This was a comparatively simple scene, with high agreement on the sad cluster, but still there was extensive use of other clusters to describe other emotions. Although the respondents seemed determined to go beyond just sadness, they had little agreement on the secondary emotions.

*Rethinking the emotions of this drama*

The respondents provided no cultural surprises in this scene. Both women were clearly sad. But even so, they drew on seven different clusters to describe each woman, indicating how complex even apparently straightforward emotional situations can be.

## SCENE 7. Hanafi abases himself before his mother

At the end of *Salah Asuhan*, Corrie has died and Hanafi comes home to his mother's Great House in the Minangkabau homeland in West Sumatra. He sees his mother for one last time and, throwing himself at her feet, asks her forgiveness. Raphia and their son are playing on the front steps of the house but there is no contact between Raphia and Hanafi, and no sense that Hanafi must also beg forgiveness from Raphia.

I chose this scene for the detail with which it explores the very Indonesian form of self-abasing begging of forgiveness. In retrospect, I should also have asked the respondents to assess the emotions of the discarded wife, who is present and is included in an indirect Indonesian way. The respondents were asked to judge Hanafi and Ibu, his mother, for the scene as a whole and then individually for five moments in the scene:

1. Ibu as she greets Hanafi;
2. Hanafi, on his knees before her;
3. Ibu, as she turns her head away from him;
4. Hanafi, as he looks up at her; and
5. Ibu, as she grimaces down at him.

# The dialogue

Hanafi enters the Great House, approaches Ibu.

| | |
|---|---|
| Ibu: You have come, Hanafi (1) | Datang juga kau, Hanafi. |
| Hanafi: Yes, mother. (Falls at her feet) (2) | Ia, Bu. |
| Raphia: (enters) Your father is home, Syafei. | Ayahrne pulang, Syafei. |
| Ibu: Everything is the same as before. Nothing has changed. | Semuanya seperti dulu, tidak ada yang berubah. |
| Hanafi: Raphia has changed. | Raphia sudah berubah. |
| Ibu: Her feelings for you haven't changed. She never blamed you. (3) | Persaannya padamu tidak berubah. Dia Tidak pernah memburuk—burukkan kau. |
| Hanafi: I know, but look at how she acts. When she pulled the child from me, I could see that she didn't want to be loved anymore. She doesn't need me anymore. (4) | Aku tau. Tapi melihat tindakkannya. yang pasti waktu die merenggut anaknya yang pangkkuanku, Aku yakin sudah, dia tidak lagi mau dikasihani, ia tidak lagi memerlukan aku. |
| Ibu: Where is your wife, Hanafi? | Nyonyamu mana, Hanafi? |
| Hanafi: She died two weeks ago. | Meninggal dua minggu yang lewak. |
| Ibu: What do you want, coming here? (5) | Apa maksudmu dating ke mari? |
| Hanafi: To see you and my child for the last time. | Melihat Ibu dan anakku untuk terakhir kali Ini. |
| Ibu: And then where will you go? | Sesudah itu mau ke mana kau, Hanafi? |
| Hanafi: I don't know. All the roads are closed. | Entahlah, semua jalan tertutup. |
| Ibu: It's best you rest first. | Sebaiknya kau istirihat dulu. |
| Hanafi: Yes. I need it badly, very badly, mother. | Ya—aku sangat memerlukannya, sangat memerlukannya, Bu |

*Table 7.12* The degree of focus on clusters. The total number of clusters used and the number of respondents agreeing on a particular cluster.

| | Number of clusters | Agreement |
|---|---|---|
| For the scene as a whole: | | |
| Hanafi | 6 | 5: depression #33 |
| | | 5: sad #10 |
| Ibu | 4 | 5: sad #10 |
| | | 3: annoyance #28 |
| | | 3: love/nurturance #6 |
| (only four respondents did the following | | |
| Cut 1. Ibu | 4 | 2: surprise #2 |
| Cut 2. Hanafi | 4 | 2: sad #10 |

(*Continued*)

118  Exploring Indonesian cinema

Table 7.12 (Continued)

|  | Number of clusters | Agreement |
|---|---|---|
| Cut 3. Ibu turns away | 3 | 2: love/nurturance #6<br>3: sad #10<br>2: Annoyance #28 |
| Cut 4. Hanafi (3 respondents) | 4 | 2: consciousness #33 |
| Cut 5. Ibu grimaces | 4 | 4: sad #10<br>2: love/nurturance #6 |

Table 7.13 Complexity and nuances. The number of respondents who make their attributions with more than one word or with words from more than one cluster, and the total number of nonkey words used.

|  | Cluster 1< | Words 1< | Nonkey words |
|---|---|---|---|
| The scene as a whole: |  |  |  |
| Hanafi | 6 | 6 | 64% 9/14 |
| Ibu | 4 | 5 | 50% 6/ 12 |
| (only 4 did the following) |  |  |  |
| Cut 1. Ibu | 1 | 1 | 80% 4/5 |
| Cut 2. Hanafi | 2 | 2 | 34% 2/6 |
| Cut 3. Ibu | 1 | 1 | 50% 3/6 |
| Cut 4. Hanafi (3 respondents) | 3 | 3 | 50% 3/6 |
| Cut 5. Ibu grimaces | 4 | 4 | 44% 4/9 |

*Analysis*

Again, although there was strong agreement on sadness (and, for Hanafi, depression), there is considerable use of other clusters for secondary emotions, but little consensus about these secondary attributions.

## SCENE 8. The servant sends the mistress to her death

The film Samiun and Dasima (also called *Njai Dasima*) is based on an Indonesian legend set in the early 19th century. It tells about Eduard, an English planter, and his mistress Dasima. Samiun, a local scoundrel, lures Dasima away from Eduard with the help of an old woman, Buyung, who has become Dasima's servant. Finally, though, Samiun tires of Dasima and has her killed. In this scene, Dasima is saying goodbye to Buyung, whom she believes is her best friend. Samiun comes to lead Dasima to her death as Buyung, knowing what is about to happen, embraces Dasima even as she betrays her.

I chose this scene for its strong depiction of fatal deception on the part of the older woman, and quite possibly self-deception on the part of the doomed Dasima. The dialogue alone gives formulaic Indonesian phrases appropriate to leave taking, but the deception is expressed nonverbally in faces, hands, and bodies.

The respondents were asked to give an overall assessment of the emotional states of Buyung and Dasima, and then to assess Buyung at two points in the scene:

1. Buyung, when Samiun arrives and the end is inevitable, and
2. Buyung, after Dasima has left, as she claps her hands together.

### The dialogue
Dasima has come to say goodbye to Buyung.

| | |
|---|---|
| Buyung: Let's hope it doesn't rain. Anyone leave anything behind? | Minta-minta jangan hujan. Nggaa ada yang ketinggalan barangnya? |
| Dasima: No, Mak, Forgive me if I did anything wrong while I was here. I made lots of trouble for you. | Engga, Mak. Mak, maafin saya kalau ada kesalahan selama saya di sini. Saya ngerepotin, Emak. |
| Buyung: No, not at all. | Ah, engga. |
| Dasima: Whenever you are around, come and visit me. | Kapan-kapan Emak mesti ke sana, nengokin saya, ya. |
| Buyung: Yes, if God grants me life and if you still want to know me. | Ya, kalau Tuhan paniangin urnur Mak san Kalau Nyai masih mau kenal sama Emak. |
| Dasima: But you are like a mother to me. | Emak kan sudah seperti ibu saya sendiri. |
| (Samiun enters.) | |
| Samiun: Ready? | 'Udah? |
| Dasima: Ready. (She and Buyung embrace. Buyung, left alone in the house, clasps her hands.) | |

*Table 7.14* The degree of focus on clusters: Scene 8. The total number of clusters used and the number of respondents agreeing on a particular cluster.

| | | Number of clusters | Agreement |
|---|---|---|---|
| (the scene as a whole) | | | |
| | Buyung: | 4 | 5: sad #10 |
| | | | 3: fear #14 |
| | | | 2: indecision #15 |
| | Dasima | 5 | 4. Sad #10 |
| | | | 3: happy #2 |
| Cut 1. | Buyung (6 respondents) | 4 | 5. Surprise #1 |
| | | | 4. fear #14 |
| Cut 2. | Buyung alone (5 respondents) | 8 | 2. fear #14 |
| | | | 2: annoyance #8 |

120   *Exploring Indonesian cinema*

*Table 7.15* Complexity and nuance. The number of respondents who make their attributions with more than one word or from more than one cluster, and the total number of nonkey words used.

|  |  | Cluster 1< | Words 1< | Nonkey words |
|---|---|---|---|---|
| (for the scene as a whole: | | | | |
| | Buyung | 4 | 4 | 28% 4/14 |
| | Dasima | 2 | 2 | 40% 4/10 |
| Cut 1. | Buyung (6 respondents) | 6 | 6 | 41% 5/12 |
| Cut 2. | Buyung alone (5 respondents) | 4 | 4 | 40% 4/10 |

*Analysis*

This scene includes strong deception, for Buyung knows or at least guesses that Sarniun is taking Dasima to her death. Even though only five respondents answered for Cut 2, when Buyung is left alone, they used a large number of clusters and showed little agreement.

*Rethinking the emotion of the drama*

The first sets of assessments are unexceptional, showing sadness on the part of both women, but then, for the older woman, strong surprise and fear when Samiun arrives to take Dasima away. The final cut, when Buyung is alone, stands out for its great complexity and low agreement. Previously, in the presence of each other, Buyung and Dasima had kept themselves under control and the respondents reached relatively easy consensus. But when Buyung is left alone, she no longer is controlling her emotion displays and different respondents pick up on different emotions in her behavior.

It would seem that this scene should be ideal for showing guilt. Buyung has betrayed Dasima from the beginning and we assume that Dasima has some inkling of this. But she is polite and affectionate toward Buyung to the end. At first glance, there is no sign of guilt. But in fact, there are no obvious words for guilt available in Indonesian. However, in the scenarios for the fear (takut) clusters, there is a strong theme of having done wrong and, usually, not being caught or exposed (Heider 1991a:77). This precisely describes Buyung, and a better gloss for Cluster #14 would be guilt. This strong guilt component of the takut cluster was a quite unexpected result of the scenario study (it had not been hinted at in the dictionary definitions) and is here confirmed.

## SCENE 9. Fitria announces her engagement

The Woman in Stocks (*Perempuan Dalam Pasungan*) tells of Fitria, who imagines that she has killed her best friend and who goes mad from guilt.

(Putting a deranged woman leg in stocks is a method of controlling and restoring order.)

This is an early scene in which Fitria bursts in on Marni, her college roommate. Andi, who has been seeing both of them socially, but who seemed to prefer Marni, has just proposed marriage to Fitria. Marni is obviously surprised but quickly rallies to support Fitria. (The wedding follows immediately.) I chose this scene as another sort of deception mixed with guilt. Although the deception is far from fatal here, in contrast to the previous scene, and is in fact done out of noble generosity, it is no less intense. And again, the script itself provides an explicit assessment of an emotion.

Respondents were asked to assess the emotions of the two women for the scene as a whole and then at six moments in the scene:

1. Marni looks up from her desk, where she has been writing, as Fitria bursts into their room;
2. Marni asks Fitria if she has been fighting with Andi;
3. Fitria says she is confused (bingung);
4. Marni looks at Fitria as she learns that Andi has proposed;
5. Fitria worries that because Andi is not Javanese, her parents will not accept him; and
6. Marni promises to intercede with Fitria's parents.

## The dialogue

Fitria bursts into their college room and throws herself weeping on the bed. Marni looks up (1)

| | |
|---|---|
| Marni: Fit, are you fighting with Andi? | Kenapa, Fit, bertengkar dengan Prasetyo? |
| Fitria: No! | Tidak! |
| Marni: Or with Andi? (2) | Atau dengan Mas Andi? |
| Fitria: But I'm not! | Tidak! |
| Marni: So, what's going on? Please say something! | Habis kenapa? Bicada, toh! |
| Fitria (embraces Marni) Marni, I'm upset. (3) | Marni, aku bingung. |
| Marni: Why? | Kenapa? |
| Fitria: Andi proposed to me. | Mas Andi mau melamarku. |
| Marni: Really? So why do you cry? Isn't it the good news we've been waiting for? | Betul? Lantas kenapa kamu nangis? Bukankan itu gembiran yang kita tunggu selama ini? |
| Fitria: Yes, but how should I tell it to Dad? Andi is not Javanese. (5) What will Mom and Dad say, and how would Andi feel | Ya, tapi bagaimana aku harus bicara sama bapak? Mas Andi bukan orang Jawa. Apa kata dan bagaimana perasaan Mas Andi kalau |

122  *Exploring Indonesian cinema*

| | |
|---|---|
| If he were rejected by Dad? | sampa ditolak dan diusir Bapak? |
| Marni: Fit, you shouldn't worry about that, | Fit, kamu tidak usah takut, nanti biar aku yang bicara |
| Just let me talk to them and I'm sure | sama Ibu Bapakmu. Aku yakin beliau pasti akan |
| They'll understand. (6) | memaharni. |

*Table 7.16* Focus on clusters. The total number of clusters used and the number of respondents agreeing on a particular cluster.

| | Clusters | Agreement |
|---|---|---|
| For the scene overall: | | |
| Fitria | 8 | 5: sad #10 |
| | | 4: indecision #16 |
| Marni | 8 | 3: surprise #1 |
| | | 3: sad #10 |
| | | 2; Depression #4 |
| | | 2: jealousy #15 |
| Cut 1. Marni looks up | 2 | 6: surprise #1 |
| Cut 2. Marni asks problem (6 respondents) | 6 | 4: surprise #1 |
| Cut 3. Fitria upset (6 respondents) | 5 | 4: sad #10 |
| | | 3: confused #17 |
| Cut 4. Marni looks at Fitn'a | 5 | 7: surprise #1 |
| Cut 5. Fitria worries | 5 | 5: sad #10 |
| | | 4: fear #14 |
| | | 2: happy #2 |
| Cut 6. Marni offers aid | 8 | 5: sad #10 |
| | | 3: depression #4 |
| | | 2: happy #2 |
| | | 2: jealousy #15 |

*Table 7.17* Complexity and nuances. The number of respondents who make their attributions with more than one word or from more than one cluster and the count of nonkey words.

| | Clusters 1< | Words 1< | Nonkey words |
|---|---|---|---|
| The scene as a whole: | | | |
| Fitria | 6 | 6 | 56% 9/16 |
| Marni | 6 | 6 | 67% |
| Cut 1. Marni looks up | 0 | 3 | 81% 9/16 |
| Cut 2. Marni asks (6 respondents) | 3 | 4 | 80% 8/10 |
| Cut 3. Fitria upset | 4 | 5 | 54% 6/11 |
| Cut 4. Marni looks | 5 | 6 | 73% 11/15 |
| Cut 5. Fitria worries | 5 | 5 | 28% 4/14 |
| Cut 6. Marni offers aid | 7 | 7 | 50% 10/20 |

## Analysis

This is a scene of greatly conflicting emotions, and the responses reflect the complexity. Andi's engagement to Fitria, instead of to Marni, was unexpected to both, and the responses are scattered widely: for three instances, they use eight different clusters. The respondents also used an exceptionally high number of nonkey words for Marni, suggesting how complex they saw her situation. Yet there is good agreement, especially on attributing surprise to Marni. For Marni, who has lost Andi, we find very little jealousy or anger, but three times pura-pura, pretend, a nonemotion word, is used for her. (To me, the most powerful emotion event was Marni's covering up her negative emotions caused by the jolt of losing Andi, but the Minangkabau respondents did not see it that way at all.)

## Rethinking the emotions of the drama

Once again, we have an instance where the script provides an emotion word which the respondents do not strongly accept. Fitria says she is bingung, confused, but only half the respondents agree, and more choose sadness. And this case is especially difficult to interpret since the scenario for bingung matches Fitria so well (it is caused by ignorance, misunderstanding, and difficulties and results in helplessness, withdrawal, and physical or mental confusion (Heider 1991a:237).

## SCENE 10. The mother unjustly punishes her son

In *Mama's Sweetheart* (*Buah Hati Mama*), a very Westernized Indonesian family has just returned to the realities of Jakarta after living for years in Holland. The mother has a terrible temper and constantly blames 12-year-old Eka for all manner of things that were not his fault.

In this scene, the mother hears a ball crash into the new television set, assumes that Eka was responsible, and beats him long and hard while the father and the two other children watch silently. Later, when Eka is still recovering in the bathroom, the rest of the family is at the dinner table. Putri, the little girl who constantly tries to mediate, tearfully blurts out the truth, that it was Indra, not Eka, who broke the television set.

The father gets Eka, the mother apologizes to him, Eka and Indra shake hands, and after the children have gone to bed, mother and father snuggle on the sofa. I chose this scene because of its intensity and complexity and clear depiction of each of the five characters. It is considerably longer, also, than the other nine scenes. And it does include many characteristic Indonesian elements. In fact, it constitutes a synopsis of the standard Indonesian sentimental movie plot, with unjust punishment, disappearance, search, reincorporation, instant conversion of agent(s) of disorder, and restored family order at the end (see Heider 1991b). And from an American emotion standpoint, it is one of the most repelling scenes I know in Indonesian movies, and so offered an opportunity to examine more deeply how Indonesian audiences understood such behavior.

Respondents were asked for emotion attributions to the characters for the scene as a whole, and then for 20 moments in the scene.

## The dialogue

| | |
|---|---|
| Mother (in the kitchen): Eka, don't play ball in the house. | Eka, jangan main bola didalam rumah. |
| (noise from off) Mother: What's happening, Eka? (1) Mother runs into the living room, sees the broken | Apa lagi itu, Eka? |
| (1) Mother runs into the living room, sees the broken TV. (2):Oh! Oh! It's broken! It's all broken! | Oh! Hancur semuanya! |
| (3) What did I tell you! What! You may not play ball in the house! | Apa tadi Mama bilang, apa! Tidak boleh main didalam rumah! |
| Now just look! The TV and everything is broken! | Sekerang lihat! TV belum lunas, Sudah hancur. |
| You have no sense! It's ruined! | Sudah hancur. Anak tidak tau diri—perusak— |
| Not paid for yet and it's broken. (She beats Eka as Indra and Putri cry. The father just watches.) (4) | perusak tidak tau diri kau. |
| Eka: It wasn't me, Mom. | Bukan saya, Ma. |
| Mother: It wasn't enough that you broke your brother's hand. | Belum puas kau hancurkan jan' tangan kakamu. |
| Now you have to break the TV! | Sekarang TV yang rusakkan! |
| Destructive, you're destructive. | Perusak, perusak! |
| What more will you break? What's next? Eh? | Apa lagi yang akan kau hancurkan? |
| Speak up! | Apa aye? Bilang! |
| Eka: It wasn't me, Mom. | Bukan saya, Ma. |
| Mother: What do you mean, it wasn't you? I should throw you out of here, you have no sense! | Apa bukan kamu? Biar aku hanjar anak ini, anak tidak tau diri. |
| If you don't want to listen to your mother, just get out of the house! | Kalau kau tidak mau dengar kata Mama, keluar dari rumah in, keluar! |
| Out, out, do you hear! | Ini, keluar! |

(The father comforts the other children while the mother beats Eka. Then, she takes him into the bathroom.)

| | |
|---|---|
| Mother: You'll stay here until you have learned your lesson. (9) | Tetapi tinggal disini sampai kau jera mengerti. |

(Cut to meal. The family, minus Eka, weepy at the table.)

*Analyzing emotion from Indonesian cinema* 125

| | |
|---|---|
| Putri: It wasn't Eka who broke the TV, Mom. | Eka Yang mecain TV bukan Bang Eka, Ma. |
| Bang Eka wanted to turn down the sound and Indra | mau kecilin suara TV, Bang Indra marah. Terus |
| got angry and threw the ball. Eka was | Bang Indra lemper pakai bola. Bang Eka kaget kakinya |
| startled and kicked the TV stand and the TV fell over | Bang Eka nyeggol meja TV. Lantas TV jatuh. |
| Father: Is that true, Indra? | Betul, Indra? |
| Mother: Why didn't you say so right away, Putri? | Kenapa Putri tidak bilang dari tadi? |
| (10, 11, 12, 13) | |
| Putri: I said so, Eka said so, but you didn't want to listen. (14) | Putri sudah bilang, Bang Eka bilang, tapi Mama tidak mau dengar. |

(Father goes to the bathroom where Eka still weeps, collapsed on the floor.)

| | |
|---|---|
| Putri: Papa and Mama know that you weren't to blame, Eka. | Papa dan Mama sudah tau Bang 'Eka tidak salah. |

(Putri helps Eka up as the father watches silently. They come slowly into the main room.) (15)

| | |
|---|---|
| Mother: Forgive me, Eka. (16) I was too upset. It was Indra who as at fault. | Maafkan mama, Eka. Mama terlalu emosi. Ternyata Indra salah. |
| Eka: It's all right. I'm used to it. | Ngga apa-apa, Ma. Eka sudah biasa begini. |
| Mother: Indra, apologize. | Indra, ayo, minta maaf. |

(Indra comes to Eka. They shake hands.) (17, 18)

| | |
|---|---|
| Indra: I apologize. (Both boys laugh.) | Maaf, ya, |
| Father: All right now, it's late. To bed everyone. | Ayo, sekarang sudah malam, semua masuk kamar. |
| (Eka and Indra: OK. (The three children leave, holding hands.) | Yu. |

(Putri between the two boys. Mother and father on the couch. They smile, then snuggle.)

*Table 7.18* Focus, complexity, and nuances. For the 5 characters in this scene as a whole, and for 20 moments in the scene: number of clusters used, number of respondents (of seven) agreeing on a particular cluster; number of respondents drawing on more than one cluster; using more than one word; and total number of nonkev words.

| | Clusters | Agreement | Clusters 1< | Words 1< | Nonkey words |
|---|---|---|---|---|---|
| For the scene overall: | | | | | |
| Mother (6 resp) | 4 | 6; anger #22 | 5 | 5 | 15% 2/13 |

(*Continued*)

126 *Exploring Indonesian cinema*

Table 7.18 (Continued)

|  | Clusters | Agreement | Clusters 1< | Words 1< | Nonkey words |
|---|---|---|---|---|---|
| Father (6 res) | 6 | 4: annoyance #28<br>3: fear #14<br>2: annoyance #28 | 4<br>4 | 4<br>4 | 34% 3/9<br>14% 2/13 |
| Eka | 4 | 6: sad #10<br>5: fear #14 | | | |
| Indra | 7 | 2: fear #14 | 3 | 4 | 55% 5/9 |
| Putri (5 resp) | 4 | 5: sad #10 | 1 | 2 | 28# 2/7 |
|  | 3 | 2: love/<br>nurturance #6<br>5: surprise #1<br>2: anger #22 | 1 | 3 | 40% 4/10 |

Cut 2 (Mother, hand to mouth, sees broken TV set)

|  | 4 | 5: surprise #1 | 1 | 3 | 40% 4/9 |
|---|---|---|---|---|---|
|  |  | 3: anger #22 | 3 | 3 | 30% 3/10 |

Cut 4 (Father sits watching mother beat Eka)

|  | 6 | 3: annoyance #28 | 5 | 5 | 25% 4/12 |
|---|---|---|---|---|---|
|  |  | 2: sad #10 | | | |
|  |  | 2: depression #34 | | | |
|  |  | 2: fear #14 | | | |

Cut 5. (Putri watches mother beat Eka)

|  | 3 | 5: sad #10 | 3 | 3 | 11% 1/9 |
|---|---|---|---|---|---|
|  |  | 3: love/<br>nurturance #6 | | | |

Cut 6. (Indra, who actually broke the TV set, watches mother beat Eka

| Eka | 6 | 3: sad #10 | 3 | 3 | 41% 5/12 |
|---|---|---|---|---|---|
|  |  | 3: fear #14 | | | |
|  |  | 2: love/<br>nurturance #6 | | | |

Cut 7. (Mother pulls Eka by the hair.)

| Mother | 4 | 6: anger #22 | 1 | 1 | 25% ¼ |

Cut 8. (Father briefly tries to intervene - 5 resp)

| Father | 5 | 2: annoyance #28 | 3 | 3 | 50% 4/8 |
|---|---|---|---|---|---|
|  |  | 2: anger #22 | | | |
|  |  | 2: sad #10 | | | |
|  |  | 2. love/<br>nurturance #6 | | | |

Cut 9. (Eka, after beating, grimaces - 5 respondents)

|  | 4 | 3: sad #10 | 2 | 3 | 11% 1/11 |
|---|---|---|---|---|---|
|  |  | 2: annoyance #28 | | | |
|  |  | 2: fear #14 | | | |

Cut 10. (Mother reacts to revelation of Eka's innocence.)

|  | 2 | 6: surprise #1 | 3 | 5 | 78% 11/14 |
|---|---|---|---|---|---|
|  |  | 4: depression #34 | | | |

Cut 11. (Indra reacts to revelation - 5 respondents)

(*Continued*)

*Table 7.18* (Continued)

|  | Clusters | Agreement | Clusters 1< | Words 1< | Nonkey words |
|---|---|---|---|---|---|
|  | 4 | 3: fear #14 | 2 | 2 | 37@ ⅜ |

Cut 12. (Father reacts to revelation - 6 respondents)

|  | 7 | 3: surprise #1 | 4 | 4 | 67% 8/12 |

Cut 13. (Mother asks why Putri didn't say it earlier - 6 respondents)

|  | 7 | 6: depression #34 | 3 | 3 | 88% 8/9 |

Cut 14. (Father throws down his napkin and stalks out to get Eka)

|  | 5 | 4: anger #22 | 4 | 4 | 38% 5/13 |

Cut 15. (Indra, his misdeeds exposed, sits rocking in chair)

|  | 6 | 3:arrogance #40 | 3 | 4 | 41% 5/12 |

Cut 16. (Mother kneels before Eka, begs forgiveness - 6 respondents)

|  | 5 | 5: depression #34 | 4 | 4 | 75% 9/12 |

Cut 17. (Eka, as the brothers shake hands - 6 respondents)

|  | 3 | 4: happy #2<br>3: sad #10<br>2: pretend (noy on emotion map) | 3 | 4 | 40% 4/10 |

Cut 18. (Indra, as the bots shake hands.)

|  | 3 | 5: happy #2<br>2: sad #10 | 3 | 4 | 44% 4/9 |

Cut 19. (Mother, snuggling on sofa after the children have gone to bed)

|  | 4 | 5: happy #2<br>2:sad #10 | 2 | 4 | 67% 8/12 |

Cut 20. (Father snuggling on sofa after children have gone to bed)

|  | 4 | 4: happy #2<br>2: sad #10 | 2 | 3 | 70% 7/10 |

## Analysis

This is an extremely complex scene from an emotion standpoint. The mother and Eka are fairly straightforward, getting high agreement on both primary and secondary emotions, using many words, but these are mainly key words. The father, who is torn between his wife and son, and Indra, who is actually the culprit, are both more complex. It is noteworthy (from an American standpoint) how unimportant the unjustness of the incident appears to be. Eka is not outraged, Indra is not ashamed, and especially the mother has little remorse. This is consistent with the general idea, developed elsewhere (Heider 1991b) that the Indonesian films are not concerned with good and evil, as are American films, but rather with order and disorder. The characteristic plot line in Indonesian sentimental drama, of which this is a prime example, introduces disorder, usually via a mistaken accusation, and eventually a female agent of order sets things right. The agent of disorder (here, the mother) instantly converts to un-derstanding and orderly behavior, at best asks forgiveness, and is instantly reintegrated into the group (usually a family). Rarely if ever are such 98 Exploring Indonesian cinema agents of disorder blamed or punished, no matter how terrible and dis-ruptive their acts have been.

*Rethinking the emotions of the drama*

Here, we have two patterns already noted above: as in Scene 4, the extremely Westernized character, discontent with Indonesia, gets extraordinarily strong anger assessments (unanimous or nearly so three times). No representative of Indonesian values ever gets so angry. Also, Indra, who, in an American film, would have to feel guilty for letting Eka be punished for his own misdeeds, is judged as fear (takut) from Cluster #14. But as discussed above, there is an undercurrent of guilt in the fear scenarios. The measure of nuances shows very low values for most characters, but is high for the mother. At the same time, relatively few clusters are used for the mother. This again points out the anomalous position of the mother.

## Conclusions

1. This study presents a promising methodology for the study of emotions. It could not be effectively used alone, but as one part of a multipart cultural approach based on knowledge of cognitive maps of emotion terms, clusters of similar emotions, and scenarios of emotions it offers insights into emotion behavior.
2. The results emphasize just how complex emotion behavior actually is. Our intuitive experience of this is often not reflected in our research. I have no quarrel with those who study single emotions or emotions singly. I do it myself. But this isolation of reality must be only a first-stage research strategy. It must be recognized that that real life is complex and people often—usually—feel conflicting complex emotions. In each of the 78 instances in this study where the respondents made judgments, they attributed emotions from more than one cluster; put another way: in no instance out of the 78 did the 7 informants agree that there was only 1 emotion, much less, emotions in only 1 cluster. Further, the respondents (usually there were seven) made a total of 512 judgments on characters in these cuts and of these judgments 44% were to 1 cluster, the rest to more than 1 cluster.
3. Dictionary definitions of emotions are sometimes misleading. When Said (Scene 1) is bangga, he is clearly pleased/proud, not arrogant/proud of his son.
4. The responses to this task suggest that the cognitive map developed in Heider (1991a) does cover the Indonesian emotion realm. Of the more than a thousand responses, only 27 are words not on the map, although some, on the basis of this new information, should perhaps have been. For example:

Analyzing emotion from Indonesian cinema    129

12 purapura (pretending)
2 sinis (from the European cynical)
2 ingin tahu (desire to know)
2 telaniur (rash)
2 groggy (from the European word?)
1 berlagak (arrogant)
1 pasrah (surrender)
1 meluan (to flare up, boil over)
1 lucu (funny)
1 sirius (from the European serious)
1 acuh-acuh (to care)
harga diri (self-value)

5. Although the overwhelming number of responses are to words in only a dozen of the 40 different clusters, this may be an artifact of the selection of scenes for the study. Although I tried to select a wide range, I was perhaps not successful enough.

One measure of the salience of the emotion clusters in this task is the number of times a cluster was cited by more than one informant (the measure of focus, or informant agreement described above). The frequency of citation of the different clusters is as follows (the maximum possible score would be 78):

39 #10 sad
26 #28 annoyed
17 #1 surprised
15 #22 anger
14 #14 fear
11 #16 love/nurturance
11 #2 happy
8 #34 depression
5 #15 jealousy
4 #40 arrogance
3 #35 mocking disapproval
1 #16 indecision
1 #17 confusion.

6. There is support for the mapping of emotion terms. In the Minangkabau Indonesian map (Heider 1991a), bangga/proud is part of the happy cluster, whose key word is gembira/happy. In Scene 1, although one character describes another as bangga, the respondents all use gembira, thus staying within the cluster but moving to the key word of the cluster.
7. There is support for the scenarios (Heider 1991a). For example, shame is attributed to the person who is at fault, and is not considered to be

shared by close relatives or onlookers. And guilt, that elusive emotion (in Indonesian) is found embedded in the fear clusters (Scenes 8 and 10).
8. An unfamiliarity factor is strong: the most un-Indonesian scene (#2), with the lovers' triangle, showed exceptionally low consensus among the respondents. On the other hand, there were two characters who showed what, for Minangkabau, is uncharacteristically strong open anger (Hanafi in Scenes 1–5 and the mother in Scene 10). Both were very Westernized and both were unanimously judged to be angry. The more typical Indonesians were never judged to be so strongly angry.
9. Avoidance of overt anger. In several scenes, where one might have expected anger, the respondents interpreted characters as sad or used the annoyance (kesal) cluster, which is a way-station to anger (Scenes 2, 4, 5, and 10).

Just how do these characters avoid anger? Do they feel anger and mask it, or do they actually substitute another emotion? Undoubtedly, both processes are at work. But the question put to the respondents presumably addressed the real feelings of the characters and not the emotions which they displayed. So the evidence here, with its very low incidence of anger (except for the two Westernized characters), supports the idea that there is substitution of one emotion for another. We can think of cultural influences on the flow of emotion coming at two moments: the culture-specific display or performance rules for masking, modulating, or neutralizing a felt emotion; and, at an earlier point, the culture-specific attribution of emotion to an event. Thus, receiving unjust punishment might make a person angry or resentful, but in Scene 10, Eka is primarily sad. These results suggest that Minangkabau attribute sadness in a wide range of different situations. The importance of sadness for Minangkabau has already been indicated. For example, the most prototypical emotions are found in the sad area. Now, we have more insight into the dynamics: we cannot say that Minangkabau lack tragic life experiences, or that Minangkabau use sad facial expressions frequently, but that Minangkabau consider as sad many experiences which in other cultures would be labeled differently.

# 8 Culture and cinema in Indonesia: Teguh Karya's *Doea Tanda Mata*

The film is *Doea Tanda Mata*, "Two Mementoes." It was directed by Teguh Karya, Indonesia's most celebrated director of the 1970s and 1980s. Since it is a historical film, we are playing back and forth with two different time horizons: the film is set in the Indonesian nationalistic movement of the early 1930s; and the film was made in the mid-1980s; and, here, we are discussing it in 1990. So, we have 1930, 1985, and 1990. We need to keep this in mind.

Now, I would like to begin by setting *Doea Tanda Mata* in the context of Indonesian cinema and then relating it to Indonesian culture, from which it emerged.

## Indonesian cinema

*Doea Tanda Mata* was one of 62 or 63 Indonesian films released in 1985. During the 1980s, Indonesia produced about 60 films a year. This is a modest rate compared with its neighbors. Thailand produced a few more, the Philippines twice as many, and Malaysia only a handful. (India produced nearly 1,000 a year, the USA nearly 500.) In terms of number of films per capita, Indonesia was far behind even Malaysia:

*(Approximate data for 1985)*

| Population in millions | | Films | Population in millions per film |
|---|---|---|---|
| Philippines | 65 | 129 | 0.5 |
| Thailand | 55 | 79 | 0.69 |
| Malaysia | 17 | 10 | 1.7 |
| Indonesia | 185 | 62 | 2.98 |

*Doea Tanda Mata* was a successful film, winning four Citras (Indonesian equivalent of Oscars) that year against strong competition, and Alex Komang won the Citra for Best Actor. Teguh Karya, who had won the Citra for Best Director two years earlier and would win it again the next year lost out in 1985 to one of his own proteges, Slamet Rahardjo.

A brief look at the history of Indonesian cinema: for all practical purposes, Indonesian film begins in 1950, the first year of peace and independence. Films had been shown in Indonesia since the turn of the century. Foreign directors—Europeans and Shanghai Chinese—had made about 100 feature films in Indonesia between 1926 and the Japanese occupation, but none of these are known to have survived. During the Japanese period, virtually no feature films were made, but many Indonesians were getting training under the Japanese and important groundwork was being laid. The late 1940s were the period of the struggle for independence. No films were released then, but something must have been brewing, for in 1950, as soon as the Dutch were gone, Indonesia produced 24 feature films! Only one of this first batch survives. It is DARAH DAN DO'A, which tells of a heroic event of the revolution. The director was Usmar Ismail, now considered the father of Indonesian cinema.

Teguh Karya worked his way into films with some of the pioneers of the 1950s. In the 1960s, he was the leader of a theater ensemble in Jakarta. And in the 1970s, he emerged as a leading film director. We might just note two things about Teguh: he was deeply committed to the ensemble principle. He not only worked with many of the same people since his Teater Populer days, but he systematically encouraged people to develop their skills. The most dramatic example of this may be Slamet Rahardjo, who began as an actor in several of Teguh's films, then became a director; meanwhile, Slamet's younger brother, Eros Djarot, who had been living in Germany, was enlisted to do the music for a Teguh film and wound up as the director of Tjut Nya Dien, the film which swept the Citras awards in 1988. The list of people who had been nurtured in Teguah's shop is long indeed—one might just mention Tuti Indra Malaon, an extraordinary actress of great depth and maturity whose untimely death in 1989 shocked the Indonesian film world.

A second thing about Teguh: he articulated more than many the moral conviction that Indonesian films must contribute to Indonesian by developing understanding and accommodation among Indonesia's many peoples.

There are several different approaches which may be taken to *Doea Tanda Mata*.

## Film as an agent of change

Despite the old Hollywood joke ("if you want to send a message, go to Western Union") films do send messages. There may be quite intentionally propaganda—for example, Asrul Sani's DESA DI KAKI BUKIT was made with the support of the national Family Planning program; or the message may be more general as, for example, in PUTRI GIOK, a sort of Romeo and Juliet story which pleads for Indonesian–Chinese harmony.

But I would suggest that Indonesian film as a whole played an even more important role: it was a powerful agent in the construction of a pan-

Indonesian culture. One of the major tasks which has always confronted Indonesia is that of building a common understanding—a common culture—out of the many disparate ethnic groups of the archipelago.

And Cinema does that. Films are made only in the national language, Indonesian. There is no regional cinema industry, not even Javanese, although the population of Javanese speakers is far greater than either the population of Thailand or the Philippines. These films, then, are made in the national language for a national audience and they present people who are not regional. The culture shown in the films is flattened out, it is a generic Indonesian culture. Here, in *Doea Tanda Mata*, for example, even those scenes set in the central Javanese village of Klaten barely hint at a central Javanese village culture. It is turned into a generalized standard Indonesian village where people speak standard modern Indonesian. There are few indicators of place, either for Bandung (in West Java) or for the village: landscape, the occasionally regional word or phrase, kinship terms of address (the Sundanese "Mang"), but even these are just gestures whose effect to say that these Central Javanese villagers or Sundanese city folk are generic Indonesians. I think that the more general feeling in Indonesia was that the regional cultures are strong, even as movies are becoming Hollywoodized. But I would suggest something very different; since the 1950s, Indonesian movies on the whole became more Indonesian and were a crucial agent for constructing a pan-Indonesian culture.

(Elsewhere I have discussed this at much greater length, suggesting that the Hollywoodization was occurring at a relatively superficial level showing overt sexuality and violence, while at the same time, the basic structures and motivations were becoming increasingly Indonesian.)

## Film as history

Somehow, whenever a feature film has a historical setting, people approach it as if it were a PhD dissertation and get carried away with questions of its historical accuracy. The reviewer for the *Jakarta Post*, Jeremy Allan, (October 12 1985) called *Doea Tanda Mata* "good cinema, bad history." It is certainly legitimate to ask about the accuracy of film. But if we acknowledge that any history must be more or less a latter day construct, then we can go beyond asking about errors of detail and look at the sort of past which is being provided for the present. In this case, two major historical errors have been pointed out (by Allan): there are the killings of nationalists by Dutch troops—that happened rarely if ever in Java—and the clandestine nature of the nationalist pamphlet publishing—in the 1930s such publications were public, if often short-lived. The effect of these "errors" is to make the 1930s movement more the PERJUANGAN—a term meaning "struggle," which is usually meant to refer to the armed resistance of the 1945–1949 period. In many Indonesian films about the Japanese occupation of the early 1940s, we see groups of Indonesian freedom fighters attacking the Japanese forces. Here, in *Doea Tanda Mata*, the "perjuangan" is given even earlier roots in the 1930s.

Teguh Karya himself does not talk about "historical accuracy." In an unpublished interview with John McGlynn about *Doea Tanda Mata*, Teguh characterized the film with two words, TAMSIL, and PERUMPAMAAN, which mean "parable," or "example," and he called it semacam metaphor (a sort of metaphor.)

## Film as art

In cinema studies, a distinction is often made between auteur and genre films. Auteur films are those films which show the unique hand of the author, while genre films are those which follow a standard formula. In these terms, *Doea Tanda Mata* is certainly an auteur film. One current in cinema debates in the US is the claim that many of the films which had previously been considered the creation of a director are actually collaborative works, and that one must acknowledge not only the writer but also the producer and even the entire studio organization. This is less relevant here, since Teguh was usually both director and writer. In any case, I am appropriating these terms not because of an interest in the process of production but because of what they say about the product. Some films are like works of art since the Renaissance: unique, recognizably individualistic constructions. Others are more predictable and formulaic, repeating with minor variations a familiar story with stock characters and cliched motifs. It is just those genre films, though less valued by critics, which are the most interesting to anthropologists. For it is those genre films which more closely reflect the culture. By the way, in Indonesian theater, Putu Widjaya's plays are greater art but the ludruk folk drama reveals more of the culture. So, we have on this panel, a linguist who does literally criticism of Putu Widjaya's plays and a cultural anthropologist who does field work with ludruk.

At this point, one may well think that I have backed myself into a corner. If *Doea Tanda Mata* is such an individualistic creation of Teguh Karya the auteur, what can an anthropological analysis do?

The answer is, of course, that no matter how original a movie may be, it emerges from a cultural matrix. And so the challenge of cultural analysis is to discover the cultural even in auteur films.

## Film as cultural text

The question, "how does *Doea Tanda Mata* reflect Indonesian culture" is actually threefold:

What is Indonesian about its structure?
What is Indonesian about its themes?
What is Indonesian about its motifs?

## Structure

Let us begin with the structure. Elsewhere (Heider 1991b), I have suggested that there is a structure which I call the "classical sentimental plot," involving family separation and reunion, which is found not only in Indonesian movies but also in other Indonesian literature, especially in the Malay epics, or kaba. In outline, the prototypical plot is:

1. Introduction of the intact social group; (ORDER)
2. Disruption of the group because of (DISORDER)
   a. unjust persecution or
   b. false information or
   c. false accusation or
   d. prejudice (social or ethnic)
3. Separation of the family
4. Search for the missing member
5. Reunion (on death bed or sick bed) (ORDER RESTORED)
6. Final freeze frame: the group reunited.

Even here, it turns out, this classic plot can be discerned through the story told by Teguh: Goenadi becomes a member of the group (the rombongon) of nationalists who run the clandestine printing press in the theater and who meet to discuss revolution. When Asep is shot down, Goenadi is blamed and he leaves the group and loses contact with Miss Ining, the singer. There is a long search, and he finally rediscovers Miss Ining, who helps him kill the Dutch officer. But that same evening, another nationalist is killed by the Dutch, and the group is convinced that Goenadi is actually a Dutch spy. He meets up with the group, but they kill him.

There is some internal evidence for this interpretation. After an introduction, the film is divided into five segments by intertitles which read:

SEMANGAT (enthusiasm)
PERPISAHAN (parting, discord)
KEHILANGAN JEJAK (losing the trail)
PERTEMUAN (meeting)
TANDA MATA (keepsake. memento).

## Theme

A major theme of Indonesian cinema is the subordination of the individual to the group. Even love stories wind up not with the couple alone at last, but with the two families of the lovers reconciled and reunited in the final freeze frame. This reflects in many ways Indonesian cultural values. In the sentimental genre films, there is little doubt about the outcome. It is rare indeed to have a resolution which suits the individual but not the groups.

*Doea Tanda Mata*, however, is a story of tension between an individual and a group. Goenadi is pulled by two groups: one is his wife and her group of nationalists in the village; and the second is the nationalistic group around the printing press in Bandung. He leaves the village for the city group, he leaves the city group to pursue his infatuation—attraction—love—for Miss Ining. He fails in both respects—he does not achieve the essentially asocial union with Miss Ining and he is not reincorporated into either group. He succeeds only in the intensely personal act of revenge, jealousy, and self-justification, shooting the Dutch officer. But in the end, he himself is killed in a way reminiscent of the ending of that first Indonesian film, DARAH DAN DO'A, where the hero also is killed and dies a solitary death. And after his death, there is an interesting coda in which his widow reads aloud a letter, thus allowing Goenadi to comment on his own fate. The final words of the film show his belated realization: "I have too much ambition but too little ability. The result is only foolishness heaped on foolishness." (… terlalu besar keinginannya tapi terlalu kecil kemampuannya. Dan buahnya sekarang ini hanyalah kekonyolan demi kekonyolan.) (This ending also recalls that of The Bridge on the River Kwai.)

*Motifs*

The signs, premonitions, and activities used in films are especially subject to convention. Black hats and white hats in cowboy movies, or banana peels in comedies, are examples of these visual clichés of American films. They are most common, of course—by definition—in genre films.

In the next chapter, I have identified nearly two dozen such motifs. For example, vomiting means pregnancy, red blouses suggest sexuality, and a broken glass presages death. I do not claim that this is an exhaustive list, and I certainly did not expect it to be any sort of measure of the Indonesian-ness of the films. But now, to my great surprise, it turns out that *Doea Tanda Mata* uses none of those motifs which I had recognized. In some manner, more or less consciously, the filmmakers—director, writers, and cameraman—were avoiding the clichés of Indonesian cinema.

To summarize: *Doea Tanda Mata* is both an auteur film and an unmistakably Indonesian film. In its structure, it recalls the Indonesian tradition; in its themes, it plays with the tension between an individual and a group, even as it comes to an untraditional conclusion; and it is at its most original in avoiding conventional Indonesian narrative motifs.

# 9 Banana peels: visual conventions in Indonesian movies

Anthropological interest in ordinary fictional feature films dated from the 1940s, when U.S. intelligence was seeking ways to understand the enemies. Ruth Benedict reported in her *The Chrysanthemum and the Sword* (1946) on the themes of 1930s Japanese movies. Gregory Bateson analyzed a Nazi propaganda film in 1945. Siegfried Kracauer, although not strictly an anthropologist, published *From Caligari to Hitler. A Psychological History of the German Film* (1947). The 1955 volume, *The Study of Culture at A Distance*, edited by Margaret Mead and Rhoda Metreaux, included film analyses by Jane Belo, Vera Schwartz, John Weakland, and Martha Wolfenstein. Weakland continued to look at Chinese Communist movies in the postwar period. He published an important note on his work (1966) but apparently no full account has been released. In such a major study, Martha Wolfenstein and Nathan B. Leites compared English, French, and American movies of the late 1940s. Their book, *Movies. A Psychological Study (1950)*, uses symbolic, psychological, and psychoanalytic approaches. It is purely a textual treatment, with no indication of any sort of audience reaction data. Their style of analysis is well summarized by the following example:

> "The GOOD–BAD GIRL"
> The difficulty of choosing between a good girl and a bad girl is one of the major problems of love life in western culture...
> Current American films have produced the image of the good–bad girl. She is a good girl who appears to be bad....
> American films, in the effort to fuse goodness and badness, take a good girl as the base and try to disguise her as bad... French films, concerned with the same problem, proceed in the opposite direction. The point of departure is a bad girl, who may appear to be good, or to be redeemed, or carry an aura of idealization.
> (1950:25, 27, 42)

The book, published in 1950, was based on data from films released between 1945 and 1948. But when the book was reprinted in 1970, the authors wrote a new preface in which they noted that the cultural norms for the three cultures that they had sketched in the 1940s had changed dramatically in two decades. They also imply that culture-specific analyses of the type that they had carried out were, by 1970, considerably more problematic:

> "Film-making has since tended to become an international mélange, and the question arises to what extent films now express a more western, or world culture, to what extent traditional cultural styles retain their distinctive qualities."
> (Wolfenstein and Leites 1970:8)

And they conclude their 1970 Preface on a puzzling and pessimistic tone:

> "Whether in a cross-cultural frame of reference, or one of merging cultures developing over time, the problem remains of analyzing the variations on the basic human themes."
> (Wolfenstein and Leites 1970:8)

More recently Darrell Williams Davis, although not an anthropologist, has taken an ethnographic approach to Japanese cinema in his *Picturing Japaneseness. Monumental Style, National Identity, Japanese Film* (1996).

My own research on Indonesian movies follows this older tradition based on textual analysis of the content of the films, ignoring audience reactions. However, it is worth noting a more recent approach, exemplified by Sara L. Friedman's paper "*Watching Twin Bracelets in China: The Role of Spectatorship and Identification In an Ethnographic Analysis of Film Reception.*" (2006). She has used this Chinese film, which is a controversial dramatization of gender and sexual roles in a Chinese community, as an elicitation device. She has screened the film for audiences within the Chinese culture depicted, as well as in Taiwan, to get their reaction. And she herself treats the film as a cultural text as she presents it to the readers of her article. By combining textual analysis with audience reaction, Friedman can get more insights than if she had used only one approach.

In the previous chapters, I laid out at some length my own analysis of how Indonesian cinema is based on Indonesian culture and need not recapitulate it all here. But in this chapter, I will present a collection of motifs and conventions fairly specific to Indonesian culture(s) that I gleaned from many Indonesian films of the pre-1990s period.

1. Ethnographic documents (In Indonesian films set in traditional areas, there is often a fairly accurate sequence of a local ceremony, authenticating the location setting.)

### Visual conventions in Indonesian movies 139

- A Minangkabau wedding (in *Salah Asuhan*)
- A Javanese wedding (in *Perempuan Dalam Pasungan*)

2. on a breezeway (a scene on a breezeway of a hospital, nurses and family pushing a bed on wheels, indicates the person is seriously ill)
3. a woman sitting with legs in stocks and her long hair loose indicates she has lost her mind, probably with some sexual connotation)

    - Buaya Putih, *Perempuan Dalam Pasungan*

4. picture glass pane breaks, presages death (*Si Doel Anak Betawi*)
5. young woman bathing in pool at foot of waterfall, spied on by man presages sexual assault (*Buaya Putih*)
6. woman drinking alcohol, long hair loose, clothing loose indicates sexual promiscuity
7. older woman hunkering, chewing betel mix, talking with young man in chair with legs crossed sums up East versus West.
8. Young woman vomits (indicates she is pregnant—audience immediately understands, but no one in the scene seems to get it).
9. anger displays

    - *Salah Asuhan, Mereka Kembali* (twice), *Rembulan dan Matahari*

10. extreme anger by Javanese–Dutch mother (*Buah Hati Mama*)
11. Anger display (extreme for Indonesian) (*Desa Di Kaki Bukit*)
12. Anger display—Chinese stereotype (three times—*Nyai Dasima*)
13. Anger played for comic effect (*Raja Copet*)
14. Anger display—brows down, then up (*Buah Hati Mama*)
15. extreme anger display sequence—false accusation beat child ineffective father looks on agent or order intervenes restoration of order without punishment
16. explosive sigh—meaning unclear—four times (*Nyai Dasima*)
17. indirection—confrontation between men, cut to rams, then to women (*Desa Di Kaki Bukit*)
18. Indirect confrontation—boys' gang leaders' seconds (*Si Doel Anak Betawi*)
19. Indirect confrontation—boy runs fight between ants (*Si Doel Anak Betawi*)
20. avoid anger (*Salah Asuhan*)
21. nonkiss (*Salah Asuhan*)
22. kiss (one of the first in Indonesian film!) (*Cintaku Di Kampus Biru*)
23. handholding without letting palms touch (four times)
24. handholding—one of the first with actual palm-to-palm contact! (*Carok*)
25. shootout in village street (inspired by American Western) (*Mereka Kembali*)

26. Shooting of crowd on steps (inspired by *Battleship Potemkin*) (*Ateis*)
   Special Songs:
27. "Indonesia" by chorus representing each ethnic group (*Putri Giok*)
28. "Mister Beniman I Love You" (using English "love" for lack of good Indonesian word) (*Raja Copet*)
29. "Anak Betawi" (rare song—and film—that actually builds on local cultural pattern) (*Si Doel Anak Betawi*).

# 10 Anger in Indonesian cinema

In this chapter, I use fictional acting to shed light on cultural patterns. Of all emotions, anger is the one most studied by anthropologists. There are several very good reasons for this:

1) In its performance, or expression, anger is the most obvious emotion ethnographically. Of course, if its expression is masked by behavior indicating another emotion, it may be difficult to recognize. But if anger is expressed directly, it is unmistakable: it fully employs the face, the body, and the voice.
2) Anger is the most dangerous emotion socially, for it is most likely to destroy, not strengthen, social ties.
3) And, following from the previous point, anger is the most managed emotion culturally. And for this reason, because culture does play such an important role in its management, anger shows particularly great cultural variation in the management patterns, or "display rules." These culturally specific intrusions, or influences, on the pancultural flow of emotion are so powerful in the case of anger that this is a particularly good locus for the study of cultural variation in emotion behavior.

For example, in the US, Northern anger is more open and less masked by smiles, than is Southern anger. In Indonesia, ethnic groups like Batak, Madura, and even Minangkabau are at the more open, expressive end of the anger spectrum, while Javanese are more likely to mask anger with a smile. Historically, anger in America today is more controlled, more a matter of concern, than it was 200 years ago (Stearns and Stearns 1986).

Here, I would like to talk about an "Indonesian" pattern of anger behavior and contrast it with an "American" pattern.

## Anger and political discourse

John Kenneth Galbraith, an economist who has served in both academia and government, proposed eight rules for bureaucratic success. Number 5 is:

> Anger and indignation may usefully be simulated but should never be real. They impair judgement. (Galbraith 1981:400)

Then Senator Joseph R. Biden Jr. was quoted in the International Herald Tribune of 18 June 1987 (p.3) saying:

> I think that there are certain things that warrant being angry... I don't know that I will ever overcome that, any more than other candidates will overcome their reputation for dullness.

Headlines in the *New York Times* indicate that it is permissible to be angry in American politics:

> AN ANGRY REAGAN ACCEPTS PROPOSAL ON SPENDING CUTS (September 27, 1987)
>
> ANGRY BORK SAYS HE WILL NOT QUIT NOMINATION FIGHT (October 10, 1987)

And note this comic strip advice for kids:

> It is OK to feel angry. Anger tells you what is important to you. If someone makes you angry, let them know how you feel so they can better understand you.

An important moment in Ronald Reagan's successful campaign for the presidency in 1980 was the famous incident in a debate in New Hampshire when Reagan, expressing great anger, grabbed the microphone and proclaimed "It's my mike, I paid for it!"

In fact, it is so good to be angry in American politics that one does not attribute anger to one's opponent (unless the opponent is a woman, in which case anger is seen as inappropriate). In the 1988 presidential campaign, when Dukakis reacted to Bush's insinuations of unpatriotism, Bush quickly defined the situation in his own favor by asking why Dukakis was "upset!" This actually served multiple purposes. Being upset is definitely not OK, and in the context of the unfounded rumors being floated in the Summer of 1988 about Dukakis' mental instability, the accusation of "being upset" was bound to strengthen doubts about Dukakis' mental state while avoiding the suggestion that he might actually be angry.

But Galbraith, you will recall, had gone a step further, talking about the effectiveness of the appearance of emotion, even while warning against the actuality. It is likely that Reagan, in the microphone incident, was using this strategy: he showed anger, in a way that he, as an old actor, could do most effectively.

But in Indonesian politics, anger plays a rather different role. It is definitely not permissible to show anger, and accusations of anger are effective offensive weapons. This pattern in national politics reflects the Javanese pattern and is evidence for the generally Javanese cast to Indonesian politics. (Perhaps, if Bataks or Madurese were the majority ethnic group in Indonesia, the national rules would be somewhat different.)

As an example, in December 1985, stories began to surface in the world press suggesting that the Live Air concert audiotapes, whose proceeds were supposed to help alleviate hunger in Africa, were being pirated in Indonesia and that perhaps Indonesian-made cassettes were being exported to the Near East in great volume. Indonesia was at that time not a signatory of the International Copyright agreement, and Indonesian officials were usually somewhat testy when this was brought up. The official answers were that paying royalties would be inconvenient, that Indonesia is a poor third-world country, and that most performing artists are too rich anyway. However, in the case of the Live Aid concert, these arguments rang a bit hollow since the money was being denied to people obviously much worse off than are most Indonesians. For a short time, Bob Geldorf, the organizer of the Live Aid project, seemed about to succeed in forcing Indonesia to make some sort of compensation. But then, becoming impatient with Indonesia's footdragging, he turned publicly angry, threatening to start an Australian tourist boycott of Bali (a potentially serious loss of hard currency for Indonesia.) Suddenly, by becoming angry, he let Indonesia off the hook. Indonesian concern with the matter vanished, and newspapers which had been attacking the cassette pirates turned instead on Geldorf for losing his temper and no more was heard of compensation. Geldorf's righteous indignation, his anger, which was so appropriate in his own culture, served to remove him from serious consideration for the Indonesian audience.

A few months later, the so-called *Sydney Morning Herald* Affair threatened relations between Indonesia and Australia. The newspaper published a story about the financial dealings of President Suharto's family. This was felt to insult the president, and Australian tourists were banned from Bali. A single planeload was turned back, and then the ban was lifted. The Australian Prime Minister expressed surprise at what he called "erratic" Indonesian behavior, whereupon the Indonesian Foreign Affairs Minister requested that the Australian control his anger. Similarly, in October 1988, when an Australian minister demanded an inquiry into the shooting death of an Australian yachtsman in Indonesian waters, headlines described him as "naik pitam," a particularly strong word in the anger region of the emotion map. But for *Kompas*, the Jakarta equivalent of the *New York Times*, to run a headline saying that President Suharto is "angry" would be quite unthinkable.

## Anger in Indonesian movies

Another way to approach anger is to look at the ways in which it is handled in Indonesian movies. Like the previous political anecdotage, the movie data can be attributed to a general, pan-Indonesian culture.

A word of explanation: most anthropologists writing on Indonesia usefully focus on one or another regional ethnic group. But both national political discourse and movies can better be considered in terms of a national Indonesian culture. This culture is strongly shaped by the dominant regional culture, Javanese, and it would be possible do a more fine-grained analysis of the way in which the regional ethnic origins of specific politicians, directors, actors, and writers give particular regional twists to their public behavior. But in both politics and cinema, the goal is behavior which will be understood and accepted throughout the nation. In movies, regional characteristics are flattened out to a sort of pan-Indonesian culture. Specific landscapes and specific regional costumes and specific regional ceremonies may be used but they are just incidental exotic touches in the films, while both language and behavior are pan-Indonesian. (e.g. it would be hard to find in films set in Minangkabau—*Salah Asuhan, Harimau Tjampa, Titian Serambut Debelah Tujuh* for example—any hint of that most famous Minangkabau institution, the matrilineal social structure. People in those films act like generalized patrilineal Indonesian villagers.)

Previously (1987), I had described the results of using some scenes from films to elicit attributions and judgments of emotions. I had selected scenes in which anger was strongly represented. However, in fact, anger is rarely shown in Indonesian cinema but when it is shown, it is clearly labeled as exceptional.

Films with much violence usually attribute it to some specific violence-prone ethnic group: *Carok*, a sort of "Godfather" film, is set in Madura; *Buah Hati Mama* is set in Jakarta but the mother who mercilessly beats her innocent child is a disaffected Eurasian; and in the sentimental college film, *Cintaku Di Kampus Biru*, when the professor finally blows up at the student rabble rouser, she switches to English to shout "Get Out!"

In short even though emotion scenarios are generally exaggerated in all Indonesian movies, the overt expression of anger is still strongly managed.

Yet more significant is the way in which anger is expressed. Much psychological research (e.g. Ekman and Friesen 1975:82) has identified a panculturally recognized anger face, involving several muscle group movements:

> brows pulled down and together
> upper eyelids raised
> lower eyelids tensed
> either: lips pressed together
> or: open squared tensed mouth.

From two sources, then we have evidence that a brows-raised anger face is used as an emblem for anger in Indonesia. We also know that anger is strongly controlled and masked in Indonesian behavior. And we know that an inadequate anger face—for example, one with the brows raised instead of lowered—does. More recent psychophysiological research (Ekman, Levenson, and Friesen 1983) has discovered a hardwired feedback system for some basic emotions involving the facial muscles, the autonomic nervous system, and the cognitive centers of the brain, such that the muscle movements of the face set off a distinct ANS response syndrome, and the person has the sensation of feeling that emotion. But for anger, this seems to work only if all the appropriate facial muscles are employed.

When I elicited Minangkabau emblems—mainly hand gestures with specific meanings—a facial emblem for anger was mentioned with some frequency. Minangkabau are mostly bilingual, and this same facial emblem appears in both their Minangkabau language repertory and their Indonesian language repertory. The interesting thing about this anger facial emblem is that although it resembles the pancultural configuration, it is done with raised brows. It is not the pancultural anger face.

And it turns out that in the Indonesian movies, about half of all strong, obvious anger faces are made with raised brows.

This does not trigger the ANS feedback pattern. Putting these different bits of information together, we come to the remarkable conclusion that the culture is playing a trick on the biology! To put it in crude anthropomorphic terms; Indonesian culture inhibits the expression of anger and as part of its management of anger, the culture provides a false facial emblem for anger. It looks impressive but has a physiological error such that the physiological feedback intensification of anger cannot begin.

Of course, we should note that Indonesians, despite the cultural management, do get angry. And that despite the availability of the "false anger" emblem, the true anger face is known, used, and recognized in Indonesia.

In summary, when looking at pan-Indonesian culture, there is considerable evidence for the cultural masking of anger. There is of course much else to be said about anger in Indonesia. There is great variation among regional cultures in the extent to which they manage anger. And even what we are calling "pan-Indonesian" culture is far from homogenous. There is good evidence (Heider 1991a) that when Minangkabau and Javanese use the national language, Indonesian; they are using it in rather different ways. Although both groups use the same Indonesian words for anger, there is much greater consensus about these words among Minangkabau—it looks as if Javanese have much less shared understandings about anger, probably because they discuss it less than do Minangkabau.

# 11 Order and disorder in Indonesian genre films and national politics

In 1965, Indonesia was rocked by an outbreak of communal violence. Leftists, supporting President Sukarno, abducted and killed six generals. The right struck back, replacing Sukarno with General Suharto. A wave of killings, centered in Java and Bali, swept across the cities and villages, claiming many tens of thousands of lives: communists, Chinese assumed to be communists, and leftists in general were particular targets. The novel and subsequent feature film, *The Year of Living Dangerously*, are fictional accounts of events leading up to the killings but the anticommunist tenor of American foreign policy during the Reagan years meant that little attention was paid to the bloodshed in Indonesia.

In 2014 and 2015, two remarkable documentary films by the American filmmaker Joshua Oppenheimer were released: *The Act of Killing* and *The Sound of Silence*. The films were made up of long interviews with perpetrators as well as relatives of the victims. The perpetrators describe in proud, even joyous detail how they captured, tortured, and killed their victims. There seems to be not the slightest hint of regret for what they did. And the statements of the survivors are equally unemotional. They do not demand justice, they do not hint at any sort of revenge. In effect, everyone says "yes, it happened but that time is past—let's move on."

It is this calm, unemotional acceptance of the murders that most surprises American audiences. The Indonesian survivors have let their American viewers down.

I suggest that we are dealing with cultural differences. Let us look at Indonesian film (following my book, *Indonesian Cinema* 1991b).

A common Indonesian plot structure begins with a social setting (a family or a village) in orderly equilibrium. Then, there is a serious disruption of order, followed by a disorderly phase instigated by an agent of disorder. But at last, an agent of order restores harmony and the social setting winds up once again in an orderly state.

The key difference between American and Indonesian plots of this sort lies in the fate of the agent of disorder. In the Indonesian films, he (or, often she) is at the end reincorporated into the group without punishment. But the disruptor, in an American plot, is a Bad Guy (rarely a Bad Girl) who is punished, removed, often killed off but not reformed at the end of the story.

In short, Americans expect to see evil that is punished where Indonesians expect to see order that is restored. And this is where the two Oppenheimer films come in: although the films push us to understand the killings of the 1960s as evil, perpetrated by Bad Guys, the interviews with Indonesians filmed decades after the fact present a calm orderly society where both perpetrators and survivors may express some regret and sadness but neither fear a just punishment nor plot a just revenge.

This has been a structural analysis linking two sets of data on Indonesian culture. Unfortunately, it is not supported by personal fieldwork in Indonesia and so questions remain. First, who are these Indonesians in Oppenheimer's films? He seems to have shot his footage in North Sumatra, but who are his subjects? Bataks, the main ethnic group in North Sumatra? Javanese transmigrants? They seem to speak a version of the national language, not either a Javanese or a Batak language.

Also, it could be argued that I have created a false picture of a generalized Indonesian culture in what I have called "Indonesian" films. The earliest such films were not made by members of the majority Javanese cultures, but by Chinese entrepreneurs from Shanghai and by Minangkabau from West Sumatra. After Independence from the Netherlands, Indonesian Chinese became prominent in the film industry. But of course, all these marginal people were trying to make films that would be viewed by masses of Indonesia. Which direction did adaptation occur? So, we can legitimately wonder just how Indonesian are those "Indonesian" films that were made not by Javanese but by members of Indonesian minorities and by Chinese.

A final note: Oppenheimer's second film, The Sound of Silence, was nominated for a 2016 Oscar in the documentary category. Oscars are the most prestigious American film awards and are voted on by the mainly American members of the Academy. The 2016 Academy award for best documentary went to another film. I suggest that The Sound of Silence lost out for cultural reasons: the American voters could not appreciate this American film that gave such an accurate account of an Indonesian event.

# Appendix
## Other uses of visuals: fragments and suggestions

This appendix includes four excerpts from research projects in visual anthropology that I never published. They are included not so much for their strength of research but for their suggestions of additional ways that visuals can support the anthropological enterprise.

### Excerpt one

*Above the fold: early 20th century front page anger*

**In this excerpt, we examine the post-Suharto fluorescence of Indonesian newspapers in 2001 as they develop banner headlines and cartoons into an art form.**

The great expansion of freedom of the press in Indonesia after the fall of President Suharto led to a proliferation of newspapers, all engaged in intense competition for circulation. Here, we examine how some of these, mainly in West Sumatra at the end of 2001, used highly visual banner headlines and editorial cartoons above the fold on their front pages to raise the intensity of political discourse. Close attention to these visual displays supports the argument that there is a very complex manipulation of anger that plays with and against Indonesian cultural rules prohibiting the ordinary expression of anger. There seem to be two related strategies: 1) suppressing anger in accordance with the cultural rules or expressing anger in violation of the cultural rules and getting away with it; and 2) accusing others of anger, of violating the cultural rules as a way of discrediting them.

Here, I am attempting to fill a gap in the analysis of Indonesian politics. Even the most culturally-sensitive observers pay little attention to emotion when they write about Indonesia. I assume that emotion is central to politics and must be taken into account. In this way, I follow the anthropologist Gregory Bateson, whose 1936 words about ethnography in New Guinea seem equally pertinent to contemporary Indonesia. He wrote that "... the emotional background is causally active within a culture, and no functional study can even be reasonably complete unless it links up the structure and pragmatic working of the culture with its emotional tone or ethos" (1936:2). This can be rephrased as "no political analysis can be complete that does not incorporate the emotional tone."

Before venturing into the Indonesian newspaper world, let us lay out some basic observations about anger, especially as used in Indonesia. Of all emotions, anger is one of the most studied by anthropologists. There are several reasons for this:

1. In its performance, or expression, anger is the most obvious emotion ethnographically. Of course, if its expression is masked by behavior indicating another emotion, it may be difficult to recognize. But if anger is expressed directly it is unmistakable: it fully employs the face, the body, and the voice and even sometimes the odd throwable object or the other's body parts.
2. Anger is the most dangerous emotion socially, for it is most likely to destroy, not strengthen, social ties.
3. And, following from the previous point, anger is the most managed emotion culturally. And for this reason, because culture does play such an important role in its management, anger shows particularly great cultural variation in the management patterns, or "display rules." These culturally-specific intrusions, or influences, on the pancultural flow of emotion are so powerful in the case of anger that this is a particularly good locus for the study of cultural variation in emotion behavior.

To make some broad generalizations: in the US, Northern anger tends to be more open and less marked by smiles than is Southern anger. In Indonesia, ethnic groups like Batak, Madura, and even Minangkabau are at the more open, expressive end of the anger spectrum, whereas Javanese are more likely to mask anger with a smile. Historically, anger in America today is more controlled, more a matter of concern, than it was 200 years ago (Stearns and Stearns 1986).

So, one can talk of an "Indonesian" pattern of anger behavior and contrast it with an "American" pattern.

In Indonesian politics, anger plays a rather different role. It is definitely not permissible to show anger, and accusations of anger are effective offensive weapons. This pattern in national politics reflects the Javanese pattern, and is evidence for the Javanese cast to Indonesian politics. (Perhaps, if Bataks, or Madurese were the majority ethnic group in Indonesia, the national rules would be somewhat different.)

As an example, in December 1985, stories began to surface in the world press suggesting that the Live Air concert audiotapes, whose proceeds were supposed to help alleviate hunger in Africa, were being pirated in Indonesia and that perhaps Indonesian-made cassettes were being exported to the Near East in great volume. Indonesia was at that time not yet a signatory of the International Copyright agreement, and Indonesian officials were usually somewhat testy when this was brought up. The official answers were that paying royalties would be inconvenient, that Indonesia is a poor third world country, and that most performing artists are too rich anyway. However, in the case of the Live Aid project, these arguments rang a bit hollow since the money was being denied to people obviously much worse off than are most Indonesians. For a short time, Bob Geldorf, the organizer of the Live Aid projects, seemed about to succeed in forcing Indonesia to pay some sort of compensation. But then, becoming impatient with Indonesia's foot-dragging, he turned publicly angry, threatening to start an Australian tourist boycott of Bali (a potentially serious loss of hard currency for Indonesia). Suddenly, with his anger, he let Indonesia off the hook. Indonesian concern with the matter vanished and newspapers which had been attacking the cassette pirates turned instead on Geldorf for losing his temper and no more was heard of compensation. Geldorf's righteous indignation, his anger, which was so appropriate in his own culture, served to remove him from serious consideration for the Indonesian audience.

A few months later, the so-called *Sydney Morning Herald* affair threatened relations between Indonesia and Australia. The newspaper published a story about the financial dealings of President Suharto's family. This was felt to insult the president, and Australian tourists were banned from Bali. A single plane load was turned back, and then the ban was lifted. The Australian Prime Minister expressed surprise at what he called "erratic" Indonesian behavior, whereupon the Indonesian Foreign Affairs Minister requested that the Australian control his anger. Similarly, in October 1988, when an Australian minister demanded an inquiry into the shooting death of an Australian yachtsman in Indonesian waters, headlines described him as "naik pitam," a particularly strong word in the anger region of the emotion map. But for *Kompas*, the Jakarta equivalent of the *New York Times*, to run a headline saying that President Suharto is "angry" would have been quite unthinkable.

### *Visualizing anger above the fold*

Let us now turn to the way some Indonesian newspapers managed the visualization of anger. A glance at the front pages reproduced below testify to the power of banner headlines and editorial cartoons in conveying powerfully simple emotions—here, especially anger. Two major events in 2001 triggered accusations of anger: on July 25, the Indonesian parliament replaced Abdurrachman Wahid as President with his Vice President, Megawati. The two had been dose allies, almost like family, and bitterness was running high. Almost immediately, there was talk of indicting him for misconduct in office—the actual charge that had been used to remove him from the presidency. And not surprisingly, there was public notice of his fits of anger. A headline in the *Padang Ekspress*, 13 August, read:

GUS DUR MASIH MARAH, TAWARAN ISLAH DITOLAK
(Gus Dur Still Angry, Rejects Offer of Islah)

Islah is an Arabic term for the formal settlement of a dispute. According to (at least some) Islamic teaching, it is a sin to carry anger for more than three days. Here, one Muslim leader, the new Vice President, Hamzah Haz, let us it be known that another Muslim leader, the former President, has refused islah. This was a serious accusation.

The second major event was the September 11th attacks on New York and Washington and the aftermath. At first, the Indonesian press covered the damage caused by the attacks. Then, a photograph of President George W. Bush with American Muslim leaders appeared on the front pages of national newspapers. But soon the 11th of September was pushed aside, overshadowed by the threat and then the reality of the American counter-attack against Taliban forces in Afghanistan. Many papers joined in a great surge of anti-American feeling in Indonesia. While the national newspaper, *Kompas*, the English language *Jakarta Post*, and the weekly, *Tempo*, maintained a balance of coverage, other papers like *Rakyat Merdeka* (Jakarta) and two West Sumatra papers, *Sumbar Mandiri* and *Padang Ekspress*, became overwhelmingly hostile to America and Americans. Their use of terms with which they attacked the US, President Bush, and the American ambassador in Jakarta are revealing.

A favorite adjective for America as "arogan," a relatively new word in Indonesian, whose meaning must be somewhat opaque for those who do not know any English. For example:

"... sikap arogan pemerintah Amerika:
(the attribute of arogan of the American government) *Rakyat Merdeka*, 29 September 2001

And

"MUI dan Ornas Islam Kecam Sikap Aragan AS"
([two Muslim organizations] criticize the arogan of the U.S.) *Padang Ekspress* 3 October 2001.

"Aragan" seems to be used as an intensification of sombong, which is itself stronger than the English word "arrogance." (see Heider 1991a:85,86) One of the outcomes of sombong in Indonesian is that a person is cut off from social contact—a particularly harsh fate.

Further,
MUI Serukan: Boikot Produk Amerika
(The MUI attempts a boycott of American products) *Rakyat Merdeka* 14 October 2001.

A common metaphor for America became "babi buta," literally "blind pig," used either as noun or verb. Babi buta means a person who is out of control with anger, and is a term with special resonance in this Muslim context.

Bagaimana tindakan yang membabi buta AS ini dapat diterima?

How are we to understand the blind pigging behavior of the US?

*Padang Ekspress* 21 September 2001

America is also labeled as crazy:

Amerika benar-benar "gila"
America is really crazy *Rakyat Merdeka* 7 October 2001

and

Simbol Kemegahannya Rontok, AS Menggila
The symbol of its glory collapsed, the US goes crazy
*Padang Ekspress* 21 September 2001

And America—or Bush—was pictured as a dead Superman (or "Supermemble," "Super Lousy") with a headline reading

Tentara Bush Bunuh Diri
Bush's army commits suicide *Rakyat Merdeka* 19 October 2001.

Bush was given a "Terrorist Award" in Surabaya (Bush dapat Terrorist Award)

*Rakyat Merdeka*, 23 September 2001.

And he was called a coward by the "big boss" of the Taliban (Bos Besar Taliban Dasar Bush Pengcut, *Rakyat Merdeka*, 2 October 2001).

Choice Arabic words were used to give the verbal assault on America a theological slant:

AS Adalah Dajjal
The US is a Dajjal, *Padang Ekspress* 20 October 2001.

A dajjal is an apocoliptic monster. Echols and Shadily give, among other translations, "irreligious person who tempts others to be irreligious and licentious."

Bush Kesetanan!
Bush is possessed! *Rakyat Merdeka*, 22 October 2001.
The root of the above is, of course, Satan.
The U.S. Is hypocritical:
Dicatat Sejarah, Amerika Negara Paling Munafik.
In the writing of history, America is the most hypocritical country
*Padang Ekspress* 8 October 2001.
And sexual identity is used:
Amerika Bencong!
America is a transvestite! *Rakyat Merdeka*, 7 October 2001.

Bencong is Jakarta slang for banci, transvestite, or third sex. (Tom Boellsdorff, personal communication.) With a doctored up picture of George W. Bush in drag, wearing lipstick. The use of gender identity to attack a person is a new tactic in Indonesian political discourse. Until recently, third genders like banci have been tolerated in Indonesia, particularly Java. It was only in the last years of the Suharto regime, and subsequently, that various interests have initiated physical attacks on gay and lesbian groups.

Even as Egypt is "The Land of the Pharaohs" to lure tourist dollars, for other Muslims, the pharaohs have other connotations:

President Bush Dituding Fir'aun Baru
President Bush accused of being a new tyrant/pharaoh.

and

*Padang Ekspress* 17 October 2001
Konteks Tertentu AS Mirip Fira'aun
In certain contexts the US Seems like a pharaoh.
*Padang Ekspress* 29 September 2001.

This word, fira'aun, has powerful reverberations, for just before his assassination, President Anwar Sadat was damned as a fira'aun, a pre- or non-Islamic tyrant, and so a legitimate target.

A banner headline in *Rakyat Merdeka* (7 October 2001) screamed in English

"Go To Hell Amerika!" evocative of President Sukarno's slogan "To Hell with your aid!" And, for good measure, the American ambassador was pictured as Donald Duck, quacking in angry frustration.

Thus, did these Indonesian newspapers go beyond text to visualize their emotional attacks on the US. In the Fall of 2001.

# Excerpt two

## Still photographs

In this excerpt, we look at some ways to make still photographs accessible for teaching.

A few decades ago, most anthropologists would take still cameras into the field and shoot more or less at random. Afterward, they might select a very few to include in a publication, or bring a slide projector into a classroom to entertain their students with color slides. But on the whole, photography was not thought out as part of even the best research plan, and boxes of photographs, mostly unlabeled, wound up on the top shelves of scholars offices, eventually to be dealt with by their survivors and literary executors.

The video slide document is one way to combine photographs with a narration into a self-standing production. Here are several examples:

## Minangkabau houses, Minangkabau identity

Over the years, I have been fascinated by roof forms in Southeast Asia, partly dating from my studies with Professor Robert Heine-Geldern at the University of Vienna, who was a connoisseur of these roofs with their many different sorts of upswept gable ends. Nowhere is this architectural feature more salient than in the Minangkabau region of West Sumatra, Indonesia. For my students in the US, I put together a 13-minute video that uses stills I have shot in many places over the years, with narration.

It allows for a simple but effective exploration of the roofs (and their inspiration):

> "The most dramatic visual marker of Minangkabau identity is the traditional great house, the rumah gadang, with its stunning upswept roof ends. This is one regional expression of a general Southeast Asian elaboration of roof shape ..."

"Minangkabau also point to the similarity between their roofs and the water buffalo."

*The grand Valley Dani pig feast*

From 1961, when I first lived with the Grand Valley Dani in the highlands of West New Guinea, I had hoped to see their great pig feast. It was one of the world's most culturally-significant ceremonies. It would be held to finally close the funerals for people who had died since the last pig feast, to initiate the boys, and was the only occasion when weddings could be held. But it was always just a few months away. Finally, in 1970, I was able to see it. I was then able to write about it in detail (1970; 1997:138–152) and illustrate the descriptions with photographs.

*Visualizing emotions in Minangkabau figurative speech*

During the years when I was studying Minangkabau emotions in West Sumatra, Indonesia, I was frustrated by not being able to think of how to photograph emotions. Spontaneously-occurring facial expressions of a wide range of emotions would have been next to impossible to capture. And in any case, the experiment with movie clips of emotion behavior described above, in Chapter 7, suggested that a still photograph would not work. But as I was working through Minangkabau figurative speech about emotions, it occurred to me that these evoked highly visual images that could well be photographed. Examples include:

Dendam "revenge"—api alam sekam. Fire inside the rice husks. (one does not see the flames of the smoldering fire.)

and

Cinta—"love"—seperti pinang dibelah dua. (As well matched as two faces of) an areca nut cut in half.

I had little trouble photographing these during my casual movements around West Sumatra. And the ability to capture these images, however much of a stretch they were, supported my arguments about the saliency of the Minangkabau saying, alam terkembang jadi guru, unfolding nature is our teacher. (Also, see Heider 2011 for a detailed discussion of this figurative speech.)

## Excerpt three

### Life story: Dr Mochtar Naim

The life story is an ethnographic genre that has somewhat gone out of style. In the post-World War II period, it was used by ethnographers particularly interested in psychological processes. Curiously, many of the leading psychological anthropologists of that generation (like Cora Du Bois, Clyde Kluckhohn, A.L. Hallowell, A.L. Kroeber) did not publish life histories of their informants. Nor did any of the British social anthropologists experiment with this genre. More recently, although "life history" per se has lost its popularity, ethnographers have often focused their analyses on the personal experiences of one or a few people in their cultural contexts. For example, Jean Briggs' account of the emotional growth of a young Inuit girl (1970); Douglas Hollan and Jane Wellenkamp presented seven Toraja (Sulawesi, Indonesia) informants going through their life crises (1996); and Unni Wikan focused her study of Balinese emotion behavior on the experiences of her Balinese landlady (1990).

I had not intended collecting a life story from a Minangkabau in the 1980s until I got to know one particular man with an especially compelling story. In 1982, I was sent to Mochtar Naim by Joanna Prindiville, who had been doing ethnographic research in West Sumatra. I had just finished the intensive Indonesian language course at Cornell, and was planning to do fieldwork among the Minangkabau. I made a quick visit to West Sumatra, and talked with Dr Naim, who was then teaching at Andalas University, the provincial university. He was most encouraging and when I returned a year later to begin my first year of research, he put me in touch with a research assistant and arranged for me to teach an anthropology course at Andalas. Over the next years, we often discussed things about Minangkabau. He had done an MA degree in sociology at New York University and a PhD degree at the National University of Singapore and was best known for his book on Merantau, the signature Minangkabau pattern of out-migration (1973). And he frequently wrote op-ed pieces in newspapers about various aspects of Minangkabau culture. (Such publications are a major outlet for Indonesian intellectuals.)

Soon I realized that his story would be very effective on video. He had an engaging manner, excellent English, and deep insights into both Indonesian and Western life. He willingly agreed. We began talking and taping at the house that he and his wife—a lawyer—had built on the coast near Padang, outside the Minangkabau heartland. We then drove up into the mountains to his native village and continued the conversation, strolling around, meeting his friends and relatives, as I worked the camera. This was just the beginning of a series of interviews with Dr Naim that took place in a variety of locations.

It is surely not surprising to find that different ethnographic methods produce different sorts of information. These may not be actually contradictory, but show different aspects of the same subjects. Certainly, in studying Minangkabau emotion behavior, my use of long semistructured interviews evoked information that my earlier sentence completion questionnaires never hinted at. And so this open-ended videotaping of conversations between Dr Naim and me produced some new insights into Minangkabau culture.

For example, the matrilineal social organization of Minangkabau puts special pressure on Minangkabau males who live and are very aware of the patterns of surrounding patrilineal cultures. These Minangkabau men may well feel locked in by the rules of matriliny. One escape route is merantau, temporarily moving away from the homeland to Java or elsewhere. And on the tape, Dr Nairn talks freely about his comfort and even pride in having his own house, belonging to himself and his wife, on the coast, away from both his village and his wife's village.

As we wandered around his village, it turned out that his matriclan had no traditional leader. "But don't clans always have leaders?" I asked. Not always. The position had been vacant for years because they could not afford the ceremony necessary to install a leader.

And it turned out that two people whose wedding Dr Naim had taken me to were of the same clan. "But I thought that there was clan exogamy?" Not necessarily. If two people are members of clan segments with different leaders, they may marry even if technically they are members of the same named clan.

There were some problems with this particular tape. By the time I shot it, my video camera was not functioning well and I could not get it adjusted locally. Also, the second tape that I had planned, talking with Mochtar Naim's wife in her village in a parallel interview did not work out, so I was left with only half of the project.

# Excerpt four

*Ethnographic shorts*

**In this excerpt, we consider two sorts of short low-cost ethnographic-type productions that are useful for teaching.**

Most productions called "ethnographic films" are carefully edited, often running an hour or more. But there is also a case for shorter, basically unedited single-subject films (or videos) that we can call "ethnographic shorts." Timothy Asch experimented with this form when he returned from the Yanomamo of Venezuela with masses of footage. After he finished his major films (The Ax Fight, The Feast, and others) he culled dozens of crudely edited films on very simple themes—a man telling a myth, a man weeding his garden—for use in his anthropology classes, where he would challenge his students to read as much as they could from what they saw. Asch called these his "slopticals," but I prefer "ethnographic shorts."

I shot material for 19 of these in 1994, when Richard Rice and I took a group of American school teachers (second grade through high school) on a five-week tour of Indonesian, supported by a Fulbright-Hayes grant. The goal was to give the teachers enough exposure to Indonesian culture so that they could infuse their courses with some particular cross-cultural insights.

We had English-speaking guides for many events, so I decided to make a series of short clips that the teachers could show to their classes. I included the teachers themselves the pictures to provide a link with the eventual student audiences. After the tour, I did minimal editing, mainly removing footage, to make the short clips, and sent copies to each teacher (and also to a dozen Southeast Asia Centers in American universities). I have never gotten any feedback from schools or universities, and so have no idea how, or if, these shorts were of any use at any level. But I have used them in my own Southeast Asia Cultures undergraduate courses. For example, some sort of betel mixture (including betel vine leaf, areca nut, and tobacco—often falsely called "betel nut") is used recreationally or ritually in many parts of Southeast Asia (and in fact from India to Taiwan and New Guinea). It is possible to describe betel in words only, but the short clip from Bali is far more memorable than a verbal description alone.

*Combining ethnographic shorts: embodied styles of learning and teaching in Java and Bali*

Jean Lave is a cognitive anthropologist, a professor emerita in the School of Education at the University of California, Berkeley. For decades, she has been studying how knowledge is transmitted: how people teach and learn. She has done ethnographic fieldwork with tailors' apprentices in West Africa, looking at how they learn to make clothes. She and her colleagues have studied learning in many different cultural contexts around the world. They have identified two major patterns of teaching and learning (see, especially, Lave and Wenger 2014.)

The pattern that is variously called "situated learning," "legitimate peripheral participation," "context-embedded," "informal," dealing with "embodied knowledge," is found especially in small scale societies. The other is the decontextualized, context-free "culture of acquisition" that shapes the bulk of teaching and learning in "modern" schools, colleges, and universities. Although this is generally associated with modern Western cultures, it seems to me likely that the Chinese imperial system, producing literati or mandarins through its nation-wide examinations, antedates anything similar in Europe.

It was in 1994, when I traveled with the Fulbright-Hayes group in Indonesia, that I saw clearly the two patterns that Lave was thinking about. I had arranged for local experts to show our American teachers various Indonesian cultural activities and I videotaped these events. But as I was editing the footage, I realized that I had good sequences of both embodied and decontextualized teaching. I later juxtaposed four examples:

1. **After the wayang performance** (at the Agastya Theater in Jogjakarta, Java).

    The performance ends and the puppeteer—the dalang—places the bilaterally symmetrical two-dimensional shadow piece against the screen. I walk the camera around to the other side of the screen as audience and performers leave. The dalang tells a boy—probably his son—to put the character puppets back into their storage box. Instead, after the dalang leaves, the boy arranges two puppets against the screen and begins his own private performance. Meanwhile, a smaller boy sits at one of the instruments to try their hands.

2. **The gamelan lesson.** In this video sequence, we see teaching through lectures and white boards. Joyce Suyenaga is an American who studied gamelan at the University of Hawaii and then came to Yogayakarta for further work. She is teaching these American teachers in American style. First, we listen in on a lecture about the gamelan instruments, illustrated by sketches on the white board. The teachers sit around a seminar table attentively taking notes. Then, we move to the room where the actual gamelan instruments are housed. Suyenaga demonstrates and tells the teachers how to strike a gong with the mallet. Each teacher has been given a written score and on another white board Suyenaga has written the same score. The teachers take their places at one or another instrument and follow Suyenaga's directions as she points to each note on the eight-beat lines and simultaneously calls out the number ("and two and three ...."

3. **The batik lesson** is held in a studio a few blocks away from the gamelan room. Here, the teachers are introduced by the artist, a man who has experience leading batik workshops in the US. Again, a white board is used to outline the history and principles of batik and the sequence of

colors to be used. Then, the teachers each get their own cloth on a frame and the equipment to lay on the hot wax. The artist circulates, answering questions. In the background, a young Indonesian woman sits quietly at her full-sized frame, perhaps listening, and working on her own batik project.

4. **The Balinese dance lesson**. We moved to Ubud, on Bali, where a famous dancer, an older woman, has given the teachers some instruction in Balinese dance. Now, she calls in a young woman who has come from Japan to study with her. She stands behind the young woman, holding her hands and moving her, shaping her movements. Then, standing in front of her, she mirrors with her own body how her pupil should move.

In conclusion, each of these clips represents a different style of teaching, more or less embodied or contextualized. The sequence is really accidental. Certainly, if I had been thinking along these lines beforehand, the results would have been more effective in illustrating Lave's ideas. But here is at least a hint of what more carefully thought-out visuals could do to support her theoretical framework.

# Bibliography

Alatas, Ismail Fajrie 2017 Sufi Sociality in Social Media in Piety, Celebrity, Sociality: A Forum on Islam and Social Media in Southeast Asia, Slama Martin and Carl Jones, Eds. American Ethnologist website, November 8.

Anderson, Benedict 1966/1990 The Language of Indonesian Politics. Indonesia 1:89-116. Reprinted pp. 123–151 in Benedict R. O'G Anderson, *Language and Power. Exploring Political Cultures in Indonesia*. Ithaca: Cornell University Press.

Anderson, Benedict 1983 *Imagined Communities. Reflexions on the Origins and Spread of Nationalism*. London: Verso.

Ayer, Pico 1988 *Video Nights in Kathmandu: And Other Reports From the Not-So-Far East*. New York: Knopf.

Barbash, Ilisa and Lucien Taylor 2007 *Cross-Cultural Filmmaking*. Berkeley: University of California Press.

Bateson, Gregory 1936/1958 *Naven: A Survey of the Problems Suggested by a Composite Picture of a New Guinea Tribe Drawn from Three Points of View*. Stanford, CA: Stanford University Press.

Bateson, Gregory and Margaret Mead 1942 *Balinese Character: A Photographic Analysis*. Special Publications of the New York Academy of Sciences. New York: New York Academy of Sciences.

Benedict, Ruth 1946 *The Chrysanthemum and the Sword: Patterns of Japanese Culture*. Boston: Houghton and Mifflin.

Briggs, Charles L. 1986 *Learning How To Ask: A Sociolinguistic Appraisal of the Role of the Interview in Social Science Research*. Cambridge: Cambridge University Press.

Briggs, Jean 1970 *Never in Anger*. Cambridge, MA.: Harvard University Press.

Bruner, Edward M. 1961 Urbanization and Ethnic Identity in North Sumatra. American Anthropologist 63:508–521.

Bruner, Edward M. 1979 Comments: Modern Indonesia? Culture? In Gloria Davis, Ed. *What is Modern Indonesian Culture?* Athens, OH: Center for International Studies.

Boas, Franz 1927 *Primitive Art*. New York: Dover Publications.

Collier, John, Jr., 1967 *Visual Anthropology: Photography as a Research Method*. New York: Holt, Rinehart and Winston.

Collier, John and Malcolm Collier 1989 *Visual Anthropology*, 2nd Edition. Albuquerque: University of New Mexico Press.

Colson, Elizabeth 1974 Introduction in Ogbu, John. *The Next Generation: An Ethnography of Education in an Urban Neighborhood*. New York: Academic Press.

Comber, Barbara and Anne Simpson 2001 *Negotiating Critical Literacies in Classrooms*. Mahway, NJ: Lawrence Eribaum Associates.
Connor, Linda, Patsy Asch and Timothy Asch 1996 *Jero Tapakan: Balinese Healer. An Ethnographic Film Monograph*, Revised Edition. Los Angeles: Ethnographic Press.
Davis, Darrell Williams 1996 *Picturing Japaneseness: Monumental Style, National Identity, Japanese Film*. New York: Columbia University Press.
Depari, Eduard 1990 Eurasian Faces in Indonesian Films. pp. 77–79 in Salim Said, Ed. *Indonesian Film Festival, 1990*. Jakarta: Foreign Relations Division, The Indonesian Film Festival Permanent Committee.
de Queljoe, David 1974 *Marginal Man in a Colonial Society. Abdoel Moeis' Salah Asuhan*. Papers in International Studies - Southeast Asia Series, no. 22. Athens: Ohio University Center for International Studies.
Dissanayake, Wimal, Ed. 1994 *Colonialism and Nationalism in Asian Cinema*. Bloomington: Indiana University Press.
Ekman, Paul 1972 Universals and Cultural Differences in Facial Expressions of Emotion. In *Nebraska Symposium on Motivation*, Lincoln: University of Nebraska Press.
Ekman, Paul 1973 Cross-Cultural Studies of Facial Expression. pp. 169–222 in Paul, Ekman, Ed. *Darwin and Facial Expression. A Century of Research in Review*. New York: Academic Press.
Ekman, Paul and Wallace V. Friesen 1975 *Unmasking the Face*. Englewood Cliffs, NJ. Prentice Hall, Inc.
Ekman, Paul, Karl Heider et al. 1987 Universals and Cultural Differences in the Judgments of Facial Expressions of Emotion. *Journal of Personality and Social Psychology* 53.4: 712–717.
Ekman, Paul and Karl G. Heider 1988 The Universality of a Contempt Expression: A Replication. *Motivation and Emotion* 12.3:303–308.
Ekman, Paul, Wallace V. Friesen, Maureen O'Sullivan, Irene Diacoyanni-Tarlatzis, Rainer Krause, Tom Pitcairn, Klaus Scheerer, Anthony Chan, Karl Heider, William Ayhan LeCompte, Pio E. Ricci-Bitti, Masatoshi Tomita and Athanase Tzavaras 1987 Universals and Cultural Differences in the Judgements of Facial Expressions of Emotion. *Journal of Personality and Social Psychology* 53.4:712–717.
Ekman, Paul, Robert W. Levenson and Wallace V. Friesen 1983 Autonomic Nervous System Activity Distinguishes Amobg Emotions. *Science* 221:1208–1210.
Foster, Robert J. 1991 Making National Culture in the Global Ecumene. *Annual Review of Anthropology* 20:235–260.
Friedman, Sara L. 2006 Watching Twin Bracelets in China: The Role of Spectatorship and Identification in an Ethnographic Analysis of Film Reception. *Cultural Anthropology* 21:603–632.
Gabler, Neal 1988 *An Empire of Their Own. How the Jews Invented Hollywood*. New York: Crown Publishers.
Galbraith, John K. 1981 *A Life in Our Times: Memoirs*. Boston: Houghton Mifflin Company.
Gardner, Robert 2006 *The Impulse to Preserve: Reflections of a Filmmaker*. New York: Other Press LLC.
Gardner, Robert 2007 *Making Dead Birds: Chronicle of a Film*. Cambridge, MA: The Peabody Museum Press.

Gardner, Robert and Okos Oster 2001 *Making Forest of Bliss. Intentions, Circumstances, and Chance in Nonfiction Film*. Cambridge, MA: A Harvard Film Archive Publication.

Gardner, Robert and Karl G. Heider 1968 *Gardens of War*. New York: Random House.

Geertz, Clifford 1983 Local Knowledge: Further Essays in Interpretive Anthropology. New York: Basic Books.

Geertz, H. 1959 The Vocabulary of Emotion. A Study of Javanese Socialization Processes. *Psychiatry* 22:225–237.

Geertz, H. 1963 *Indonesian Cultures and Communities* in McVey, Ruth, Ed. Indonesia/New Haven: HRAF Press.

Ginsburg, Faye D., Lila Abu-Lughod and Brian Larkin, Eds. 2002 *Media Worlds. Anthropology in New Terrain*. Berkeley: University of California Press.

Hanan, David 2017 *Cultural Specificity in Indonesian Film*. Cham, Switzerland: Palgrave Macmillan.

Hannerz, Ulf 1989 Cultures Between Center and Periphery: Towards a Macro-anthropology. *Ethos* 54.3-4: 200–216.

Heider, Karl G. 1970 *The Dugum Dani. A Papuan Culture in the Highlands of West New Guinea*. Chicago: Aldine Publishing Co.

Heider, Karl G. 1972 On the Making of Dead Birds. pp. 31–35. New York: Warner Modular Publications, Inc.

Heider, Karl G. 1975a. *Ethnographic Film*. Austin: University of Texas Press, 2006, Second Edition, Revised.

Heider, Karl G. 1975b Societal Intensification and Cultural Stress as Determining Factors in the Innovation and Conservatism of Two Dani Cultures. *Oceania* 46.1:53–67.

Heider, Karl G. 1976 *Ethnographic Film*. Austin: University of Texas Press.

Heider, Karl G. 1977 From Javanese to Dani: The Translation of a Game. From *Studies in the Anthropology of Play: Papers in Memory of B. Allan Tindall*. Stevens, Phillips, Jr., Ed. pp. 72–81. West Point, NY: The Leisure Press.

Heider, Karl G. 1988 The Rashomon Effect: When Ethnographers Disagree. *American Anthropologist* 90.1:73–81.

Heider, Karl G. 1991a *Landscapes of Emotion: Three Maps of Emotion Terms in Indonesia*. New York: Cambridge University Press.

Heider, Karl G. 1991b *Indonesian Cinema. National Culture on Screen*. Honolulu: University of Hawaii Press.

Heider, Karl G. 1994 National Cinema, National Culture: The Indonesian Case. 173–176 in Dissanayake Wimal, Ed. *Colonialism and Nationalism in Asian Cinema*. Bloomington: Indiana University Press.

Heider, Karl G. 1997 *Grand Valley Dani. Peaceful Warriors*. Fort Worth: Harcourt Brace.

Heider, Karl G. 2006 *Seeing Anthropology*, 2nd Edition. Boston: Pearson Allyn and Bacon.

Heider, Karl G. 2007 *Seeing Anthropology*, 4th Edition. Boston: Pearson Allyn and Bacon.

Heider, Karl G. 2011 *The Cultural Context of Emotion. Folk Psychology in West Sumatra*. NY: Palgrave Macmillan.

Heryanto, Ariel 2014 *Identity and Pleasure. The Politics of Indonesian Screen Culture*. Singapore: NUS Press.

Hollan, Douglas W. and Jane C. Wellenkamp 1996 *The Thread of Life: Toraja Reflections on the Life Cycle.* Honolulu: The University of Hawaii Press.
Home, Elinor Clark 1974 *Javanese-English Dictionary.* New Haven: Yale University Press.
Iyer, Pico 1988 *Video Nights in Kathmandu. And Other Reports from the Not-So-Far- East.* New York: Random House.
Kato, Tsuyoshi 1981 *Matriliny and Migration: Evolving Minangkabau Traditions in Indonesia.* Ithaca: Cornell University Press.
Keeler, Ward 1987 *Javanese Shadow Plays, Javanese Selves.* Princeton: Princeton University Press.
Koch, Christopher 1979 *The Year of Living Dangerously.* NY: St. Martin's Press.
Kracauer Siegfried 1947 *From Caligari to Hitler.* Princeton, NJ: Princeton University Press.
Kushel, Rolf 1975 Games on a Polynesian Outlier Island: A Case Study of the Implications of Culture Change. *Journal of the Polynesian Society* 84.1: 25–66.
Lave, Jean and Etienne Wegner 2014 *Situated Learning: Legitimate Peripheral Participation.* Cambridge, UK: Cambridge University Press.
Lemelson, Robert and Annie Tucker 2017 *Afflictions. Steps Toward a Visual Psychological Anthropology.* New York: Palgrave Macmillan.
Levenson, Robert W., Laura L. Carstensen, Wallace V. Friesen and Paul Ekman 1991 Emotion, Physiology, and Expression in Old Age. *Psychology and Aging* 6.1:28–35.
Levenson, Robert W., Paul Ekman and Wallace V. Friesen 1990 Voluntary Facial Action Generates Emotion-Specific Autonomic Nervous System Activity. *Psychophysiology* 27.4:363–384.
Levenson, Robert W., Paul Ekman, Karl Heider and Wallace Friesen 1992 Emotion and Autonomic System Activity in the Minangkabau of West Sumatra. *Journal of Personality and Social Psychology* 62.6:972–988.
Lukens-Bull, Ronald A. 2001 Two Sides of the Same Coin: Modernity and Tradition in Islamic Education in Indonesia. *Anthropology and Education Quarterly* 32.3:350–372.
Lutze, Lothar 1985 *From Eharata to Bombay: Change and Continuity in Hindu Aesthetics.* pp. 3–15 in Pfleiderer and Lutze.
Maccoby, Michael et al. 1964 Games and Social Character in a Mexican Village. *Psychiatry* 27:150–162.
Matt, Susan J. and Peter N. Stearns 2014 *Doing Emotion History.* Urbana: University of Illinois Press.
Mead, Margaret 1928 *Coming of Age in Samoa.* NY: William Morrow.
Mead, Margaret and Frances Cook MacGregor 1951 *Growth and Culture: A Photographic Study of Balinese Childhood.* NY: G.P.Putnam' Sons.
Mead, Margaret and Rhoda Metreaux 1953 *The Study of Culture at a Distance.* Chicago: University of Chicago Press.
Mischler, Craig 1985 Narrativity and Metaphor in Ethnographic Film: A Critique of Robert Gardner's Dead Birds. *American Anthropologist* 87:68–72.
Naim, Mochtar 1973 Merantau: Minangkabau Voluntary Migration/Migration (Doctoral dissertation). Singapore: University of Singapore.
Naim, Mochtar 1983 Minangkabau Dalam Dialektika Kebudayaan Nusantara in Navis, A.A., Ed., *Dialektika Minangkabau Dalam Kemulut Sosial dan Politik.* pp. 56–67. Padang: Genta Singgalang Press.

## Bibliography

Ness, Sally Ann 2008 Bali, the Camera, and Dance: Performance Studies and the Lost Legacy of the Mead/Bateson Collaboration. *Journal of Asian Studies* 67.4:1251–1276.

Patton, Michael Quinn 2001 *Qualitative Research and Evaluation Methods*, 3rd Edition. Thousand Oaks, CA: Sage.

Peacock, James L. 1968 *Rites of Modernization. Symbolic and Social Aspects of Indonesian Proletarian Drama*. Chicago: University of Chicago Press.

Peacock, James L. 1973 *Indonesia: An Anthropological Perspective*. Pacific Palisades, CA: Goodyear Publishing Company.

Peacock, James L. 1987 *Second Edition, 1968 Rites of Modernization. Symbolic and Social Aspects of Indonesian Proletarian Drama*. Chicago: University of Chicago Press.

Pflederer, Beatrix and Lothar Lutze, Eds. 1985 *The Hindu Film. Agent and Re-Agent of Cultural Change*. New Delhi: Manohar.

Roberts, John M., Malcolm Arth and Robert Bush 1959 Games in Culture. *American Anthropologist* 61.4:597–605.

Roberts, John M. and Brian Sutton-Smith 1962 Child Training and Game Involvement. *Ethnology* 2:166–185.

Ruby, Jay 1991 An Anthropological Critique of the Films of Robert Gardner. *Journal of Film and Video* 43.4:3–17.

Said, Salim 1982 Profil Dunia Film Indonesia/Jakarta: Grafitipers. (1991 English Translation by Toenggoel P. *Siagian as Shadows on the Silver Screen: A Social History of Indonesian Film*. Jakarta: The Lontar Foundation.

Seigel, James 1966 Prayer and Play in Atjeh. A Comment on Two Photographs. *Indonesia* 36:1–14.

Sen, Krishna 1988 Filming "History" under the New Order in Krishna Sen, Ed. *Histories and Stories: Cinema in New Order Indonesia*. Clayton: Monash University.

Sen, Krishna 1989 Power and Poverty in New Order Cinema: Conflicts on Screen, 1–20 in Paul Alexander Ed. *Creating Indonesian Cultures*. Sydney: Oceania.

Sen, Krishna 1994 *Indonesian Cinema. Framing the New Order*. London and New Jersey: ZedBooks.

Shaver, Philip 1987 Emotion Knowledge: Further Exploration of a Prototype Approach. *Journal of Personality and Social Psychology* 52.6:1061–1086. 10.1037/0022-3514.52.6.1061.

Simons, Ronald C. 1996 *Boo! Culture, Experience, and the Startle Reflex*. New York: Oxford Press.

Sorenson, E. Richard 1976 *The Edge of the Forest. Land, Childhood and Change in a New Guinea Protoagriculturaal Society*. Washington: Smithsonian Institution Press.

Stearns, Carol Z. and Peter Stearns 1986 *Anger: The Struggle for Emotional Control in Americaas History*. Chicago: University of Chicago Press.

Strong, Mary and Laena Wilder, Eds. 2009 *Viewpoints. Visual Anthropologists at Work*. Austin: University of Texas Press.

Sullivan, Gerald 1999 *Margaret Mead, Gregory Bateson and Highland Bali: Fieldwork Photographs of Bayung Gede, 1936-1939*. Chicago: University of Chicago Press.

Tobin, Joseph J., David Y. H. Wu and Dana H. Davidson 1989 *Preschool in Three Cultures. Japan, China, and the United States*. New Haven: Yale University Press.

Tobin, Joseph, Hsueh Yeh and Mayumi Kurosawa 2009 *Preschool in Three Cultures Revisited. China, Japan and the United States.* Chicago: The University of Chicago Press.

Trigger, Bruce 1989 *A History of Archeological Thought.* Cambridge: Cambridge University Press.

Whiting, Robert 1977 *The Chrysanthemum and the Bat. Baseball Samurai Style.* New York: Dodd, Mead.

Wikan, Unni 1990 *Managing Turbulent Hearts. A Balinese Formula for Living.* Chicago: University of Chicago Press.

Wilson, Pamela and Michael Stewart, Eds. 2009 *Global Indigenous Media: Cultures, Poetics, and Politics.* Durham, NC: Duke University Press.

Wierzbicka, Anna 1993 A Conceptual Basis for Cultural Psychology. *Ethos* 21.2:205–231.

Wolfenstein, Martha and Nathan Leites 1950 *Movies: A Psychological Study.* Glencoe, IL: The Free Press.

# Index

Note: *Italicized* page numbers refer to figures, **bold** page numbers refer to tables

abortion 71
abstinence 71–3
*The Act of Killing* (documentary) 146
*adat* houses 86
*Afflictions: Steps Toward a Visual Psychological Anthropology* (Lemelson/Tucker) 3
Alatas, Ismail Fajrie 84
Allan, Jeremy 133
Anderson, Benedict 23–4, 84–5, 89
anger: diagnostic elements 67–71; elicitations 66–7, 78; expression of 64–6; in Indonesian cinema 144–5; in newspapers 148–53; observations on 149; and political discourse 141–2; visualizing 150–3
anthropologists, cameras 1–2
Anwar, Khaidir 16
aragan 151
arogan 151
Asch, Patsy 2, 3
Asch, Timothy 2, 159

babi buta 151–2
Bali 150
*Balinese Character* (Bateson/Mead) 1–2
Balinese dance 160–1
banci 152–3
Batak 149
Bateson, Gregory 1–2, 18, 39, 137, 148
batik 160–1
Belo, Jane 137
bencong 152
Benedict, Ruth 93, 137
Biden, Joseph R., Jr. 143
Birdwhistell, Ray 13

blue shift phenomenon 23
Boas, Franz 1, 8
*bodoh* 23–7
Briggs, Jean 35, 157
Broekhuise, Jan 33
Bruner, Edward 85
*Buah Hati Mama* (film) 123–7, 144
Bukittinggi 5, 39, 41–2
Bush, George W. 151

cameras 1–2, 8, 33, 37, 41, 66, 74
Cancian, Frank 2
*Carok* (film) 144
CBSA (*cara belajar siswa aktif* - active learning) 49
center time 45
Chagnon, Napoleon 2
children, Minangkabau 39; ages of 29; Derwita 24–5; education of parents 30; emotion behavior of 13–32; Eva 20–1; Indra 27–8; microcultural incidents in emotion behavior of 13–32; Murni 25–7; Nasrul 21–2; Reni 21, 22; schedule of visits 29; visits 31–2
Chinese preschools 53
*The Chrysanthemum and the Bat* (Whiting) 59
*The Chrysanthemum and the Sword* (Benedict) 93, 137
classical sentimental plot 135
Collier, John, Jr. 3, 95
Colson, Elizabeth 48
Connor, Linda 2, 3
contraception 71
copyright 143, 149

culture of acquisition 160
*Culture Specificity in Indonesian Film* (Hanan) 84

dajjal 152
dalang 160
Dani 2, 4, 5; anger expression 64–71; funeral 33–8; game 55–63; sexual expression 64–71, 71–8
Dani game 55–63; casualness 60–1; competition in 59–60; flip-the-stick 57; Javanese version 62; Micronesian version 63; origin of 57; overview 55–6; quantification 60; rules of 57–9; translation 59; variations 58–9
Daniels, Timothy P. 83
*Darah Dan Do'a* (film) 132
Davis, Darrell Williams 138
*Dead Birds* (film) 4, 33–8, 62; background 33; battle between Dani and Widaia 37; funeral scene 34–8; nonsync wild sound 34; Rashomon effect in 37
*Desa di Kaki Bukit* (film) 91; "ex-girlfriend confronts the present girlfriend" scene 102–6; "father hears his son praised" scene 99–102; "lovers are interrupted by her little brother" scene 106–8; as propaganda for Family Planning program 132; Indonesian cinema
direct command and comment 15
direct threat 15; microcultural incidents
disgust: diagnostic elements 67–71; elicitations 66–7, 78
disingenuousness 14–5
Djarot, Eros 132
*Djyut Nya Dien* (film) 87
*Doea Tanda Mata* (film) 131–6, 134; awards 131; central village culture in 133; classical sentimental plot 135; historical accuracy of 133–4; motifs 136; perjuangan in 133–4; structure of 135; themes 135–6; Indonesian cinema
Du Bois, Cora 35, 157
Dugum Dani 65, 71
*durung Jawa* 23
*durung mengerti* 23

Ekman, Paul 17, 64, 65
elicitations 66–7, 78
embodied knowledge 160

emotions in Indonesian cinema 93–130; analysis of 97, 101, 107, **107**, 109–10, 113–14, 116, 118, 120, 123; bangga-scene 99; "bridegroom explodes at the wedding" scene 111–14; choosing the scenes 98–9; cognitive map 97; complexity 97, 101, **104, 107, 110, 113, 116, 118, 120, 122, 125**–7; dialogue 100, 102–3, 106, 109, 112, 115, 117, 119, 121–2, 124–5; ethnography of 94–5; "ex-girlfriend confronts the present girlfriend" scene 102–6; "father hears his son praised" scene 99–102; "Fitria announces her engagement" scene 120–3; focus on clusters 97, 101, 102–3, **104, 107, 109**–10, **112**–13, **115**, 117, **117**–18, **119, 122, 125**–7; "Hanafi abases himself before his mother" scene 116–18; informant agreement 97, 101; "lovers are interrupted by her little brother" scene 106–8; methodology in study of 95–6; "mother unjustly punishes her son" scene 123–7; and national culture 99; nuances 97, 101, **104, 107, 110, 113, 116, 118, 120, 122, 125**–7; overview 93–4; "Raphia and Ibu read Hanafi's letter" scene 115–16; rethinking emotions of drama 101–2, 105–6, 107–8, 111, 114, 116, 120, 123, 127; "servant sends the mistress to her death" scene 118–20; "young man rejects his cousin" scene 108–11
empty threats 15; microcultural incidents
ethnographers, cameras 1
*Ethnographic Film* (Heider) 6
ethnographic films 3
ethnographic shorts 159

Facial Expression Reaction Test 74–5, 79–80
facial expressions 64–6; diagnostic elements 67–71; elicitations 66–7
fear 78
figurative speech 156–7
film: as agent of change 132–3; as art 134; ethnographic 159–61; as history 133–4
*Films For Anthropological Teaching* (Heider) 6

## Index

fira'aun 153
flip-the-stick 57; casualness 60–1; competition in 59–60; Javanese version 62; Micronesian version 63; origin of 57; quantification 60; rules of 57–9; translation 59; variations 58–9
Fore 2
*Forest of Bliss* (film) 7
free play 52
Friedman, Sarah L. 138
*From Caligari to Hitler: A Psychological History of the German Film* (Kracauer) 137

Gabrel, Neal 92
Galbraith, John Kenneth 142
gamelan 160
games, definition of 56
Gardner, Robert 2, 4, 7, 33–8, 62
Geertz, Clifford 36
Geertz, Hildred 23, 85
Geldof, Bob 143, 150
Gesell-Ilg 2
Gilbert Islands 57
global indigenous media 3
*goblog* 23–4
Goettingen Film Archive 63
Grand Valley Dani 4, 5, 86; anger/disgust expression 64–71; eliciting phrases 78; in the film *Dead Birds* 33; game 58, 61; pig feast 156; Western Dani
groupism 53–4

Hallowell, A.I. 157
Hanan, David 84
Hannerz, Ulf 84
happiness 78
Harvard- Peabody Expedition 2, 33–8
Haz, Hamzah 151
head aversion 67–71
Head Start 51
head thrust 67–71; anger
Heider, Karl G. 39, 43, 97
Heine-Geldern, Robert 155–6
Heryanto, Ariel 83–4
Hollan, Douglas 157

*Identity and Pleasure* (Heryanto) 83–4
image-capitalism 85
imagined communities 84–5
individualism 53–4

Indonesian cinema 83–92; anger in 141–5; brief history 132; classical sentimental plot 135; culture in 131–6; emotions in scenes from 93–130; film as agent of change 132–3; film as art 134; film as cultural text 134–6; film as history 133–4; history 86–7; Islam in 83–4; motifs 136, 138–40; non-Indonesian influences 92; order and disorder in 146–7; production in 1985 131; structure of 135; themes 135–6; visual conventions in 137–40
*Indonesian Cinema, Framing the New Order* (Sen) 83
*Indonesian Cinema. National Culture on Screen* (Heider) 93
Indonesian language 86, 87, 93, 95, 99, 145, 157
infanticide 71
informant agreement 97, 101; emotions in Indonesian cinema
Irian Jaya, Indonesia 90
islah 150
Islam 19, 83
Iyer, Pico 84

*jahe* 22–3
*Jakarta Post* 151
Japanese preschools 53
Javanese: anger expression 141, 145, 149; in cinema 87, 90, 96, 99, 101, 133, 145; and emotions in Indonesian cinema 99, 101–2; expressions 23–4; game 57, 60, 62; and national politics 143, 149; transmigrants 147
Jennings, Louise 41–2, 44, 45, 51–2
*Jero Tapakan: Balinese Healer: An Ethnographic Film Monograph* (Connor et al.) 2

Karya, Teguh 131, 132, 134
Keeler, Ward 23
*kilek jo bayang* 16
kindergartens 42–51
Kluckhohn, Clyde 157; nonsync wild sound 34
Koch, Gerd 63
Komang, Alex 131
*Kompas* (newspaper) 94, 151, *153*
Kracauer, Siegfried 137
Kroeber, A.L. 157

Kurosawa, Akira 37

latah 3
Lave, Jean 159–60
legitimate peripheral participation 160
Leites, Nathan B. 93, 137–8
Lemelson, Robert 3
Levenson, Robert 17
lies 15
lip suck/bite/press 67–71
Live Air concert audiotapes 143, 149–50
*ludruk* 87
Lukens-Bull, Ronald 49
Luthfi, Habib 84
Lyon, David 40

Macgregor, Frances Cooke 2
macroanthropology 84
Madjapahit 90
Madura 149
*Majapahit* (film) 90
*Making Forest of Bliss* (Gardner/Otor) 7–8
Malaon, Tuti Indra 132
Malinowski, Bronislaw 1
*Mama's Sweetheart* (film) 123–7
Marshall, John 2
Martin, David 66
Matthiessen, Peter 33
Maxey, Buzz 62
Mead, Margaret 1–2, 18, 39, 137
Megawati 150
merantau 18
Metreaux, Rhoda 137
microcultural incidents 13–32; children, choosing 17–9; definition of 13; direct command and comment 15; direct threat 15; disingenuousness 14–5; empty threats 15; engagement 16; *kilek jo bayang* 16; lie 15; naturalistic observation 19–20; nonverbal dissimulation 15; sarcasm 15; third party 15; videotaping versus pencil and notebook records 16–7
*Microcultural Incidents in Ten Zoos* (Birdwhistell) 13
Micronesian game 63
Minangkabau 5, 86, 87–8, 92; emblems 145; and emotions in Indonesian cinema 99, 101–2; expression of anger 149; figurative speech 156–7;

houses 155–6; identity 155–6; matrilineal social organization 158
Minangkabau children 39; ages of 29; Derwita 24–5; education of paremts 30; emotion behavior of 13–32; Eva 20–1; Indra 27–8; microcultural incidents in emotion behavior of 13–32; Murni 25–7; Nasrul 21–2; Reni 21, 22; schedule of visits 29; visits 31–2
*Movies: A Psychological Study* (Wolfensetin/Leites) 93, 137–8
*Mr. Baseball* (film) 59
multivocalic analysis 42–51; American tapes 51; American teachers' reactions to Indonesian tapes 45–8; groupism 53–4; individualism 53–4; Indonesian teachers' reactions to American tapes 48; Indonesian teachers' reactions to Indonesian tapes 48–51; researchers' view 42–3; students' reactions to Indonesian tapes 44–5; US versus Indonesian kindergartens 42–51

*nafsu* 23
Naim, Mochtar 157–8
naturalistic observations 19–20
Netherlands, independence from 147
*Never in Anger* (Briggs) 35
New Guinea 148
newspapers 143, 148–53, 153–4
*Njai Dasima* (film) 118–20
nonverbal dissimulation 15
nose wrinkle 67–71

O'Brien, D. 65
Ogbu, John 48
Orang Padang 86
Ostor, Akos 7–8

Padang 41, 86
*Padang Ekspress* (newspaper) 150–3
*Padang Metropolis* (newspaper) *154*
*pandai* 26
pan-Indonesian culture 145
Peacock, James 87, 94
pencil and notebook records 16–7
*Perempuan Dalam Pasungan* (film) 120–3
*Performance, Popular Culture, and Piety in Muslim Southeast Asia* (Daniels) 83

perjuangan 133–4
Pfaff, Gunther 3
photography 1
*Picturing Japaneseness: Monumental Style, National Identity, Japanese Film* (Davis) 138
pig feast 156
Ploeg, A. 65
Pratt, Mary Louise 84
*Preschool in Three Cultures Revisited* (Tobin) 40
*Preschool in Three Cultures* (Tobin) 39, 44
*Primitive Art* (Boas) 8
*Principles of Visual Anthropology* (Hockings) 93
Prindiville, Joanna 157
print-capitalism 85
*Putri Giok* (film) 88–9, 132

radical diffusionism 84
Rahardjo, Slamet 131, 132
*Rakyat Merdeka* (newspaper) 151, *154*
*rancak* 26
*rantau* 86
Rashomon effect 37
Rice, Richard 159
*Rites of Modernization* (Peacock) 94
Roberts, John M. 56, 61
Rockefeller, Michael 33, 34
Rosch, Eleanor 64

Sadat, Anwar 153
sadness 78
Said, Edward 86
Said, Salim 83
*Salah Asuhan* (film) 87–8; "bridegroom explodes at the wedding" scene 111–14; "Hanafi abases himself before his mother" scene 116–18; "Raphia and Ibu read Hanafi's letter" scene 115–16; "young man rejects his cousin" scene 108–11; Indonesian cinema
*Samium and Dasima* (film) 118–20
Sani, Asrul 91, 132
sarcasm 15; microcultural incidents
*Saur Sepuh* (film) 90
Schwartz, Vera 137
semacam metaphor 134
Sen, Krishna 83
September 11 attacks (2001) 151
sexual abstinence 71–3
sexual expression 64–71, 71–8; facial expression reaction test 74–5; stimuli 73
*Shadows on the Silver Screen* (Said) 83
Simons, Ronald C. 3
situated learning 160
*sombong* 151
Sorenson, E. Richard 2
*The Sound of Silence* (documentary) 146–7
Southern Valley Dani 65
startle reflex 3
still cameras 155
still photographs 155
Strong, Mary 3, 8
Suharto 143, 150, 153
Sukarno 146, 153
*Sumbar Mandiri* (newspaper) 151
Surabaya (East Java) 87
surprise 78
Sutton-Smith, Brian 61
Suyenaga, Joyce 160
*Sydney Morning Herald* 143, 150

Tapakan, Joe 2–3
*Tempo* (newspaper) 94, 151
third party 15
Tjut Nya Dien 132
Tobin, Joseph 39–40, 53
Toraja 157
Torres Straits Expedition 1
Trigger, Bruce G. 90

University of South Carolina 44–5
Unni Wikan 157
upper lip raised 67–71

video cameras 16, 25, 41, 45, 66, 74
video ethnography 64–80; anger expression 64–71; sexual expression 71–8
*Video Nights in Kathmandu* (Iyer) 84
video-cued multivocalic ethnography 39–54; American tapes 51; American teachers' reactions to Indonesian tapes 45–8; groupism 53–4; individualism 53–4; Indonesian teachers' reactions to American tapes 48; Indonesian teachers' reactions to Indonesian tapes 48–51; multivocalic analysis 42–51; overview 39–40; research schedule 40–2; researchers' view 42–3; students' reactions to Indonesian tapes 44–5; US versus Indonesian kindergartens 42–51; in

year 2000 40–1; in year 2000-2001 41; in year 2001 42
videotaping 16–7
*Viewpoints. Visual Anthropologists At Work* (Strong/Wilder) 3, 8
visual anthropology: overview 1–4; principles of 6–8; scope of 8
*Visual Anthropology: Photography as a Research Method* (Collier) 3, 95
visual data 9

Wahid, Abdurrachman 150
wayang 160
Weakland, John H. 93, 137
Wellenkamp, Jane 157
West Irian 65
West New Guinea 156
West Sumatra 5, 17, 31, 37, 147, 148, 157; in cinema 83, 93, 108, 116, 147; kindergartens 39–51; Minangkabau identity 155, 156; newspapers 148, 151
Western Dani 65–6; anger/disgust expression 64–71; eliciting phrases 78; Grand Valley Dani
Whiting, Robert 59
Widjaya, Putu 134
Wilder, Laena 3
Wolfenstein, Martha 93, 137–8
*Woman in Stocks* (film) 120–3

Yanomano 159
*The Year of Living Dangerously* (film) 146
Yogayakarta 160

Printed in the United States
by Baker & Taylor Publisher Services